Peterson's
MASTER
TOEFL
READING
SKILLS

PETERSON'S

About Peterson's, A Nelnet Company
Peterson's (www.petersons.com) is a leading provider of education information and advice, with books and online resources focusing on education search, test preparation, and financial aid. Its Web site offers searchable databases and interactive tools for contacting educational institutions, online practice tests and instruction, and planning tools for securing financial aid. Peterson's serves 110 million education consumers annually.

For more information, contact Peterson's, A Nelnet Company, 2000 Lenox Drive, Lawrenceville, NJ 08648; 800-338-3282; or find us on the World Wide Web at: www.petersons.com/about.

© 2007 Peterson's, A Nelnet Company

Portions of this book were previously published as *Reading and Vocabulary Workbook for the TOEFL® Exam*

Editor: Wallie Hammond; Production Editor: Bernadette Webster; Manufacturing Manager: Ivona Skibicki

ISBN-13: 978-0-7689-2327-8
ISBN-10: 0-7689-2327-1

Printed in the United States of America

10 9 8 7 6 5 4 3 2   07

First edition

OTHER TITLES IN SERIES:

Peterson's Master TOEFL Vocabulary

Peterson's Master TOEFL Writing Skills

Contents

121847

Contents

Before You Begin

HOW THIS BOOK IS ORGANIZED

If you are preparing for any version of the TOEFL, you are not alone. Almost a million people all over the world took the TOEFL last year. A high score on this test is an essential step in being admitted to graduate or undergraduate programs at almost all colleges and universities in North America. But preparing for this test can be a difficult, often frustrating experience.

Peterson's Master TOEFL Reading Skills, used as a self-tutor, will help you improve your reading skills. You'll find:

- **Top 10 Strategies to Raise Your Score** gives you test-taking strategies.
- **Part I** includes everything you need to know about the Reading Section of the TOEFL.
- **Part II** provides a diagnostic test to determine your strengths and weaknesses.
- **Part III** provides the basic reading comprehension review. The reading passages progress from relatively simple to relatively difficult as you continue through the book. Various skills, such as finding the main idea and supporting details, are reviewed.
- **Part IV** includes two additional practice reading tests. They will show you how well you have mastered the reading skills presented in this book.
- The **Appendixes** provide a word list, as well as important college selection information for international students.

SPECIAL STUDY FEATURES

Peterson's Master TOEFL Reading Skills is designed to be user-friendly. To this end, it includes features to make your preparation much more efficient.

Overview

The reading review chapter begins with a bulleted overview, listing the topics to be covered in the chapter. This will allow you to quickly target the areas in which you are most interested.

Note

Notes highlight critical information about improving your reading skills.

Tip

Tips draw your attention to valuable concepts, advice, and shortcuts for tackling the reading passages.

Summing It Up

The review chapter ends with a point-by-point summary that captures the most important concepts. They are a convenient way to review the chapter's key points.

Practice Tests

The three practice tests, including the diagnostic test, are designed to help you prepare with little anxiety.

YOU'RE WELL ON YOUR WAY TO SUCCESS

Remember that knowledge is power. By using *Peterson's Master TOEFL Reading Skills* as a supplement to your other TOEFL test preparation, you will fine tune your reading comprehension skills.

GIVE US YOUR FEEDBACK

Peterson's publishes a full line of resources to help guide you and your family through the college admission process.

We welcome any comments or suggestions you may have about this publication and invite you to complete our online survey at http://www.petersons.com/booksurvey. Or you can fill out the survey at the back of this book, tear it out, and mail it to us at:

> Publishing Department
> Peterson's
> 2000 Lenox Drive
> Lawrenceville, NJ 08648

Your feedback will help us to provide personalized solutions for your educational advancement.

TOP 10 STRATEGIES TO RAISE YOUR SCORE

1. As with other sections of the TOEFL, **be familiar with the directions and examples so you can begin work immediately.**

2. **For each passage, begin by briefly looking over the questions** (but not the answer choices). Try to keep these questions in mind during your reading.

3. **Scan passages to find and highlight the important facts and information.**

4. **Read each passage at a comfortable speed.**

5. **Answer the questions,** referring to the passage when necessary.

6. **Eliminate answers that are clearly wrong** or do not answer the question. If more than one option remains, guess.

7. **Mark difficult or time-consuming answers** so that you can come back to them later if you have time.

8. **Timing is an important factor.** Don't spend more than 10 minutes on any one passage and the questions about it.

9. **Concentration is another important factor.** The reading section is one of the longer sections of the test. Your practice and hard work will help you.

10. **Relax** the night before the exam.

PART I

TOEFL READING BASICS

CHAPTER 1   All About TOEFL Reading

All About TOEFL Reading

OVERVIEW

- What does the reading section contain and how long does it last?
- To read or not to read
- Summing it up

WHAT DOES THE READING SECTION CONTAIN AND HOW LONG DOES IT LAST?

The Reading section contains passages on a variety of subjects. Following each passage are several questions about the passage. You will answer from 36 to 70 questions in this section, and you will have 60 to 100 minutes to read the passages and answer the questions. Before you begin this section, you will be shown how to answer the questions with the computer screen and mouse.

The reading passages are similar to the ones you will probably read and study in North American universities and colleges. There are three important differences between the Reading section and the other sections of the exam:

- The Reading section is not computer adaptive. When you answer question number 1, the computer does not select a more difficult (or less difficult) question for number 2.

- In the Reading section, you are allowed to return to questions you have already answered and can change your answers. You are also permitted to skip a question and return to it later, which you can't do in the other sections of the exam.

- You will see the Reading passage and the question on the monitor screen at the same time. The Reading passage will appear on the left side of your screen, and the questions will appear on the right side of the screen.

TO READ OR NOT TO READ

You will not be scored on whether you read the entire passage. You will be scored on whether you answer the question correctly. It is not only probable that you can answer all questions correctly without reading the entire passage; it is imperative that you read only what is necessary to answer the questions.

So that you do not underestimate the importance of this advice, it will be repeated:

**DO NOT READ THE ENTIRE PASSAGE BEFORE
YOU START ANSWERING THE QUESTIONS!**

Most questions will indicate which part of the reading passage is being asked about. Work through each passage answering the questions, using the process we describe in the following pages.

Read the First Sentence of Each Paragraph and the Last Sentence in the Passage

In the following passage, read only the sentences in boldface.

The American composer, George Gershwin, was born in 1898 in Brooklyn, New York, the son of Russian-Jewish immigrants. He began his musical education at age 11, when his family bought a second-hand piano. The piano was not bought for him, but for his older brother, Ira. However, George surprised everyone
(5) when he played a popular song, which he had taught himself by following the keys on a neighbor's player piano, and his parents decided that George should receive lessons. He studied piano with a famous music teacher at the time, Charles Hambitzer. He was so impressed with Gershwin's talent that he gave him lessons for free.

Gershwin dropped out of school at age 15 and earned a living by making
(10) **piano rolls for player pianos and by playing in New York nightclubs.** His most important job in this period was his work as a song plugger, who promoted interest in the sheet music of popular songs by playing and singing those songs in stores. At that time, sheet-music sales were the measure of a song's popularity, and song pluggers had to work long hours for the music publishers who employed them.
(15) As a result of his hard work, Gershwin's piano technique improved greatly, so much so that, while still in his teens, Gershwin became known as one of the most talented pianists in New York City. As a result, he worked as an accompanist for popular singers and as a rehearsal pianist for Broadway musicals.

His knowledge of jazz and popular music grew quickly, and one of his
(20) **songs was included in the Broadway musical *The Passing Show of 1916*.** George became friends to many prominent Broadway composers. He particularly admired the music of Irving Berlin whom Gershwin called "America's Franz Schubert." Jerome Kern, another Broadway composer, demonstrated to George how popular music was inferior to material in Broadway shows. In 1919, enter-
(25) tainer Al Jolson performed Gershwin's song *Swanee* in the musical *Sinbad*. **The song became a hit, and Gershwin became an overnight celebrity when his song sold more than 2 million recordings and a million copies of sheet music.**

Questions About the Main Idea of the Passage

After you have read the sentences in boldface type, answer the following question:

> **Q** Which of the following statements best expresses the main idea of the passage?
>
> **(A)** Russian immigrants in America were all musical and creative.
>
> **(B)** The Gershwins were school dropouts who became successes in show business.
>
> **(C)** George Gershwin became a famous composer before he was 30.
>
> **(D)** Musical training on Broadway did not prepare the Gershwins for success.
>
> **A** **The correct answer is (C).** By reading those four sentences in bold type, you have not only saved yourself time, you have also learned what the passage is about. In addition, you have gotten the information necessary to answer the question.

TIP

Main idea questions are usually asked first.

Vocabulary Questions

Vocabulary questions are found in the parts of the reading passage that will be highlighted to correspond with a question. This is another reason why it is unnecessary for you to read the entire passage. See the following examples:

Highlighted Words

You will answer three kinds of vocabulary questions. In the first kind, you will see a word or phrase highlighted in the text on the screen. This highlights the word or phrase that is the subject of the question. Look at the example. You will see the passage and the question on the monitor screen arranged this way:

> Gershwin dropped out of school at age 15 and earned a living by making piano rolls for player pianos and by playing in New York nightclubs. His most important job in this period was his work as a song plugger, who promoted interest in the sheet music of popular songs by playing and singing those songs in stores. At that time, sheet-music . . .

Look at the word highlighted in the text. Click on the answer choice that is closest in meaning to the words dropped out of.

(A) Graduated from college

(B) Stopped attending secondary school

(C) Scattered sheet music on the street

(D) Dropped by his school frequently

"Dropped out of" is an idiomatic expression, and if you are not acquainted with it, you can still figure out the correct answer by looking at the other words in the sentence. You can do this by mentally removing the words "dropped out of" from the sentence and reading the sentence this way:

> Gershwin _____ school at age 15 and earned a living by making piano rolls for player pianos and by playing in New York nightclubs.

Then, you fill in the blank with a verb that completes the sentence so that it is logical and grammatically correct. The other words in the sentences contain clues. Look at the words:

> school at age 15 and earned a living by making piano rolls for player pianos and by playing in New York nightclubs.

A 15-year-old person who earns a living by playing in New York nightclubs is not likely to stay in high school at the same time. So, you choose a word or words that will finish the sentence correctly. It's not important what the words are; they can even be words in your native language. The word or phrase you came up with is probably "quit" or "withdrew from."

Then, you compare your word to the answer choices:

Q
- **(A)** Graduated from college
- **(B)** Stopped attending secondary school
- **(C)** Scattered sheet music on the street
- **(D)** Dropped by his school frequently

A **The correct answer is (B).** The answer closest in meaning to "quit" or "withdrew from." Choice (A) is incorrect, because college is not mentioned in the sentence. Choice (C) is incorrect, because the sentence is not about sheet music. Choice (D) is incorrect and a tricky one, because "dropped out" is close in sound to "dropped by," which means visited.

Highlighted Sentences

Another type of vocabulary question asks you to read a boldface sentence, and choose the correct definition of the highlighted word or phrase in that sentence.

> Gershwin dropped out of school at age 15 and earned a living by making piano rolls for player pianos and by playing in New York nightclubs. **His most important job in this period was his work as a song plugger, who promoted interest in the sheet music of popular songs by playing and singing those songs in stores. At that time, sheet-music sales were the measure of a song's popularity, and song pluggers had to work long hours for the music publishers who employed them.**

Look at the words "promoted interest in the sheet music" in the passage. Click on the word or phrase in the bold text that the words refer to.

    (A) Sheet music sales

    (B) A song's popularity

    (C) Song plugger

    (D) Music publishers

On the computer screen, you will highlight those words and click them as your choice. Which words would you choose?

     (A) Sheet music sales

    (B) A song's popularity

    (C) Song plugger

    (D) Music publishers

The correct answer is (C). The highlighted words "who promoted interest in sheet music" identify what song pluggers do.

Pronouns

Another kind of Reading question deals with pronouns. You will see a sentence in boldface with a highlighted pronoun, and you will be asked to identify the noun that the highlighted pronoun refers to. Look at the example:

> However, George surprised everyone when he played a popular song, which he had taught himself by following the keys on a neighbor's player piano, and his parents decided that George should receive lessons. **He studied piano with a famous music teacher at the time, Charles Hambitzer. He was so impressed with Gershwin's talent that he gave him lessons for free.**

Look at the highlighted word. Click on the word or phrase in the bold text that the word refers to.

     (A) Piano

    (B) Charles Hambitzer

    (C) The Time

    (D) Gershwin

The correct answer is (B). The pronoun "he" refers to a person, not to a thing ("piano" and "time" are things). "He" also does not refer to Gershwin, because Gershwin did not give lessons to himself, so "he" must refer to Charles Hambitzer.

Detail Questions

You will have to answer detail questions at least twice per reading passage. In these types of questions, you are asked about specific information in the text. First, read the question to find out what information you have to find. Then, search for it in the text.

The American composer, George Gershwin, was born in 1898 in Brooklyn, New York, the son of Russian-Jewish immigrants. He began his musical education at age 11, when his family bought a second-hand piano. The piano was not bought for him, but for his older brother, Ira. However, George surprised everyone when he
(5)   played a popular song, which he had taught himself by following the keys on a neighbor's player piano, and his parents decided that George should receive lessons. He studied piano with a famous music teacher at the time, Charles Hambitzer. He was so impressed with Gershwin's talent that he gave him lessons for free.

Q According to the passage, who did the Gershwin parents buy the piano for?

   (A)   George Gershwin

   (B)   Charles Hambitzer

   (C)   Other Russian immigrants

   (D)   Ira Gershwin

A **The correct answer is (D).** In lines 3–4 above, the passage states that Gershwin's parents bought the piano for George's brother Ira.

Look for the Important Words

Detail questions contain important words that will lead you to the answer. They are not words such as "George Gershwin" or "composer." They are words that specify the information that will answer the question for you.

In the question, the words "buy the piano" are the most important words to help you find the answer. Instead of reading the entire passage, scan the passage for those words. You find it at the end of the second sentence and see that the correct answer is (D).

Look at the next example:

The American composer, George Gershwin, was born in 1898 in Brooklyn, New York, the son of Russian-Jewish immigrants. He began his musical education at age 11, when his family bought a second-hand piano. The piano was not bought for him, but for his older brother, Ira. However, George surprised everyone when he
(5)   played a popular song, which he had taught himself by following the keys on a neighbor's player piano, and his parents decided that George should receive lessons. He studied piano with a famous music teacher at the time, Charles Hambitzer. He was so impressed with Gershwin's talent that he gave him lessons for free.

Q According to the passage, why did George's piano teacher give him lessons for free?

    (A) His parents were too poor to pay for the lessons.

    (B) The teacher was impressed with George's talent.

    (C) Famous piano teachers never received money from their students.

    (D) Popular music was more important than classical music.

A **The correct answer is (B).** The most important words in the question are "lessons for free." When you scan for those words, you will find them in the last sentence of the paragraph.

Once again, repeat to yourself the most important strategy of answering questions in the reading section:

DO NOT READ THE ENTIRE PASSAGE BEFORE
YOU START ANSWERING THE QUESTIONS!

Questions with *Except* and *Not*

The following is an example of "Except/Not" questions:

Q All of the following are mentioned as members of the French Impressionist group EXCEPT

    (A) Edgar Dégas.

    (B) Camille Pissaro.

    (C) Rembrandt van Rijn.

    (D) Mary Cassat.

A In this question, you look for the answer that names a painter who is NOT a French Impressionist. In this case, it is choice (C), Rembrandt van Rijn.

Whenever you see this kind of question, remember that the answer is the one that is *different* from the others. Sometimes an answer has nothing to do with the main topic. In the above example, choice (C) might have been "Honore de Balzac," who was French but not a painter.

These kinds of questions will be asked at least four times per passage. Look at the following example:

    The American composer, George Gershwin, was born in 1898 in Brooklyn, New York, the son of Russian-Jewish immigrants. He began his musical education at age 11, when his family bought a second-hand piano. The piano was not bought for him, but for his older brother, Ira. However, George surprised everyone when he
(5) played a popular song, which he had taught himself by following the keys on a neighbor's player piano, and his parents decided that George should receive

lessons. He studied piano with a famous music teacher at the time, Charles Hambitzer. He was so impressed with Gershwin's talent that he gave him lessons for free.

(10)   Gershwin dropped out of school at age 15 and earned a living by making piano rolls for player pianos and by playing in New York nightclubs. His most important job in this period was his work as a song plugger, who promoted interest in the sheet music of popular songs by playing and singing those songs in stores. At that time, sheet-music sales were the measure of a song's popularity, and song pluggers *(15)* had to work long hours for the music publishers who employed them. As a result of his hard work, Gershwin's piano technique improved greatly, so much so that, while still in his teens, Gershwin became known as one of the most talented pianists in New York City. As a result, he worked as an accompanist for popular singers and as a rehearsal pianist for Broadway musicals.

(20)   His knowledge of jazz and popular music grew quickly, and one of his songs was included in the Broadway musical *The Passing Show of 1916*. George became friends to many prominent Broadway composers. He particularly admired the music of Irving Berlin whom Gershwin called "America's Franz Schubert." Jerome Kern, another Broadway composer, demonstrated to George how popular music *(25)* was inferior to material in Broadway shows. In 1919, entertainer Al Jolson performed Gershwin's song *Swanee* in the musical *Sinbad*. The song became a hit, and Gershwin became an overnight celebrity when his song sold more than 2 million recordings and a million copies of sheet music.

Q All of the following are reasons that George Gershwin became a success while he was young EXCEPT

    (A) He studied piano with a famous teacher.

    (B) He learned about jazz and popular music while he worked as a song plugger.

    (C) He graduated from high school when he was only 15.

    (D) He worked as an accompanist for popular singers in New York.

A **The correct answer is (C).** To answer this question correctly, you have to determine the time period of each answer. In the text, in what order were the answers stated? If you scan the passage you will see that the order is (A), (C), (B), and (D).

Choices (A) and (C) appear in the first paragraph, where you read that Gershwin studied with a famous teacher, which is the statement in choice (A). You also read that Gershwin's parents bought a piano for his brother, which means that Gershwin's parents did NOT give him a piano.

Choices (B) and (D) give reasons why Gershwin became a success while he was young.

Questions with *Imply* and *Infer*

To *imply* something is to "communicate an idea without stating it directly." To *infer* something is to "understand the idea that is being communicated by another person, even though the other person does not say it directly."

For example:

> Mildred said to Mark, "Harry is moving to Japan permanently, but he doesn't know how to speak Japanese."

Mildred *implied* that Harry would have to learn Japanese. Mark *inferred* that Harry would have to learn Japanese.

> During the Reading section, you will be asked questions that begin in the following way:
>
> It can be inferred from the passage that . . .
>
> The author implies that . . .
>
> The passage suggests that . . .
>
> Based on the information in the passage, what can be inferred about . . .

The answer to these questions is always in the form of a paraphrase. It repeats an idea found in the passage but expresses it in a different way.

To answer these questions, first eliminate as a possible correct answer anything that is ridiculous and illogical. Also, eliminate any answer choice that introduces material not discussed in the passage. Answer choices that contain words such as "always," "never," and "completely" are usually incorrect, so you can eliminate them. If an answer choice simply repeats word-for-word a lot of material from the passage, you can eliminate that answer as well. Answer choices that are longer than the other answer choices are often a trap.

Answer the following question:

> His knowledge of jazz and popular music grew quickly, and one of his songs was included in the Broadway musical *The Passing Show of 1916*. George became friends to many prominent Broadway composers. He particularly admired the music of
> (5) Irving Berlin whom Gershwin called "America's Franz Schubert." Jerome Kern, another Broadway composer, demonstrated to George how popular music was inferior to material in Broadway shows. In 1919, entertainer Al Jolson performed Gershwin's song *Swanee* in the musical *Sinbad*. The song
> (10) became a hit, and Gershwin became an overnight celebrity when his song sold more than 2 million recordings and a million copies of sheet music.

> Q It can be inferred from the passage that
>   (A) Gershwin became a famous jazz pianist in Russia.
>   (B) Gershwin admired the music of Franz Shubert.
>   (C) Gershwin disliked music by Kern and Berlin.
>   (D) Gershwin never became a well-known musician.
>
> A **The correct answer is (B).** Choices (A), (C), and (D) are not true. Gershwin compared the music of Jerome Kern, who was his friend, to that of Franz Shubert's.

Questions with Black Squares

During the reading section of the computer-based test, you will have to answer questions with black squares. On the left side of the screen, you will see the reading passage with the following black-square mark located throughout the text: ■

On the right side of the screen, you will read a sentence followed by the question:

> Where in the passage would the sentence best fit in the passage? Click on the square ■ to add the sentence in the passage.

When you point to the square and click the mouse, the sentence in the question will appear in the passage.

This is a very difficult kind of question to answer, and you should not answer it *until you have answered all other kinds of questions!* To answer this kind of question, carefully read the sentence and determine the most important words, usually found at the end of the sentence. Then, scan the passage for the squares. Look at the sentences before the square and particularly after the square. You will find that in the sentence to be inserted, the words at the end contain information that introduces ideas in the beginning of the next sentence that is in the passage.

The American composer, George Gershwin, was born in 1898 in Brooklyn, New York, the son of Russian-Jewish immigrants. He began his musical education at age 11, when his family bought a second-hand piano. The piano was not bought for him, but for his older brother, Ira. However, George surprised everyone when he
(5) played a popular song, which he had taught himself by following the keys on a neighbor's player piano, and his parents decided that George should receive lessons. ■ He studied piano with a famous music teacher at the time, Charles Hambitzer. He was so impressed with Gershwin's talent that he gave him lessons for free.
(10) Gershwin dropped out of school at age 15 and earned a living by making piano rolls for player pianos and by playing in New York nightclubs. His most important job in this period was his work as a song plugger, who promoted interest in the sheet music of popular songs by playing and singing those songs in stores. At that

time, sheet-music sales were the measure of a song's popularity, and song pluggers
(15) had to work long hours for the music publishers who employed them. ■ As a result
of his hard work, Gershwin's piano technique improved greatly, so much so that,
while still in his teens, Gershwin became known as one of the most talented
pianists in New York City. As a result, he worked as an accompanist for popular
singers and as a rehearsal pianist for Broadway musicals.
(20)   His knowledge of jazz and popular music grew quickly, and one of his songs was
included in the Broadway musical The Passing Show of 1916. George became
friends to many prominent Broadway composers. He particularly admired the
music of Irving Berlin whom Gershwin called "America's Franz Schubert." Jerome
Kern, another Broadway composer, demonstrated to George how popular music
(25) was inferior to material in Broadway shows. In 1919, entertainer Al Jolson
performed Gershwin's song Swanee in the musical Sinbad. ■ The song became a
hit, and Gershwin became an overnight celebrity when his song sold more than 2
million recordings and a million copies of sheet music.

The following sentence can be added to the passage:

> **However, Gershwin's income rose, and he worked harder and harder.**

Where would it best fit in the passage? Click on the square ■ to add the sentence to the
passage.

Look at the ideas at the end of the sentence:

> However, Gershwin's income rose, and *he worked harder and harder.*

This sentence best fits at the place marked by the second square. With the new sentence
inserted, the passage would read as follows:

> At that time, sheet-music sales were the measure of a song's popularity, and song pluggers had to work long hours for the music publishers who employed them. ***However, Gershwin's income rose, and he worked harder and harder.*** As a result of his hard work, Gershwin's piano technique improved greatly, so much so that, while still in his teens, Gershwin became known as one of the most talented pianists in New York City.

SUMMING IT UP

- Do not read the entire passage. Begin each passage by reading the first sentence in each paragraph and the last sentence of the last paragraph.

- You should answer the questions not in numerical order but in the following order (as they were presented in this chapter) according to kind of question:

  All vocabulary questions

  All questions that ask you to identify a noun or a pronoun

  All questions that ask for detailed information in the passage

  All questions that ask about the main idea of the passage

  All questions with EXCEPT and NOT

  All questions with IMPLY and INFER

  All questions with black squares

PART II

DIAGNOSING STRENGTHS AND WEAKNESSES

CHAPTER 2   Practice Test 1: Diagnostic

ANSWER SHEET PRACTICE TEST 1: DIAGNOSTIC

1. Ⓐ Ⓑ Ⓒ Ⓓ 11. Ⓐ Ⓑ Ⓒ Ⓓ 21. Ⓐ Ⓑ Ⓒ Ⓓ 31. Ⓐ Ⓑ Ⓒ Ⓓ 41. Ⓐ Ⓑ Ⓒ Ⓓ
2. Ⓐ Ⓑ Ⓒ Ⓓ 12. Ⓐ Ⓑ Ⓒ Ⓓ 22. Ⓐ Ⓑ Ⓒ Ⓓ 32. Ⓐ Ⓑ Ⓒ Ⓓ 42. Ⓐ Ⓑ Ⓒ Ⓓ
3. Ⓐ Ⓑ Ⓒ Ⓓ 13. Ⓐ Ⓑ Ⓒ Ⓓ 23. Ⓐ Ⓑ Ⓒ Ⓓ 33. Ⓐ Ⓑ Ⓒ Ⓓ 43. Ⓐ Ⓑ Ⓒ Ⓓ
4. Ⓐ Ⓑ Ⓒ Ⓓ 14. Ⓐ Ⓑ Ⓒ Ⓓ 24. Ⓐ Ⓑ Ⓒ Ⓓ 34. Ⓐ Ⓑ Ⓒ Ⓓ 44. Ⓐ Ⓑ Ⓒ Ⓓ
5. Ⓐ Ⓑ Ⓒ Ⓓ 15. Ⓐ Ⓑ Ⓒ Ⓓ 25. Ⓐ Ⓑ Ⓒ Ⓓ 35. Ⓐ Ⓑ Ⓒ Ⓓ 45. Ⓐ Ⓑ Ⓒ Ⓓ
6. Ⓐ Ⓑ Ⓒ Ⓓ 16. Ⓐ Ⓑ Ⓒ Ⓓ 26. Ⓐ Ⓑ Ⓒ Ⓓ 36. Ⓐ Ⓑ Ⓒ Ⓓ 46. Ⓐ Ⓑ Ⓒ Ⓓ
7. Ⓐ Ⓑ Ⓒ Ⓓ 17. Ⓐ Ⓑ Ⓒ Ⓓ 27. Ⓐ Ⓑ Ⓒ Ⓓ 37. Ⓐ Ⓑ Ⓒ Ⓓ 47. Ⓐ Ⓑ Ⓒ Ⓓ
8. Ⓐ Ⓑ Ⓒ Ⓓ 18. Ⓐ Ⓑ Ⓒ Ⓓ 28. Ⓐ Ⓑ Ⓒ Ⓓ 38. Ⓐ Ⓑ Ⓒ Ⓓ 48. Ⓐ Ⓑ Ⓒ Ⓓ
9. Ⓐ Ⓑ Ⓒ Ⓓ 19. Ⓐ Ⓑ Ⓒ Ⓓ 29. Ⓐ Ⓑ Ⓒ Ⓓ 39. Ⓐ Ⓑ Ⓒ Ⓓ 49. Ⓐ Ⓑ Ⓒ Ⓓ
10. Ⓐ Ⓑ Ⓒ Ⓓ 20. Ⓐ Ⓑ Ⓒ Ⓓ 30. Ⓐ Ⓑ Ⓒ Ⓓ 40. Ⓐ Ⓑ Ⓒ Ⓓ 50. Ⓐ Ⓑ Ⓒ Ⓓ

answer sheet

PRACTICE TEST 1: DIAGNOSTIC

50 Questions • Time: 25 Minutes

Directions: Each passage is followed by a series of questions. Answer the questions based on the information you gathered from the passage. Choose the best answer to each question and answer each question based on what is *stated* or *implied* in the passage.

QUESTIONS 1–10 REFER TO THE FOLLOWING PASSAGE.

The cabildo, which is Spanish for "municipal council," was the fundamental unit of local government in colonial Spanish America. Following a tradition going
(5) back to the Romans, the Spanish considered the city to be of paramount importance, with the surrounding countryside directly subordinate to it.

In local affairs, each municipality in
(10) Hispanic America was governed by its cabildo, or council, in a manner reminiscent of Castilian towns in the late Middle Ages. A council's members and magistrates, together with the local judge ap-
(15) pointed by the king, enjoyed considerable prestige and power. The size of a council varied but was always small. The cabildos of important cities, such as Lima and Mexico, had about 12 members.
(20) The cabildo was in charge of all ordinary aspects of municipal government— e.g., policing, sanitation, taxation, the supervision of building, price and wage regulation, and the administration of
(25) justice. To assist them in these responsibilities, the city councilors appointed various officials, such as tax collectors, inspectors of weights and measures and the markets, and peace officers. In spite
(30) of royal decrees to promote honest and efficient city government, the cabildos were often corrupt and rapacious.

By the mid-sixteenth century, appointments to cabildos were ordinarily made
(35) by the Spanish crown and sometimes became hereditary. Occasionally, the propertied class in a city elected some of the councilors. Sometimes citizens were asked to attend a open town meeting on
(40) important matters. Such open meetings became very important to the movement for the independence of Hispanic America in the early nineteenth century.

1. Which choice does the word "paramount" as used in line 6 refer to?
   (A) Fundamental
   (B) Government
   (C) Tradition
   (D) Surrounding

2. Where was the cabildo used as a form of government?
   (A) In Roman colonies
   (B) In Spanish colonies
   (C) In Roman provinces
   (D) In Spanish provinces

3. Which of the following answer choices is closest in meaning to the word "reminiscent" as used in lines 11–12?
   (A) Suggesting something in the past
   (B) Suggesting a schedule or agenda
   (C) Suggesting a small village
   (D) Suggesting an odor

4. According to the passage, how was a local judge in Hispanic America selected?
   (A) He was elected by the council.
   (B) He was appointed by the king.
   (C) He was chosen by the town's wealthy citizens.
   (D) He was the richest man in the town.

5. According to the passage, how many councilors did Lima have?

   (A) Ten

   (B) Eleven

   (C) Twelve

   (D) Thirteen

6. From the passage it can be inferred that some cabildos were

   (A) poorly educated

   (B) important

   (C) corrupt

   (D) independent

7. What word does the phrase "peace officers" as used in line 29 refer to?

   (A) Sanitation

   (B) Policing

   (C) Assist

   (D) Tax collectors

8. Which is closest in meaning to the word in the passage "responsibilities" as used in lines 25–26?

   (A) Duties

   (B) Wages

   (C) Sanitation

   (D) Inspections

9. From the passage it can be inferred that by the mid-sixteenth century, the cabildo was all of the following EXCEPT:

   (A) Elected by all registered voters

   (B) Appointed by the king

   (C) Came from the propertied class

   (D) Was an inherited office

10. Where can the following sentence best be added to the passage?

    Debates were sometimes heated, and the wealthy landowners had to defend their positions by arresting their opponents.

    (A) At the end of paragraph 1

    (B) At the end of paragraph 2

    (C) After the words "peace officers" in paragraph 3

    (D) After the words "important matters" in paragraph 4

QUESTIONS 11–20 REFER TO THE FOLLOWING PASSAGE.

    Annie Oakley, an intriguing figure in American entertainment, was a markswoman who starred in Buffalo Bill's Wild West Show, where she was

(5) often called "Little Sure Shot." She was born in 1860 in Darke County, Ohio, and her original name was Phoebe Ann Moses. As a child, she hunted game with such success that, according to legend,

(10) by selling it in Cincinnati, Ohio, she was able to pay off the mortgage on the family farm. When she was 15 she won a shooting match in Cincinnati with Frank E. Butler, a vaudeville marks-

(15) man, and they were married a year later.

    For the next ten years they toured the country and performed in theaters and circuses as "Butler and Oakley." In April 1885, Annie Oakley, now under her

(20) husband's management, joined "Buffalo Bill" Cody's Wild West Show. Billed as "Miss Annie Oakley, the Peerless Lady Wing-Shot," she was one of the show's star attractions for sixteen years.

(25)   Oakley never failed to delight her audiences, and her feats of marksmanship were truly incredible. At 30 paces she could split a playing card held edge-on, and she hit dimes tossed into the air.

(30) She shot cigarettes from her husband's lips, and, when he threw a playing card into the air, she would shoot it full of holes before it touched the ground. She was a great success on the Wild West

(35) Show's European trips.

In 1887, she was presented to Queen Victoria, and later in Berlin she performed her cigarette trick with, at his insistence, Crown Prince Wilhelm (later
(40)   Kaiser Wilhelm II) holding the cigarette. A train wreck in 1901 left her partially paralyzed for a time, but she recovered and returned to the stage to amaze audiences for many more years.

11. Which of the following is closest in meaning to the word "intriguing" as used in line 1?

    (A) Frightening

    (B) Fascinating

    (C) Fabulous

    (D) Funny

12. What was Oakley often called while performing in Buffalo Bill's Wild West Show?

    (A) Little Orphan Annie

    (B) Little Phoebe Ann

    (C) Little Sure Shot

    (D) Little Phoebe Butler

13. Which of the following is the closest in meaning to the word "mortgage" as used in line 11?

    (A) A debt left by a deceased property owner

    (B) A bank-loan contract using property as security

    (C) A measurement of debts owed

    (D) A piece of furniture loaned to a neighbor

14. What does the word "it" as used in the phrase "by selling it" in line 10 refer to?

    (A) Child

    (B) Game

    (C) Legend

    (D) Mortgage

15. The passage implies that Oakley and Butler were married in

    (A) 1873

    (B) 1874

    (C) 1875

    (D) 1876

16. According to the passage, Frank E. Butler was all of the following EXCEPT:

    (A) Annie Oakley's assistant in her act

    (B) Annie Oakley's husband

    (C) Annie Oakley's teacher

    (D) Annie Oakley's manager

17. Which of the following is closest in meaning to the word "feats" as used in line 26?

    (A) Jokes

    (B) Accomplishments

    (C) Displays

    (D) Mistakes

18. Where can the following sentence best be added to the passage?

    Her story was made into a Broadway musical called *Annie Get Your Gun*, but the real life of Annie Oakley is just as interesting.

    (A) After the phrase "Little Sure Shot" in paragraph 1

    (B) After the phrase "Butler and Oakley" in paragraph 2

    (C) At the end of paragraph 3

    (D) At the beginning of paragraph 4

19. According to the passage, who performed the cigarette trick with her in Europe?

    (A) Queen Victoria

    (B) Crown Prince Wilhelm

    (C) Buffalo Bill Cody

    (D) Princess Anne

20. Which of the following can be inferred from the passage?

    (A) Annie Oakley was a talented and popular entertainer.

    (B) Frank E. Butler was jealous of his wife's talent and popularity.

    (C) Queen Victoria was brave when she held a cigarette for Annie Oakley.

    (D) Buffalo Bill Cody was not as good a marksman as Annie Oakley.

QUESTIONS 21–30 REFER TO THE FOLLOWING PASSAGE.

Edward Patrick Eagan was born April 26, 1897, in Denver, Colorado, and his father died in a railroad accident when Eagan was only a year old. He and his
(5) four brothers were raised by his mother, who earned a small income from teaching foreign languages.

Inspired by Frank Merriwell, the hero of a series of popular novels for boys,
(10) Eagan pursued an education for himself as well as an interest in boxing. He attended the University of Denver for a year before serving in the U.S. Army as an artillery lieutenant during World War
(15) I. After the war, he entered Yale University and, while studying there, won the U.S. national amateur heavyweight boxing title. He graduated from Yale in 1921, attended Harvard Law School,
(20) and received a Rhodes scholarship to the University of Oxford where he received his A.M. in 1928.

While studying at Oxford, Eagan became the first American to win the Brit-
(25) ish amateur boxing championship. Eagan won his first Olympic gold medal as a light heavyweight boxer at the 1920 Olympic Games in Antwerp, Belgium. Eagan also fought at the 1924 Olympics
(30) in Paris as a heavyweight but failed to get a medal. Though he had taken up the sport just three weeks before the competition, he managed to win a second gold medal as a member of the four-man
(35) bobsled team at the 1932 Olympics in Lake Placid, New York. Thus he became the only athlete to win gold medals at both the Summer and Winter Olympics.

Eagan was a member of the first group
(40) of athletes inducted into the U.S. Olympic Hall of Fame in 1983. Eagan became a respected attorney, serving as an assistant district attorney for southern New York and as chairman of the New
(45) York State Athletic Commission (1945–51). He married soap heiress Margaret Colgate and attained the rank of lieutenant colonel during World War II.

21. What is the main idea of the passage?

(A) Eagan's life shows how a wealthy student can achieve as much as a poor one.

(B) Eagan's life shows that military experience makes athletes great.

(C) Eagan's life shows that a man can be an athlete and a well-educated person.

(D) Eagan's life shows how easy it is to win two gold medals in different Olympic sports.

22. According to the passage, who was Frank Merriwell?

(A) A teacher at Yale

(B) A fictional character

(C) A student at Oxford

(D) A bobsledder at the Olympics

23. According to the passage, how did Eagan's mother earn a living?

(A) Renting rooms to immigrants

(B) Teaching foreign languages

(C) Doing laundry and cleaning

(D) Writing fiction for women's magazines

24. Which of the following is the closest in meaning to the word "artillery" as used in line 14?

(A) Large weapons such as cannons

(B) Small weapons such as pistols

(C) Shoulder weapons such as rifles

(D) Tension weapons such as crossbows

25. According to the passage, Eagan won all of the following EXCEPT:

(A) Light heavyweight boxing, Olympic gold medal

(B) U.S. national amateur heavyweight boxing title

(C) British amateur boxing championship

(D) Heavyweight boxing, Olympic gold medal

26. According to the passage, where were the 1920 Olympic Games held?

    (A) Antwerp, Belgium

    (B) Paris, France

    (C) London, England

    (D) Lake Placid, New York

27. Where can the following sentence best be added to the passage?

    He continued to be active in amateur athletics for the rest of the decade.

    (A) At the end of paragraph 1

    (B) After the word "boxing" in paragraph 2

    (C) After the phrase "get a medal" in paragraph 3

    (D) At the end of paragraph 4

28. Which word or phrase does the word "competition" as used in lines 32–33 refer to?

    (A) Sport

    (B) Gold medals

    (C) 1932 Olympics

    (D) Summer Olympics

29. According to the passage, what was Eagan's profession?

    (A) He was a boxing trainer.

    (B) He was an attorney.

    (C) He was an army officer.

    (D) He was president of Colgate.

30. According to the passage, what special honor did Eagan receive in 1983?

    (A) He was inducted into U.S. Olympic Hall of Fame.

    (B) He was promoted to lieutenant colonel in the U.S. Army.

    (C) He received a gold medal in four-man bobsledding.

    (D) He was appointed assistant district attorney for Southern New York.

QUESTIONS 31–40 REFER TO THE FOLLOWING PASSAGE.

The first folio edition of the collected works of William Shakespeare was originally published in 1623 as *Mr. William Shakespeares Comedies, Histories & Tragedies*. This folio edition is the major (5) source for contemporary texts of his plays.

The publication of drama in the early seventeenth century was usually left to (10) the poorer members of the Stationers' Company and to outright pirates. The would-be publisher only had to get hold of a manuscript, legally or illegally, register it as his copy, and have it printed. (15) Sometimes the publisher dispensed with the formality. Such a man was Thomas Thorpe, the publisher of Shakespeare's sonnets in 1609.

Titus Andronicus was the first play by (20) Shakespeare to be published and was printed by a notorious literary pirate, John Danter, who also brought out, anonymously, a defective *Romeo and Juliet*, largely from shorthand notes (25) made during performance. Eighteen of Shakespeare's plays were printed in quartos (books about half the size of a modern magazine) both "good" and "bad" before the First Folio (a large-format (30) book) was published in 1623. The bad quartos are defective editions, usually with badly garbled or missing text.

For the First Folio, a formidable project of more than 900 pages, five men formed (35) a partnership, headed by Edward Blount and William Jaggard. The actors John Heminge and Henry Condell undertook the collection of 36 of Shakespeare's plays, and about 1,000 copies of the First (40) Folio were printed by Isaac Jaggard, William's son. In 1632, a second folio was issued and in 1663, a third. The latter included *Pericles* and several other plays that may not have been written by (45) Shakespeare. These included *The Two Noble Kinsmen*, which is now thought to have been a collaboration of Shakespeare and John Fletcher.

31. From the passage it can be inferred that the First Folio of Shakespeare's plays is important because it

    (A) was registered at the Stationer's Office by Thomas Thorpe

    (B) is the major source for contemporary texts of Shakespeare's plays

    (C) is twice the size of the quarto editions that were badly printed by many publishers

    (D) was published three years after the establishment of the Plymouth Colony

32. Which of the following is closest in meaning to the word "outright" as used in line 11?

    (A) Unfairly judged as something

    (B) Proved to be something without question

    (C) Imprisoned without a trial

    (D) Opposing the rights of an enemy

33. The passage implies that many publishers

    (A) were unsuccessful authors themselves

    (B) printed the work of only the best writers.

    (C) used an author's work without permission

    (D) paid the author very well for his writing

34. Which of the following is closest in meaning to the phrase "dispensed with" as used in line 15?

    (A) Gave away to customers

    (B) Managed without something

    (C) Wrote a denial to an accusation

    (D) Compensated another's loss

35. According to the passage, when were Shakespeare's sonnets published?

    (A) 1609

    (B) 1610

    (C) 1611

    (D) 1612

36. Which word is closest in meaning to the phrase "brought out" as used in line 22?

    (A) Published

    (B) Printed

    (C) Performed

    (D) Defect

37. According to the passage, how many of Shakespeare's plays were printed in quartos?

    (A) 17

    (B) 18

    (C) 19

    (D) 20

38. The passage implies that John Danter acquired the text of *Romeo and Juliet* by

    (A) paying an actor for a copy of the script

    (B) buying the copyright from Shakespeare

    (C) taking notes during a performance

    (D) hiring an actor to recite the lines to him

39. According to the passage, all of the following were involved in the publishing of the First Folio EXCEPT:

    (A) Edward Blount

    (B) Henry Condell

    (C) William Jaggard

    (D) John Danter

40. Where can the following sentence best be added to the passage?

    They sold quickly to a public anxious to have accurate copies of the master dramatist's plays.

    (A) At the end of paragraph 1

    (B) After the word "formality" in paragraph 2

    (C) After the word "performance" in paragraph 3

    (D) After the phrase "William's son" in paragraph 4

QUESTIONS 41–50 REFER TO THE FOLLOWING PASSAGE.

Steamboats were shallow-draft boats propelled by steam-driven paddle wheels. In the nineteenth century, they could be seen every day on rivers, par-
(5) ticularly on the Mississippi River and its principal tributaries in the United States.

The development of the steamboat as a practical means of transportation began
(10) in America in 1787, but it wasn't until 1811 that a steamboat was built specifically to travel along the lower Mississippi River. The boat, called appropriately the *New Orleans*, was built at
(15) Pittsburgh, Pa., for Robert Fulton and Robert R. Livingston. In 1812, the two men began operating a regular steamboat service between New Orleans and Natchez, Mississippi. Their vessels trav-
(20) eled at eight miles per hour downstream and three upstream.

In 1816, Henry Miller Shreve launched his steamboat *Washington*, and soon became known as the father of Missis-
(25) sippi navigation, because he adapted steamboat design to fit the shallow waters of the river. He installed the engine high up above the water line and mounted it on a hull that was as shallow
(30) as that of a barge. He also added a tall second deck, and afterwards all Mississippi steamboats copied Shreve's design. From then on and until about 1870, the steamboat dominated the economy, ag-
(35) riculture, and commerce of the middle area of the United States.

By 1834, there were 1,200 steamboats, carrying not only cotton and sugar, but also passengers who enjoyed luxuriously
(40) appointed lounges with rich rugs, oil paintings, and chandeliers. Many steamboats were famous for their chefs, orchestras, and large staffs of maids and butlers to assist their cabin passengers.
(45) Steamboat pilots had to memorize or guess at the depths of the river and its potential obstacles along long stretches of river in order to navigate safely. The average life span of a steamboat was
(50) only four to five years, because most of the vessels were poorly constructed and maintained. They sank after hitting sand bars and hidden rocks in the river, and many of their boilers exploded, causing
(55) many deaths among their passengers. By the 1870s, railroads had become more efficient modes of transport and gradually caused the retirement of almost all the steamboats from the river.

41. In the passage, it is implied that steamboats were used mainly

(A) in New Orleans

(B) in Washington, D.C.

(C) along the Hudson River

(D) in the Mississippi River valley

42. Which of the following is closest in meaning to the word "tributaries" as used in line 6 of the passage?

(A) A party honoring a famous person

(B) A stream that flows into another

(C) A three-wheeled vehicle

(D) A state that has a border on three other states

43. According to the passage, in what year were steamboats operating regularly on the Mississippi?

(A) 1810

(B) 1811

(C) 1812

(D) 1813

44. Which of the following does the phrase "means of transportation" as used in line 9 refer to?

(A) Steamboat

(B) America

(C) Built specifically

(D) Travel

45. According to the passage, how fast did the *New Orleans* travel downstream between New Orleans and Natchez?

    (A) 3 miles per hour

    (B) 8 miles per hour

    (C) 13 miles per hour

    (D) 18 miles per hour

46. According to the passage why was Henry Shreve called the "father of Mississippi navigation"?

    (A) He designed a steering mechanism that other steamboats used.

    (B) He was born and raised in a small village on the banks of the Mississippi.

    (C) He printed maps for the steamboat captains and pilots.

    (D) He adapted steamboat design to fit the shallow waters of the river.

47. Which of the following is the closest in meaning to the phrase "from then on" as used in line 33 in the passage?

    (A) Subsequently

    (B) Consequently

    (C) Apparently

    (D) Thoroughly

48. According to the passage, after the 1830s, steamboats had all of the following EXCEPT:

    (A) Orchestras

    (B) Chefs and maids

    (C) Chandeliers

    (D) Air conditioning

49. According to the passage, how long did the average steamboat remain afloat?

    (A) Two to three years

    (B) Three to four years

    (C) Four to five years

    (D) Five to six years

50. Where can the following sentence best be added to the passage?

    Mark Twain, a steamboat pilot who became one of America's greatest writers, told about his brother's death in a steamboat explosion in his book *Life on the Mississippi*.

    (A) After the words "Mississippi River" in paragraph 2

    (B) After the phrase "Shreve's design" in paragraph 3

    (C) After the word "chandeliers" in paragraph 4

    (D) After the phrase "their passengers" in paragraph 5

ANSWER KEY AND EXPLANATIONS

1.	A	11.	B	21.	C	31.	C	41.	D
2.	B	12.	C	22.	B	32.	B	42.	B
3.	A	13.	B	23.	B	33.	C	43.	C
4.	B	14.	B	24.	A	34.	B	44.	D
5.	C	15.	D	25.	D	35.	A	45.	B
6.	D	16.	C	26.	A	36.	A	46.	D
7.	B	17.	B	27.	D	37.	B	47.	A
8.	A	18.	A	28.	C	38.	C	48.	D
9.	A	19.	B	29.	B	39.	D	49.	C
10.	B	20.	A	30.	A	40.	D	50.	D

1. **The correct answer is (A).** The other choices are incorrect definitions.

2. **The correct answer is (B).** The answer is stated in the first paragraph.

3. **The correct answer is (A).** The other answer choices do not relate to the meaning of the word.

4. **The correct answer is (B).** The answer is stated in the second paragraph.

5. **The correct answer is (C).** The answer is stated in the second paragraph.

6. **The correct answer is (D).** Choice (D) can be inferred from the final two sentences in the passage. There is nothing in the passage to indicate the educational level of cabildos, so choice (A) cannot be inferred. The work of cabildos was important, so there is no basis to consider that only "some" cabildos were important. Choice (C) is directly stated in the third paragraph.

7. **The correct answer is (B).** A police officer keeps the peace.

8. **The correct answer is (A).** Only choice (A) makes sense and is general enough in the context of the sentence. Choice (B) does not make sense. Choices (C) and (D) are only two of the various responsibilities that cabildos might be in charge of.

9. **The correct answer is (A).** It is NOT true. Sentence 2 in the fourth paragraph disproves this answer.

10. **The correct answer is (B).** Paragraph 2 describes the functioning of cabildos, so it is the best place to add a sentence that provides more details about this aspect. Choice (A), paragraph 1, discusses the background of cabildos, not their functions. Inserting the sentence into paragraphs 3 or 4 would interrupt the flow of ideas in either paragraph.

11. **The correct answer is (B).** *Fascinating* means to hold the attention of someone by being interesting. *Fabulous* means hard to believe or incredible. Neither choices (A) or (D) are correct definitions.

12. **The correct answer is (C).** The answer is stated in the first paragraph.

13. **The correct answer is (B).**

14. **The correct answer is (B).** Omit the phrase "according to legend" and it is easier to see that the antecedent is *game*.

15. **The correct answer is (D).** Sentence 2 of the first paragraph states that Oakley

was born in 1860. The final sentence in the paragraph states both that she was 15 when she worked with Butler and that she married him a year later. Add 15 plus 1 to find that she was 16 when she married Butler. Sixteen plus 1860 equals 1876 when they married.

16. **The correct answer is (C).** It is not true. Choice (A) can be inferred from the third paragraph. Choice (B) is stated in the first paragraph. Choice (D) is stated in the second paragraph.

17. **The correct answer is (B).** Substitute the answers into the sentence and answer (B) makes the most sense in context.

18. **The correct answer is (A).** The sentence sums up Oakley's life. If it were inserted in any of the other choices, it would not make sense because it would interrupt the description of what she did in her life.

19. **The correct answer is (B).** The answer is stated in the fourth paragraph.

20. **The correct answer is (A).** There is no information in the passage to support either choices (B) or (D). Choice (C) is contradicted in the fourth paragraph.

21. **The correct answer is (C).** Only choice (C) includes both Eagan's education and athletic ability. Choice (A) is not supported by information in the passage. Choices (B) and (D) are misreadings of the passage.

22. **The correct answer is (B).** The answer is stated in the second paragraph.

23. **The correct answer is (B).** The answer is stated in the first paragraph.

24. **The correct answer is (A).** Eliminate choice (D) immediately because Eagan served in World War I.

25. **The correct answer is (D).** It is NOT true. Paragraph 3 states that Eagan did not win this medal.

26. **The correct answer is (A).** The answer is stated in the third paragraph.

27. **The correct answer is (D).** Adding the sentence to the end of paragraph 4 picks up and adds to the information in the preceding sentence. There is no reference to athletics in the first paragraph, so adding the sentence there makes no sense. The sentence would interrupt the sense of the paragraphs if added where either choice (B) or (C) indicate.

28. **The correct answer is (C).** The answer is stated at the end of the sentence.

29. **The correct answer is (B).** The answer is stated in the fourth paragraph.

30. **The correct answer is (A).** The answer is stated in the first sentence of the fourth paragraph.

31. **The correct answer is (C).** The First Folio had twice as many plays as had been printed previously and the inclusion of the two actors in the publishing team implies that good texts were used. Choice (B) is stated in the first paragraph and the question asks for an inference. There is no information to support either choices (A) or (D).

32. **The correct answer is (B).** The other answer choices are incorrect definitions.

33. **The correct answer is (C).** Statements in the second and third paragraphs support this answer.

34. **The correct answer is (B).** The other answer choices are incorrect.

35. **The correct answer is (A).** The answer is stated in the final sentence of the second paragraph.

36. **The correct answer is (A).** To publish means to issue books, whereas to print means to imprint letters onto paper. **[Very fine distinction and difficult for an ELL person to figure out from the context which uses both *publish* and *print* in the same sentence.]**

37. **The correct answer is (B).** The answer is stated in the third paragraph.

38. **The correct answer is (C).** The answer is supported by sentence 1 of the third paragraph.

39. **The correct answer is (D).** It is NOT true. Paragraph 4 supports this answer as being not true, but correct.

40. **The correct answer is (D).** The word "they" is a clue to the best place to insert this sentence. The antecedent for choice (A) is "folio edition," which is singular. The antecedent for choice (B) is singular, "formality," which also does not make sense. The antecedent for choice (C) is *Romeo and Juliet,* which is also singular. Only choice (D) provides a plural antecedent "1,000 copies" and also makes sense.

41. **The correct answer is (D).** The first paragraph supports this inference. Also, mention is not made in the passage of the other areas.

42. **The correct answer is (B).** The other answer choices use some form of the word *tributary,* but only choice (B) is correct. Choice (A) refers to tribute, choice (C) refers to tricycle, and choice (D) refers to tri-state.

43. **The correct answer is (C).** The reference in lines 17–18 to "regular steamboat service" supports this answer.

44. **The correct answer is (D).** Substitute the answer choices into the sentence and the only one that makes sense is choice (D).

45. **The correct answer is (B).** The answer is stated in the second paragraph.

46. **The correct answer is (D).** The answer is stated in the third paragraph.

47. **The correct answer is (A).** The other answer choices do not make sense.

48. **The correct answer is (D).** It is NOT true. The other answer choices are supported by information in paragraph 3.

49. **The correct answer is (C).** The answer is supported by the phrase "average life span of a steamboat" in line 49.

50. **The correct answer is (D).** Adding the sentence as indicated in choices (A), (B), and (C) would interrupt the flow of thought. Choice (D) inserts the sentence as an example to illustrate the detail about explosions on steamboats.

answers diagnostic test

PART III

TOEFL READING REVIEW

CHAPTER 3 Developing Reading
Comprehension Skills

Developing Reading
Comprehension Skills

OVERVIEW

- Finding main ideas and supporting details
- Skimming for specific information
- Making inferences
- Understanding advertisements
- How thoughts are related
- Understanding contemporary reading passages
- Reading history textbooks
- Summing it up

FINDING MAIN IDEAS AND SUPPORTING DETAILS

The most valuable reading comprehension skill is probably the ability to determine the most important thing an author is saying. Read the following paragraph to see if you can distinguish between essential and nonessential information and between the *main idea* and the *supporting details*.

Sample Reading Passage 1

Left-handed people suffer more from stress than their right-handed peers, according to a study of 1,100 adults by University of Michigan researchers. As a result, they smoke and drink more. Fifty-five percent of the lefties
(5)   smoked, whereas fewer than half of the righties smoked. Furthermore, the lefties consumed more alcohol per year than their right-handed counterparts.

The main idea is _____

_____

Notice that in this paragraph, it was the first sentence that told you the main idea. This sentence, called a "topic sentence," usually appears at the beginning. Sometimes, however, the paragraph's main idea is expressed in the last sentence, and sometimes readers must determine the main idea of a paragraph by summarizing the author's message themselves.

chapter 3

Answer

The main idea of the passage is that left-handed people suffer more from stress than right-handed people.

> **Directions:** Underline the main idea and circle the supporting details as you read the paragraph below. Then write them in note form in the space provided.

Sample Reading Passage 2

You ought to know what to do to help a person who is choking. First, you stand behind the choking victim and put your arms around his or her waist. Second, you make a fist and place the thumb side against the person's stomach just above the navel, *(5)* but below the ribs. Third, grasp your fist with your other hand and press into the victim's abdomen with a quick upward thrust. Repeat this action if necessary.

Main idea: _____

_____

Supporting details:

(A) _____

(B) _____

(C) _____

(D) _____

Answer

Main idea: You should know how to help a person who is choking. Supporting details:

(A) Stand behind the victim and put your arms around his or her waist.

(B) Make a fist and place the thumb side against the person's stomach.

(C) Grasp your fist with your other hand and press into the abdomen with a quick upward thrust.

(D) Repeat if necessary.

> **Directions:** Now, read the following paragraph to determine what the main idea means to a passage.

Sample Reading Passage 3

What's the best way for you, as an employer, to deliver bad news to an employee? First of all, you have to break the news yourself, face to face with the recipient. You can't write memos to tell people they will not get raises this year or that they have *(5)* made an error or are not performing as well as expected. You have to show them how you feel about the matter and that you are personally sorry and sympathize with them. If you indicate that you are ready to listen to their reactions to your bad news, you will undoubtedly save yourself from their wrath. Above all, *(10)* you must be ready for an emotional reaction from the recipient of bad news. Give people time to digest your news and to control the emotion they invariably feel. Although it is never easy to break bad news, if you follow these steps, you will at least soften the blow.

1. The author's main idea is that
   (A) bad news is hard to impart
   (B) all employers have to criticize their employees
   (C) there are ways of softening the impact of bad news
   (D) people respond emotionally to bad news

2. Where is the main idea expressed?
   (A) In the first sentence
   (B) In the last sentence
   (C) In the middle of the paragraph
   (D) Nowhere

3. The main idea is supported by
   (A) examples of employers giving bad news
   (B) a list of reasons for having to break bad news
   (C) sympathy for both the employer and employee
   (D) instructions on how to soften the blow of bad news

Answers

1. **The correct answer is (C).**

2. **The correct answer is (B).**

3. **The correct answer is (D).**

In addition to finding the main idea and supporting details in a reading passage, it is also important to understand an author's intent or purpose. When you read *critically*, you must:

- Understand what the author is saying
- Distinguish fact from opinion
- Determine the author's attitude toward the topic

> **Directions:** Read the paragraphs that follow. Then answer the questions about the author's intent and attitude.

Sample Reading Passage 4

Yogurt has as much nutritional value as a glass of milk, yet dieters and health food fanatics claim that yogurt will prolong your life and reduce your girth. Their claims are backed by reports that yogurt eaters over the years have lived longer and (5) healthier lives than non-yogurt eaters. However, what proof is there that rural life and its ensuing greater physical activity rather than consumption of yogurt are not the cause of these people's longevity?

1. The author's intent is to show that
   - **(A)** yogurt is good for your health
   - **(B)** eating yogurt will prolong your life
   - **(C)** yogurt is the same as milk
   - **(D)** there is no proof that yogurt increases longevity

2. The paragraph advises the reader that
   - **(A)** yogurt will help a person to live to be 100
   - **(B)** the author has little faith in yogurt lovers' claims
   - **(C)** yogurt may be harmful to dieters and health food lovers
   - **(D)** people in rural areas eat a lot of yogurt

Answers

1. **The correct answer is (D).**
2. **The correct answer is (B).**

Sample Reading Passage 5

Most of us believe that the death of a spouse often leads to the premature death of the bereft partner. After twelve years of study involving 4,000 widows and widowers, Johns Hopkins University researchers have perceived that it is the husbands, (5) and not the wives, whose lives are shortened by the loss of their spouses. However, the study indicates that widowers who remarry enjoy greater longevity than men the same age who continue to live with their first wives.

1. The main idea is that
   - **(A)** men live longer than their wives
   - **(B)** widowers live longer than single men
   - **(C)** remarriage after a spouse's death prolongs men's lives
   - **(D)** the death of a spouse shortens the life of the surviving partner

2. The author's intent is to

    (A) discuss a medical discovery

    (B) make a conjecture regarding death

    (C) correct a generally held misconception

    (D) advise widowers to live alone

Answers

1. **The correct answer is (C).**

2. **The correct answer is (C).**

SKIMMING FOR SPECIFIC INFORMATION

It is not always necessary to read every word of a passage. Your purpose for reading something determines how closely you should read it. Once you know what your purpose is, *skimming* is a valuable procedure. Skimming through a passage involves reading very fast in order to recognize main ideas and supporting details while skipping (not reading) parts that are not relevant to your reading purpose. Although skimming should never replace careful reading, it can save you time in deciding what or what not to read, in getting the general content of a passage, and in finding the author's main point without having to deal with details. You read the morning newspaper, for example, quite differently from the way you read a detective story, an assignment for a class, or a letter from a friend. Skimming to find a specific piece of information such as a number or the answer to a question is often called *scanning*.

The readings you will encounter in the next few pages are the kinds of things you are likely to find in a newspaper. News items are usually set up in such a way that each sentence is its own paragraph; they normally follow the pattern *who, what, where, when, why*.

> **Directions:** Scan the following paragraphs for information about who, what, where, when, and why.

Sample Reading Passage 6

  A. Mexican conservationists are wondering how to get rid of killer piranhas that were found yesterday in a lake near Puebla.

    Who _____

    What _____

    Where _____

    When _____

    Why _____

B. The Commodities Futures Trading Commission today designated four commodities exchanges to trade options on futures contracts, as part of a three-year pilot program beginning October 1.

Who _____

What _____

Where _____

When _____

Why _____

C. On October 14, workers at the Lenin shipyard in the Baltic seaport of Gdansk put down their tools in protest against poor working conditions.

Who _____

What _____

Where _____

When _____

Why _____

NOTE

Titles are often useful indicators of what the article is about.

Answers

A. Mexican conservationists are wondering how to get rid of killer piranhas that were found yesterday in a lake near Puebla.

Who Mexican conservationists

What trying to get rid of piranhas

Where in a lake near Puebla

When yesterday

Why killers

B. The Commodities Futures Trading Commission today designated four commodities exchanges to trade options on futures contracts, as part of a three-year pilot program beginning October 1.

Who the Commodities Future Trading Commission

What designated for commodities exchanges

Where information not given

When today

Why to trade options on Futures' contracts

C. On October 14, workers at the Lenin shipyard in the Baltic seaport of Gdansk put down their tools in protest against poor working conditions.

Who workers

What put down their tools

Where in Baltic seaport of Gdansk

When October 14

Why to protest against poor working conditions

When you have found the *who, what, where, when,* and *why* information in the beginning of a news story, decide whether or not to continue reading. If you do read the rest of the article, skim it by skipping to places where words are capitalized or where there are numbers, or to any points that particularly interest you. Most importantly, don't get lost in all the words; practice reading only what you need to read within a selection.

MAKING INFERENCES

There are two basic kinds of reading comprehension.

1. When you are able to use the author's words to answer a comprehension question, it is your *factual comprehension* that is being tested.

2. Sometimes, however, the information is not directly stated, so you must infer a meaning using your own reasoning and logic. This type of understanding is sometimes referred to as *inferential comprehension*.

Imagine that you are at a friend's house. It is 11:00 p.m. and your host starts to look at his watch and yawn out loud. Although he never actually tells you to leave, he implies and you infer that it is time for you to go home.

Daily newspapers publish advice columns for everything from successful vegetable gardening to curing yourself of high blood pressure. The following passage answers questions about car problems.

> **Directions:** Read the following passage and answer the questions that follow.

Sample Reading Passage 7

    Q. My engine cranks all right. But why won't it start up?

    A. Think twice. Are you following the exact starting procedure given in your owner's manual? Next, pin down the trouble area by checking these possibilities: (1) gasoline, (2) spark, and (3) air-gasoline ratio.

(5)   1. First make sure you have gasoline in the tank. If that's not the problem, maybe you have flooded the engine. Hold the gas pedal to the floor for 10 seconds (do not pump it) as you crank the engine.

    Still no start? Maybe the problem is a stuck needle valve. Tap the carburetor bowl lightly near the gas line, using pliers or a screwdriver handle. This should free the

(10)   valve so you can start. But if nothing has done the trick so far, move to the next step.

    2. Check to see if the engine is getting the spark it needs to start. First look for loose or broken spark plug wires. Fix what you can.

    If the wires look all right, make a detailed check for a spark. Twist one spark plug boot away from its plug. Push an insulated screwdriver into the boot.

(15)   Hold the shank of the screwdriver about $\frac{1}{8}$ inch away from a metal engine part. Have someone crank the engine. (Be sure you keep your hands away from the

screwdriver shank and the wire to avoid shock.) You'll see a small spark if the ignition system is working. No spark? Get help. (Caution: If there is any gasoline *on* the engine, be sure you let it evaporate before you try this test.) If you see a

(20)   spark, you have eliminated that as a possibility. Move on to the next step.

3. Finally, find out if the carburetor is feeding sufficient air and gasoline to the engine. Remove the top of the air cleaner so you can see the choke plate. If the plate is stuck open, push it shut (only if the engine is cold) and try to start again. Still no start? Hold the choke wide open and peer deep inside as someone else

(25)   pumps the gas pedal. (Make sure he doesn't crank the engine.) If you can't see gas squirting, you need professional help.

1. This type of passage can be described as
    (A) scientific reading
    (B) a "how-to" article
    (C) editorial writing
    (D) automobile advertising

2. The author's intent in this article is to
    (A) explain why cars break down
    (B) warn you about the dangers involved in do-it-yourself car repairs
    (C) describe the method of checking spark plugs
    (D) instruct you how to deal with a car problem

3. From the context of the word *crank* (line 16) it must mean
    (A) complain
    (B) start
    (C) turn around
    (D) shut off

4. List briefly the steps involved in checking the starting mechanism.
    (A) _____
    (B) _____
    (C) _____
    (D) _____

5. If you check for a spark and don't get one, what should you do?
    (A) Check the carburetor next.
    (B) Get an auto mechanic.
    (C) Clean the gas off the motor.
    (D) Get a shock.

6. What is the first thing to do when your car doesn't start?
   (A) Check your gas.
   (B) Flood the engine.
   (C) Contact your automobile salesperson.
   (D) Be sure you're following the rules for starting the car.

7. If you are testing for a spark, gas on the engine is dangerous
   (A) because it might start the car
   (B) when it has evaporated
   (C) after it leaks out of the carburetor
   (D) because the spark might ignite the gas

8. You should use an insulated screwdriver to
   (A) protect the engine
   (B) avoid scratching the metal
   (C) avoid getting a shock
   (D) twist the spark plug boot

9. You can unstick a valve by
   (A) taking it out
   (B) hitting it
   (C) loosening it
   (D) twisting it

10. You have to hold the screwdriver shank away from metal to
    (A) prevent fire
    (B) avoid cutting yourself
    (C) avoid getting a shock
    (D) check for a bad spark plug

11. Presumably a spark plug *boot* (line 14) is a
    (A) covering
    (B) shoe
    (C) trunk
    (D) plug

12. It can be inferred that a carburetor
    (A) is connected to the spark plugs
    (B) cranks the engine
    (C) regulates gas and air flow
    (D) has an open plate

13. If the engine is cold, it is all right to
    (A) try to start the car
    (B) close the choke plate
    (C) take off the air cleaner
    (D) pump the gas pedal

14. The choke plate is
    (A) next to the gas tank
    (B) above the air cleaner
    (C) beneath the air cleaner
    (D) inside the spark plugs

15. Do you think a person with no understanding of the mechanism of a car could follow these instructions?

    Why or why not? _____

    _____

Answers

1. **The correct answer is (B).**

2. **The correct answer is (D).**

3. **The correct answer is (C).**

4. (A) Make sure you have gasoline.

   (B) Check the valves.

   (C) See if the engine is getting a spark. Check the spark plugs.

   (D) Find out if the carburetor is feeding enough air and gas to the engine.

5. **The correct answer is (B).**

6. **The correct answer is (D).**

7. **The correct answer is (D).**

8. **The correct answer is (C).**

9. **The correct answer is (B).**

10. **The correct answer is (C).**

11. **The correct answer is (A).**

12. **The correct answer is (C).**

13. **The correct answer is (B).**

14. **The correct answer is (C).**

15. **The correct answer is no**. The author assumes that the reader knows something about a car's mechanism.

Sample Reading Passage 8

Questions 1–10 refer to the following restaurant review.

> The Banyan Tree, 2 East Monopoly Street ☆
> A small sidewalk restaurant on a peaceful back street with a green and white striped awning, rattan chairs, and glass-topped tables. The menu is limited to exotic East Indian specialties, savory curries of all varieties being featured. Full luncheon comes to about $25. Open daily for lunch only.
>
> The Boathouse, 433 River Road ☆
> A delightful, convivial eating place decorated with sea urchin lamps, fishermen's nets, and seaweed wall coverings. Very informal atmosphere. A lighthouse bar. Specialties are, of course, seafood, my favorite being the *moules marinières* served in steaming black pots. A five-course dinner at $11. Open daily.
>
> Café Henri, 17 Lorraine Street ☆
> Soft lighting and muted decorator shades of beige and bronze give the dining room an intimate atmosphere. Basically French, the cuisine represents aromatic country fare, with rich, nutritious soups and assorted platters of sausages, patés, and cheeses. Wholesome fare at reasonable prices. Entrées $12.50 to $20.75.
>
> Little Old San Juan, 62 Fortaleza Boulevard ☆☆☆
> A cozy Spanish decor, enhanced by mellow, red clay floor tiles, wrought-iron street lanterns, and walls lined with rows of painted pottery, gives this 100-year-old landmark an aura of romantic old Spain. Gazpacho sprinkled with chopped onion, green pepper, rice and garlic croutons, and an irresistible array of Spanish dishes are exceptional. The paella laden with shell-fish is more than worth the 30-minute wait. Wines both fine and *ordinario* from the vineyards of Spain. Entrées from $20. Closed Sundays.
>
> No stars—Fair
> ☆ Good
> ☆☆ Very good
> ☆☆☆ Excellent
> ☆☆☆☆ Extraordinary

1. You may infer that this guide is
   (A) a paid-for advertisement
   (B) written by a restaurant critic
   (C) an introduction in a cookbook
   (D) None of the above.

2. The author's intent is to
   (A) describe gourmet restaurants
   (B) give the reader a price list for dining out
   (C) recommend good places to eat
   (D) warn people about restaurants

3. Which restaurant serves the least expensive meals? _____

4. Which restaurant is recommended most highly? _____

5. Which restaurant is the most expensive? _____

6. Where could you get Indian food? _____

7. Where would you go for shrimp au gratin? _____

8. Which restaurant would most likely have a guitarist? _____

9. Which restaurant sounds like a good place for lovers? _____

10. You would infer that these restaurants are
    (A) in the United States
    (B) in Europe
    (C) for the wealthy only
    (D) informal

Answers

1. **The correct answer is (B).**

2. **The correct answer is (C).**

3. **The correct answer is The Boathouse.**

4. **The correct answer is Little Old San Juan.**

5. **The correct answer is Little Old San Juan.**

6. **The correct answer is The Banyan Tree.**

7. **The correct answer is The Boathouse.**

8. **The correct answer is Little Old San Juan.**

9. **The correct answer is Café Henri.**

10. **The correct answer is (A).**

UNDERSTANDING ADVERTISEMENTS

1. List all the places you can think of where you see and hear advertisements for products and services.

    _____

    _____

    _____

    _____

    Did you name advertising billboards and posters? Where might you see them?

    _____

    _____

2. Do you have a favorite television commercial? Why do you like it?

    _____

    Is there a commercial that you particularly dislike? What is it that bothers you about the commercial?

    _____

    Make a list of at least three features that you consider necessary for a good television commercial.

    _____

    _____

    _____

Writers of advertising copy are amateur psychologists. They know just what will appeal to our instincts and emotions. In general, there are three major areas in our nature at which advertising aims—preservation, pride, and pleasure. Preservation, for example, relates to our innate desire to live longer, know more, and look better. Pride encompasses all sorts of things—our desire to show off, to brag about our prosperity or our good taste, to be one of the élite. We all want to enjoy the fruits of our labors, and this is where the pleasure principle comes in. We want to be entertained, to eat and drink well, and to relax in comfortable surroundings.

As you read the following advertisement from the 1980s, look for the means, both *overt* and *subtle*, employed to sell an expensive car.

A CAR SO SWIFT, SILENT
AND LUXURIOUS, THAT IT IS, IN EVERY SENSE . . .
BEYOND COMPARISON

This car stands alone as a class of one. It is, to begin with, the only V-12 powered motorcar for sale in America. Car and Driver described the engine this way: "Its turbinelike smoothness and awesome torque simply set it apart from everything that might attempt to compete, even at half again the price.

The dramatically powerful engine is teamed with sports car engineering. Power rack and pinion steering is quick and precise. Four wheel independent suspension maintains balance and stability. And four wheel power disc brakes are both smooth and decisive.

The inner world offers an experience of luxury on a level that few drivers will ever know. From the exotic burled elm veneers that enhance the dashboard and doors to the supple hides that cover virtually all of the passenger compartment, opulence is everywhere. Electronic conveniences pamper you: self adjusting heating and air conditioning; power window, doorlocks and antenna; cruise control and a stereo with signal scanning tuner are all standard.

Standard too is the best warranty we have ever offered. For two years or 36,000 miles, whichever comes first, we will replace or repair any part which proves defective. The tires are covered by the tire manufacturer's warranty. Your dealer has full details on the limited warranty.

Now look back at the advertisement and use note form to fill in the specific things offered to the purchaser of this car.

_____

_____

_____

_____

_____

_____

_____

1. Show others your wealth.
2. Show your good taste.
3. Get a quality product.
4. Save money.
5. Look beautiful.
6. Be comfortable.
7. Enjoy entertainment.

Advertisements for exotic places to go on your vacation are very different from ads for luxury cars. They must appeal to another side of your nature. After reading the following ad by the Jamaica Tourist Board, answer the questions.

Sample Reading Passage 9

Questions 1–2 refer to the following advertisement.

JAMAICA

There's no place like home.

Here's you, at home in Jamaica in your very own villa, all pastels and privacy.
With Evangeline to pamper you: she's going shopping soon, to
surprise you with a lobster for dinner. Madly extravagant? Not at all.
There are hundreds of villas for rent, all over Jamaica.
Bring your family, or share one with your best friends, and the cost becomes
insidiously attractive. And what nicer way to experience the bountiful wonders of
Jamaica than to have your own special place to return to each evening,
where you can sit back with a rum punch, talk about tomorrow,
and say to yourself, "There's no place like home."
Make it Jamaica. Again.

Courtesy of the Jamaica Tourist Board

1. The ad implies that you
   (A) require entertainment by well-known singers
   (B) enjoy sightseeing in foreign places
   (C) don't want to spend a lot of money
   (D) need a lot of excitement on your vacation

2. The ad appeals to your need for
   (A) quiet pleasure
   (B) delicious food
   (C) relaxation
   (D) All of the above.

Answers

1. The correct answer is (C).
2. The correct answer is (D).

Sample Reading Passage 10

Questions 1–5 refer to the following advertisement.

ONCE-A-YEAR SUMMER SALE!
SAVE $100 OR MORE!

This month only, every membership plan is substantially reduced. That's great! But the real excitement at HRC comes from what people do.

Nautilus
Ours is the most complete and advanced equipment available.

Free Classes
We offer over 120 free classes each week including aerobic and tap dance, calisthenics, yoga and more. You'll also enjoy free clinics in racquetball, squash and tennis. Don't forget about our whirlpools, saunas and swimming pools either.

Guarantee
Come to HRC for 3 days. If all that action leaves you less than satisfied you'll get a full refund.

5 Locations
By the way, your membership allows you to use all 5 locations in Manhattan 7 days a week.

Give us a call or drop by for more information.

Sale Ends Aug. 31st!

NEW YORK HEALTH & RACQUET CLUB

Courtesy of the New York Health & Racquet Club

1. The advertisement emphasizes
    (A) locations
    (B) a trial membership
    (C) reduced cost
    (D) opening hours

2. It can be inferred that if you join the club
    (A) the sale ends on August 31
    (B) you will go to all five club locations
    (C) your body will improve
    (D) you will get a refund

3. This ad appeals to people's
    (A) pleasure
    (B) pride
    (C) preservation
    (D) All of the above.

4. From the context of the expression *free clinics*, it must mean
    (A) cost-free medical care
    (B) no charge for lessons
    (C) liberated movement
    (D) games

5. Membership in the club enables you to enjoy _____ in winter.
    (A) the cold
    (B) a full refund
    (C) dropping by
    (D) swimming

Answers

1. **The correct answer is (C).**
2. **The correct answer is (C).**
3. **The correct answer is (D).**
4. **The correct answer is (B).**
5. **The correct answer is (D).**

EXERCISES: READING COMPREHENSION SKILLS

Directions: The passages are followed by questions based on their content. Answer the questions on the basis of what is *stated* or *implied* in the passages.

QUESTIONS 1–5 ARE BASED ON THE FOLLOWING PASSAGE.

The business of tennis clothes has grown astoundingly in the past few years. Over $250 million is spent annually on the trappings of tennis. Apparently ev-
(5) eryone wants to look like a pro, even though 20% of the clientele has never even played the game.

Manufacturers pay the stars lucrative fees for wearing their brands of clothes
(10) and wielding their racquets on center court. Chris Evert-Lloyd, for example, was rumored to have signed a five-year contract for $5 million with Ellesse, a producer of fancy, expensive tennis wear.
(15) John McEnroe received a reported $600,000 for playing with a Dunlop racquet, $330,000 for sporting Tacchini clothes, and $100,000 for tying his Nike tennis shoes. Obviously, in a bad year,
(20) these stars would have made more as fashion models than as athletes.

Not only tennis players get free clothing, but also all the people involved in the game—the referees, linespeople, ball
(25) boys and girls—are living advertisements for tennis wear producers. Where, traditionally, conservative white clothing was required for the entire tennis coterie, changing times have seen a new vogue
(30) in tennis outfits. Flamboyant colors, designers' nameplates, geometric figures, and bold lines distinguish the new tennis togs from their predecessors.

1. It can be inferred from the passage that
   (A) tennis clothing appeals to the wealthy
   (B) tennis stars get huge sums for endorsements
   (C) the price of tennis racquets has remained stable
   (D) bright colors entice people to buy tennis wear

2. The author's intention is to
   (A) explain why the cost of tennis clothes has risen
   (B) defend tennis wear manufacturers from complaints about their high prices
   (C) describe the means of advertising expensive tennis clothes
   (D) describe the new tennis clothing

3. A good title for this passage would be
   (A) The Stars at Play
   (B) Big Business in Tennis Wear
   (C) The High Cost of Playing Tennis
   (D) Tennis Stars' Flamboyant Clothes

4. It is stated that John McEnroe
   (A) wore flamboyant clothing on the court
   (B) must have earned over $1 million for endorsing tennis products
   (C) was a fashion model more than he was a tennis player
   (D) had had a bad year in tennis competition

5. It is implied that
   (A) tennis clothing is bought by the well-to-do
   (B) everyone who wears expensive tennis wear plays tennis
   (C) tennis officials would prefer to wear traditional white clothing
   (D) fashion models wear tennis clothing

The oil embargoes of 1973–1975 caused vast chagrin among the manufacturers of automobiles around the world. In particular, American companies were (5) obliged to create innovations in producing small cars that would compete in the market with those flowing into the American market from Japan and Europe. No longer could Americans afford (10) ostentatious, gas-guzzling vehicles.

Of paramount importance to today's car owner is the cost of gasoline. American manufacturers have collaborated to supply their clientele with small cars (15) that provide the amenities of the stereotyped large American car, yet get better mileage than any other car in the history of American car production. It has become a question of ardently compet-(20) ing with foreign car manufacturers or succumbing to the intense competition and losing a lucrative business through apathy. The American car industry has been rejuvenated. The fuel consumption (25) of the new cars has decreased by 49% since 1977; mileage has risen from an average 17.2 miles per gallon to 25.6 miles per gallon. These figures are indicative of a major turnaround in engi-(30) neering, manufacturing, and design. The industry has made pertinent use of the computer by installing a microprocessor, a thin piece of silicon about the size of an aspirin, in new cars. This minia-(35) ture computer measures engine speed, engine load, and other functions, and sends messages to the fuel system and other parts of the car's mechanism, thus producing lower gas consumption and (40) cleaner exhaust.

By designing sleek, roomy, beautiful, sporty models, the automobile industry has enticed both the average-income and the affluent car buyer into purchasing (45) small cars. In addition to saving on gas, today's car is built to save on maintenance and repair expenses. Furthermore, the manufacturer is including the costs of maintenance in the buyer's pur-(50) chase price. New car advertisers now claim that all the buyer has to pay for is gas. To fight corrosion, new coatings have been developed that protect against the havoc caused by road salts, gravel, (55) and other materials. Hence, when car owners are ready to turn in last year's car for a new one, they will find that their well-preserved used cars will have an unusually high trade-in value.

(60) Fuel efficient, safe, emission free, economical, and beautiful, today's cars are better bargains than any ever produced before.

6. What significance did oil embargoes have in the automobile industry?

   (A) Car manufacturers worldwide had to produce fuel-efficient automobiles.

   (B) Automobile manufacturers had to make smaller cars.

   (C) The Japanese exported cars to America.

   (D) Americans continued to drive American cars.

7. In the second paragraph, there is a statement that implies that

   (A) Americans love large cars

   (B) American auto manufacturers had been indifferent to the need for smaller cars

   (C) Americans will not buy uncomfortable small cars

   (D) All of the above.

8. The microprocessor is

   (A) responsible for the American car industry's rejuvenation

   (B) a major turnaround in American car manufacturing

   (C) a computer that saves gas and helps create cleaner emission

   (D) a pertinent use of fuel consumption

9. According to the passage, small American cars are being bought

    (A) by middle-class and rich clientele

    (B) because they save fuel

    (C) because of inflation

    (D) by Americans who want to help American business

10. According to the passage, new cars are a better bargain than those manufactured in years past because they

    (A) cost less to run and are built to last longer

    (B) have a built-in computer

    (C) save fuel, have more safety features, cost less to maintain, and have a higher trade-in value

    (D) are a lot smaller and don't rust because of better coatings

11. From the information given in the reading, you can infer that anticorrosive coatings will not only protect a new car's body, but also

    (A) make the car run better

    (B) increase the trade-in value of the car

    (C) increase the car's mileage

    (D) make the car safer to drive

12. From the passage you can infer that

    (A) new cars are fuel efficient, sleek, and beautiful

    (B) Americans want their cars to be both beautiful and practical in terms of comfort and cost

    (C) Americans will continue to buy European and Japanese cars because they are cheaper

    (D) if oil becomes plentiful and cheap again, Americans will not return to buying large cars

13. Another inference from the article is that

    (A) the most important consideration in buying a car is the cost of gas

    (B) gas shortages caused American manufacturers to change their production methods

    (C) today's cars are more sensible buys than those in the past

    (D) large cars are more comfortable than small cars

ANSWER KEY

1.	B	6.	A	11.	B
2.	C	7.	D	12.	B
3.	B	8.	C	13.	C
4.	B	9.	A		
5.	A	10.	C		

answers exercises

HOW THOUGHTS ARE RELATED

In the preceding section, we talked about various aspects of reading comprehension: finding the main idea and supporting details, getting meaning from context, determining the author's intent or purpose, scanning for specific information, and vocabulary building through knowledge of common word elements and recognition of synonyms. Besides providing you with a thorough review, this section of readings will concentrate on thought relations within sentences, paragraphs, and longer passages. It is important to be able to recognize and understand signal words or *connectives*, which introduce, connect, order, and relate individual ideas to larger and often more general concepts.

Study these connectives, paying close attention to their function.

Connectives	Function
and, also, as well as, besides, finally, furthermore, in addition to, in conclusion, moreover	more information will follow
examples, for example, kinds, types, sorts, ordinal numbers (1, 2, 3, etc.), others, several, some, such as, the following, ways	examples will follow
even if, however, in spite of, instead of, nevertheless, on the other hand, rather, still, yet, despite	an opposite idea will follow
all but, except	exceptions will follow
as a result of, because, due to, in order to, on account of, since	cause
as a consequence, as a result, consequently, so, so as to, so that, therefore	effect
after, as soon as, before, if, provided that, should, while, without, unless, until, following	conditions to be met
as, before. . .after, like some. . .other, than, once. . .now	comparison

Look at the following example. Note that the connectives are underlined and the ideas connected are boxed. Can you determine the function of each connective? If necessary, refer back to the table.

> Mr. Green had sent his secretary to pick up his car, which he had taken to the garage <u>in order to</u> have the brakes repaired. While returning with Mr. Green's car, the secretary, driving on Main Street, entered the intersection at Elm after the light changed from green to red. She sounded her horn <u>but nevertheless</u> collided with a car that had entered the intersection from Elm Street after the light had turned green.

Directions: As you read the following passage, underline the signal words and box the related ideas. Then give the function of each. Answer the following questions about main ideas and supporting details.

Sample Reading Passage 11

When a death occurs, the family has religious, social, and legal responsibilities. If the deceased has left an explicit set of papers in an accessible file, arrangements will be much easier for the family to make. For example, such papers should include the deed for a burial plot (if there is one), a statement as to whether
(5) cremation or burial is desired, a copy of the birth certificate, and the names and addresses of all family members and friends who should be notified. Furthermore, the papers should include information on bank accounts, safe deposit boxes, and insurance policies, as well as the will. The person in charge of the funeral will need to know how much money is available in order to determine the expenses he or she
(10) may reasonably incur for the family.

If feasible, the person who makes the funeral arrangements should not be one of the bereaved. A melancholy widow may not be able to make objective decisions regarding expenses, such as for a coffin. Whoever makes the funeral arrangements realizes that he or she is deputized to make legally binding contracts with a funeral
(15) director and others, which will probably be honored some months later when funds from the estate are released.

One of the duties of the person in charge of the funeral is to prepare a death notice for the newspapers. Often the mortician arranges for the insertion of the notice. Included in the information should be the date of death, the names of the family
(20) members, and the time and place of the forthcoming interment.

1. The main idea of paragraph 1 is that
    (A) funerals are melancholy occasions
    (B) everybody should leave a will so that survivors will know how much property they inherit
    (C) everybody should put important papers together for his or her survivors
    (D) all friends and relatives of the deceased should be advised of the funeral arrangements

2. The supporting details of paragraph 1
    (A) give instructions about making funeral arrangements
    (B) specify the types of papers required to make funeral arrangements simpler
    (C) explain why a birth certificate is an important requisite for a death certificate
    (D) None of the above.

3. The main idea of paragraph 2 is
   (A) in the first sentence
   (B) implied
   (C) in the last sentence
   (D) not clearly stated

4. The supporting details in paragraph 2
   (A) tell why widows spend too much on funeral arrangements
   (B) explain the duties of a funeral director
   (C) emphasize the unpleasant nature of funeral arrangements
   (D) explain why a disinterested person should make funeral arrangements

5. What is the main idea of paragraph 3? Is it stated or implied?

   _____

   _____

6. List the supporting details of paragraph 3.
   (A) _____
   (B) _____
   (C) _____

Answers

1. The correct answer is (C).

2. The correct answer is (B).

3. The correct answer is (A).

4. The correct answer is (D).

5. The person in charge of the funeral should prepare a death notice for the newspapers. (It is stated.)

6.   (A) Information should include date of death.

   (B) Information should include names of the family members.

   (C) Information should include time and place of the interment.

Sample Reading Passage 12

Questions 1–10 are based on the following passage.

Divorce settlements attempt to make an equitable distribution of a couple's assets. Wrangles are common over who gets the car, the furniture, or the dog, but people overlook future needs and income. Two important issues will have to be decided by the courts. Can the divorced wife continue to have health coverage
(5) under her former husband's policy? Is the divorced wife entitled to a share of her ex-husband's pension?

So far the subject of health insurance has created much dissension. Most insurance companies exclude former wives from their definition of a worker's dependents. In order to circumvent his ex-wife's exclusion from his health plan, (10) many a husband has concealed his divorce from his employer. Divorced spouses of military men anticipate that a newly approved bill will allow them 180 days' medical coverage and continued coverage for serious ailments if they were married for at least 20 years during their husbands' service career.

Ex-wives are faring better in the pension-sharing dilemma than they are in (15) obtaining health coverage. The courts have set a precedent in awarding pension funds to divorced women, particularly if there are defaults in alimony and child-support payments. Nevertheless, the Employee Retirement Income Security Act prohibits the payment of a pension to anyone other than the worker. Litigation of ex-wives seeking a share in their former husbands' pensions contends that the (20) ERISA was passed for the purpose of protecting workers from creditors' attempts to attach pensions, not from their ex-wives. In a recent decision, the Supreme Court gave exclusive pension rights to the military retiree whose retirement plan is not under the jurisdiction of state property laws. On the other hand, the former wives of retired foreign service personnel are legally entitled to a share of these (25) retirees' pensions in proportion to the length of their marriage.

Obviously, there is no panacea for the ills besetting the legal system. Divorced women can only pray for significant benefits from future legislation.

Directions: Mark the following statements *true* or *false.* Then, indicate how you got your answer by adding on the blank line *stated, implied,* or *no info* if there is no information given.

1. _____ Divorce settlements make fair distributions of couples' property. _____

2. _____ In the emotional atmosphere of getting a divorce, wives seldom plan for the distant future. _____

3. _____ Health insurance companies cover ex-wives in the workers' policies. _____

4. _____ A divorced man can continue his wife's health insurance coverage by observing the "silence is golden" rule. _____

5. _____ The author of this selection has no sympathy for divorced women and their demands. _____

6. _____ Sailors' former wives will get some health insurance benefits under any conditions. _____

7. _____ Ex-wives have gone to court and have failed to get a share of their ex-husbands' pensions. _____

8. _____ There is a specific law that prohibits ex-wives from legally attaching their former husbands' pensions. _____

9. _____ A pension must be paid to the retired person and to no other person. _____

10. _____ Some laws regarding pensions favor ex-wives while other laws discriminate against them. _____

Answers

1. **The correct answer is false/implied.**

2. **The correct answer is true/implied.**

3. **The correct answer is false/stated.**

4. **The correct answer is true/stated.**

5. **The correct answer is false/implied.**

6. **The correct answer is false/stated.**

7. **The correct answer is false/stated.**

8. **The correct answer is no information given.**

9. **The correct answer is true/stated.**

10. **The correct answer is true/implied.**

Now read these short passages for general comprehension and vocabulary practice.

Sample Reading Passage 13

Questions 1–10 are based on the following passage.

The 1982 baptism of His Royal Highness Prince William Arthur Phillip Louis of Wales was a brief, quiet ceremony at Buckingham Palace in London. The little prince shared the honors of the day with his great-grandmother, who was celebrating her 82nd birthday. Thousands of her ardent admirers outside the palace sang
(5)　"Happy Birthday" to the accompaniment of the Coldstream Guards band.

Clad in a lace and silk christening dress first worn by the future Edward VII in 1841, Prince William affably responded to the baptismal water poured over his head by the Archbishop of Canterbury. Instead of the fierce cry that the superstitious believe expels the Devil from the infant, the prince managed only a squeak
(10)　or two. His parents and godparents promised to bring him up "to fight against evil and follow Christ."

Following a session with photographers, the baby was removed from the scene by his nanny. The parents and guests celebrated with a palatial luncheon of champagne and christening cake, the top layer of Prince Charles and Princess Diana's
(15)　wedding cake. Godparents include ex-King Constantine of Greece, Princess Alexandra, Lord Romsey, the Duchess of Westminster, Sir Laurens de Post, and Lady Susan Hussey.

Directions: Mark the following *true* or *false* according to the article. If the statement is false, go back to the reading and find the word or words that make it false and write the word or words in the space provided.

1. _____ The baptism was a lengthy ceremony.
_____

2. _____ The baby cried when the baptismal water was poured on him.
_____

3. _____ Crowds outside the palace sang to celebrate the baby's baptism.
_____

4. _____ The Coldstream Guards band played "Happy Birthday."
_____

5. _____ The prince wore a new christening robe.
_____

6. _____ The ceremony was very private.
_____

7. _____ The christening cake was made especially for the baptismal ceremony.
_____

8. _____ A nanny is a person who takes care of children.
_____

9. _____ The prince's godparents are titled people.
_____

10. _____ It is a superstition that godparents bring a child up to fight against evil and follow Christ.
_____

Answers

1. **The correct answer is false.** Brief

2. **The correct answer is false.** Affably responded—only a squeak or two.

3. **The correct answer is false.** They sang "Happy Birthday" to the prince's great-grandmother.

4. **The correct answer is true.**

5. **The correct answer is false.** First worn by Edward VII in 1841.

6. **The correct answer is true.**

7. **The correct answer is false.** Top layer of Prince Charles and Princess Diana's wedding cake.

8. **The correct answer is true.**

9. **The correct answer is true.**

10. **The correct answer is false.** Not a superstition—part of the ceremony.

Sample Reading Passage 14

Questions 1–10 are based on the following announcement.

Flora Jones Wed in Forest Hilltop to Francis Smith

Two well-known residents of Forest Hilltop, Flora Jones and Francis Smith, were married in a meadow near Smith's cabin on Sunday, August 4.

The double-ring nuptials were performed by Horace Dooley, minister of his own Church of the True Faith.

(5)   The bride was attended by Colleen Jones, the bride's daughter by a previous marriage, and Kristina Svenson, a longtime resident of Forest Hilltop. Verity Smith, the groom's daughter by a previous marriage, acted as flower girl.

The duties of best man were shared by Daniel Lion and Rory Whitney. Mr. Lion read a selection of poetry by Shakespeare, and Mr. Whitney read a selection from
(10) Wordsworth's *Prelude*. Music for the ceremony was provided by the bride's brother, James, from London, who accompanied vocalist Marilyn Horn, a Forest Hilltop neighbor.

Also performing at the ceremony was Samuel Cantor, a friend of the groom from Los Angeles, who sang several of his own compositions, accompanied by James
(15) Guidry, of Washington, D.C., and William Morris, of New York City.

Playing the flute, James Guidry led a procession of wedding guests and the groom's party from the groom's cabin to the meadow site of the wedding. Following the ceremony, the wedding party and guests strolled back to the cabin, where a reception was held for over 100 guests.

1. What type of place is Forest Hilltop?

    (A) Urban

    (B) Suburban

    (C) Rural

    (D) Metropolitan

2. This wedding would be considered

    (A) traditional

    (B) original

    (C) lovable

    (D) familial

3. The wedding was performed by

    (A) a man who has formed his own sect

    (B) a friend of the family

    (C) the bride's brother

    (D) the bride and groom

4. Apparently a vocalist is a
   (A) female
   (B) wedding guest
   (C) singer
   (D) neighbor

5. Apparently Mr. Cantor is noted for
   (A) his friendship with the groom
   (B) his attendance at the wedding
   (C) writing music
   (D) his residence in Los Angeles

6. Included in the wedding ceremony was a
   (A) dance
   (B) cabin
   (C) welcome speech
   (D) poetry recital

7. The wedding took place
   (A) in a cabin
   (B) in a church
   (C) outdoors
   (D) in a city

8. The reader knows that this is not the first marriage for both bride and groom because
   (A) it included two daughters
   (B) the guests came from many different places
   (C) it took place in a meadow
   (D) the minister was of the Church of the True Faith

9. Because a cabin is usually a small building, the reader infers that
   (A) it is constructed of wood
   (B) the reception was held outside the cabin
   (C) it was a temporary residence
   (D) the bride and groom will not live in it

10. Presumably this wedding announcement appeared in a(n)
    (A) metropolitan newspaper
    (B) alumni bulletin
    (C) musical review
    (D) small-town newspaper

Answers

1. The correct answer is (C).
2. The correct answer is (B).
3. The correct answer is (A).
4. The correct answer is (C).
5. The correct answer is (C).
6. The correct answer is (D).
7. The correct answer is (C).
8. The correct answer is (A).
9. The correct answer is (B).
10. The correct answer is (D).

EXERCISES: HOW THOUGHTS ARE RELATED

Directions: The passages below are followed by questions based on their content. Answer the questions on the basis of what is *stated* or *implied* in the passages.

QUESTIONS 1–12 ARE BASED ON THE FOLLOWING PASSAGE.

The Audubon Society operates a summer camp for adults on Hog Island, Maine, a 333-acre wildlife sanctuary. Singing paeans to nature and the wilds
(5) of Maine, campers delight in meandering down nature trails overhung with spruce and moss. The average age of the campers is 45–50, but the amenities provided are reminiscent of those at
(10) summer camps for children—dormitories divided for men and women, wake-up bells at 6:30, sharing chores, and communal meals in a dining room overlooking the rugged Maine coast.
(15) A routine day of exploration begins at 8:30, when instructors, all qualified naturalists, lead small groups of campers around Muscongus Bay, the habitat of prolific lobsters and the site of island
(20) homes for terns, gulls, and cormorants. Deer, seals, and occasional whales and porpoises enliven the scene. Each daytrip encompasses a specific theme in nature, such as the weather, birds, or animal
(25) and plant ecology. Most of the campers are not stereotyped ecology fanatics but, rather, city dwellers exhilarated by this opportunity to gain a rudimentary insight into the wonders of the natural
(30) world.
An all-day boat trip to Eastern Egg Rock, a remote island, elicits the campers' greatest enthusiasm. Once the habitat of innumerable puffins whose eggs
(35) were pilferred by poachers, the island currently has very few birds. Since 1974, the Audubon Society has been bringing puffins from Newfoundland to augment the population, but it wasn't until 1981
(40) that any produced young.
The campers' program continues without cessation into the evening hours. Lectures, slide shows, films, and "how-

to" courses complement the day's adven-
(45) tures. Compatible campers end their day seated placidly before a blazing fire, discussing their life together in the great outdoors.

1. Would the Audubon camp be a good place for a devoted bird watcher to go?

   Why or why not?_____

   _____

   _____

2. The instructors at the camp are

   (A) young people

   (B) middle-aged

   (C) trained in nature subjects

   (D) inclined to spend too much time instructing

3. Presumably the camp's facilities are

   (A) rugged but comfortable

   (B) damp and dirty

   (C) built for children

   (D) modern

4. A common practice at a summer camp is to

   (A) separate the instructors and campers

   (B) take turns doing household work

   (C) take boat trips to islands

   (D) provide for adults

5. Where is there a multitude of lobsters?

   _____

6. Why are there so few puffins on Eastern Egg Rock?_____

   _____

   _____

7. How successful has the Audubon Society been in increasing the puffin population?

_____

8. True or false? The campers eat dinner and then relax after the day's exploration. _____

9. True or false? There are numerous whales and porpoises along the coast of Maine.

_____

10. At the end of a busy day in the outdoors, most campers are

    (A) ready for bed

    (B) eager for more information

    (C) cold and hungry

    (D) stereotyped ecology fanatics

11. We may infer that Newfoundland is

    (A) distant from Maine

    (B) only an all-day boat trip from the camp

    (C) increasing its population

    (D) a habitat for puffins

12. We may infer that puffins

    (A) augment their numbers regularly

    (B) take a long time to get used to a place

    (C) are native to Maine

    (D) emigrate from Newfoundland every spring

Earlier on we talked about signal words or connectives. The author of the next selection makes frequent use of pronouns and other words that refer to something mentioned in another part of the text. Note that the style of this selection is very different from the others presented in this book, so don't worry if you don't understand everything in it. After all, the paragraph was taken from a novel by Anthony Trollope entitled *The American Senator*. Trollope was a prolific British writer known for his satirical novels, in which he criticized the upper middle class in England. *The American Senator* was first published in 1877.

QUESTIONS 13–24 ARE BASED ON THE FOLLOWING PASSAGE.

On the Monday afternoon the Trefoils arrived. Mr. Morton, with his mother and both the carriages, went down to receive them—with a cart also
(5) for the luggage, which was fortunate, as Arabella Trefoil's big box was very big indeed, and Lady Augustus, though she was economical in most things, had brought a comfortable amount of
(10) clothes. Each of them had her own lady's maid, so that the two carriages were necessary. How it was that these ladies lived so luxuriously was a mystery to their friends, as for some time
(15) past they had enjoyed no particular income of their own. Lord Augustus had spent everything that came to his hand, and the family owned no house at all. Nevertheless Arabella Trefoil
(20) was to be seen at all parties magnificently dressed, and never stirred anywhere without her own maid. It would have been as grievous to her to be called on to live without food as to go
(25) without this necessary appendage. She was a big, fair girl whose copious hair was managed after such a fashion that no one could guess what was her own and what was purchased. She certainly
(30) had fine eyes, though I could never imagine how any one could look at them and think it possible that she should be in love. They were very large, beautifully blue, but never bright; and
(35) the eyebrows over them were perfect. Her cheeks were somewhat too long and the distance from her well-formed nose to her upper lip too great. Her mouth was small and her teeth excel-
(40) lent. But the charm of which men spoke the most was the brilliance of her complexion. If, as the ladies said, it was all paint, she, or her maid, must have been a great artist. It never betrayed
(45) itself to be paint. But the beauty on which she prided herself was the grace of her motion. Though she was tall and big she never allowed an awkward movement to escape from her. She cer-
(50) tainly did it very well. No young woman

could walk across an archery ground with a finer step, or manage a train with more perfect ease, or sit upon her horse with a more complete look of being at
(55) home there. No doubt she was slow, but though slow she never seemed to drag. Now she was, after a certain fashion, engaged to marry John Morton and perhaps she was one of the most unhappy
(60) young persons in England.

13. After reading this passage, we can infer that
   (A) Arabella Trefoil is the heroine of Trollope's novel
   (B) the author does not especially like Miss Trefoil
   (C) Miss Trefoil is very rich
   (D) Miss Trefoil has a maid

14. After describing each of Miss Trefoil's features, the author
   (A) tells us how beautiful they are
   (B) makes us admire her
   (C) adds something to negate their beauty
   (D) discusses her attitude toward her maid

15. Miss Trefoil's full hair, it is implied, is
   (A) exceedingly pretty
   (B) not entirely natural
   (C) dyed
   (D) very fashionable

16. True or false? The author thinks Miss Trefoil's eyes are beautiful._____

17. What nasty remark do the women make about Arabella Trefoil?

   _____

18. Miss Trefoil's complexion appears brilliant because she
   (A) gets plenty of fresh air
   (B) is a horseback rider
   (C) is a great artist
   (D) uses makeup skillfully

19. Apparently Miss Trefoil and Lady Augustus
   (A) have plenty of money
   (B) live beyond their means
   (C) like to visit friends
   (D) have limited wardrobes

20. Lord Augustus, it is implied, has
   (A) provided his wife and daughter with luxury
   (B) moved from the family home
   (C) wasted his inheritance
   (D) become a mystery to his friends

21. Presumably the ladies' maids show that
   (A) the ladies are helpless without service
   (B) the ladies are wealthy
   (C) a large group visited the Mortons
   (D) two carriages were needed to transport the group

22. The reader can infer that Miss Trefoil is planning to marry for
   (A) new clothes
   (B) love
   (C) money
   (D) position

23. Miss Trefoil considers her maid more essential than her
   (A) mother
   (B) fiancé
   (C) dinner
   (D) clothes

24. The reason Miss Trefoil is unhappy is that
   (A) her clothes are expensive
   (B) she did not want to visit the Mortons
   (C) she and her mother do not get along well
   (D) she does not love her fiancé

ANSWERS AND EXPLANATIONS

1. Yes. The passage mentions several kinds of birds: terns, gulls, and cormorants.

2. C

3. A

4. B

5. Muscongus Bay

6. The puffin eggs were pilferred by poachers.

7. The Audubon Society had very little luck until 1981, when the puffins brought from Newfoundland began to produce young.

8. True

9. False

10. B

11. D

12. B

13. B

14. C

15. B

16. False

17. They said her brilliant complexion was due to paint (make-up).

18. D

19. B

20. C

21. B

22. C

23. C

24. D

UNDERSTANDING CONTEMPORARY READING PASSAGES

It is impossible to open a newspaper or magazine today without finding information pertaining to our health. Changes and developments in almost every area, from the social sciences and economics to science, medicine, and technology, are related to the condition of the human body and mind.

In this section you will encounter various styles of writing about contemporary health issues. Note that you will be given the opportunity to review a great many of the concepts you have learned thus far.

Sample Reading Passage 15

Drug abuse is the taking of any substance for any purpose other than the one for which it was intended and in any way that could damage the user's health. The most generally used drugs are the most generally abused. Many people treat aspirin, for example, as if it were candy. On the principle that if two aspirins are recommended to make them feel

(5) better, four will give them even more relief, people exceed the recommended dosage—no more than two tablets every 4 hours and eight within 24 hours. Without question, aspirin is a widely abused drug.

Cold capsules, laxatives, cough syrups—all the drugs sold in drugstores and supermarkets—are frequently abused, but their use, when compared to that of other drugs, does

(10) not incur the public's concern. The major source of drug abuse is alcohol, a common and easily acquired drug. A group of prohibitionists once asked Abraham Lincoln to support their cause. Sagely, he refused, replying that drunkenness is rooted not in the use of a bad thing, but in the abuse of a good thing.

1. A person who exceeds the recommended dosage of aspirin
   (A) is guilty of drug abuse
   (B) likes candy
   (C) is taking aspirin for a headache
   (D) is in for a treat

2. If a person takes a dozen aspirins within 24 hours, he or she
   (A) is aiding the aspirin manufacturers
   (B) can relieve the pain
   (C) is endangering his or her health
   (D) is concerned with his or her health

3. The author's reference to Abraham Lincoln
   (A) shows that Lincoln was a wise man
   (B) emphasizes the relation between alcohol and alcoholism
   (C) conveys the idea that alcohol may be harmless
   (D) indicates that alcohol leads to drunkenness

4. True or false? The public is not concerned with addiction to nonprescription drugs. _____

5. Presumably, this selection comes from a
   (A) scientific journal
   (B) health book
   (C) drug company advertisement
   (D) psychology textbook

Answers

1. The correct answer is (A).

2. The correct answer is (C).

3. The correct answer is (C).

4. The correct answer is true.

5. The correct answer is (B).

Sample Reading Passage 16

Vitamins are complex compounds that the body requires to function normally. The word *vitamin* was coined in the 1990s, but the therapeutic value of certain foods in combating disease was recognized as early as 3,000 years ago by the ancient Egyptians. They knew that night blindness could be circumvented by
(5) eating liver, a source of vitamin A. In the 1700s, an Austrian doctor discovered that eating citrus fruits sufficed to cure scurvy, a disease that affects the blood. In 1795, the British Navy began to give sailors lime juice to prevent scurvy. The Japanese Navy learned that too much polished rice in the diet causes beriberi, a painful nerve disease, and that meat and vegetables, which contain thiamine,
(10) prevent the disease.

In the early 1900s, as the causes of an increasing number of diseases were identified as vitamin deficiencies, vitamins were labeled with the letters of the alphabet. Researchers discovered more than twenty-six vitamins, which are now referred to by both letter and chemical names. For example, the vitamin B
(15) complex includes twelve vitamins.

1. True or false? Vitamin deficiencies first developed in the twentieth century.

   _____

2. If you were planning to cross the ocean in your own boat, what would you take with you to prevent beriberi? _____

   _____

3. Name a food other than liver that will prevent night blindness because it contains vitamin A. _____

4. True or false? Some diseases are caused by vitamin deficiencies.

   _____

Answers

1. The correct answer is false.

2. The correct answer is meat and vegetables.

3. The correct answer is milk, eggs, butter, vegetables. Answers will vary.

4. The correct answer is true.

Sample Reading Passage 17

Joan is fourteen years old, a bright student, and suffering from self-imposed starvation. She has anorexia nervosa. *Anorexia* means "without appetite," and *nervosa* means "of nervous origin." One morning six months ago Joan looked at herself in the mirror and decided she needed to lose a few pounds. Then five feet three inches
(5) tall and weighing 110 pounds, she presently weighs 81 pounds and is in the hospital where she is undergoing psychiatric treatment and being fed intravenously.

What happened to Joan? Why has she ruthlessly starved herself nearly to death? Joan is a typical anorexic—an adolescent girl who refuses to eat for the purpose of rebelling against the pressures imposed upon her by the adult environment.
(10) Family members—sometimes the mother, sometimes the father, sometimes both—require her to achieve more than they have in their lives. In her mind, school unites with her family to push her forward. Submissive for years, what does she finally do? She refuses food, says no to the two forces that are pushing her. Instead of growing into a mature woman, she holds back her physical growth by self-
(15) imposed starvation. In fact, she regresses to childhood, to the stage when she lacked curves, no one expected much from her, and she was dependent upon adults who gave her love and approval without demanding anything from her in return.

Anorexia nervosa, formerly not recognized as a disease, has become common among adolescent girls. Today the cure is prolonged treatment by a psychiatrist
(20) who initiates discussion among family members and the patient to determine the causes and ways to eliminate them in the future.

1. The main purpose of paragraph 1 is to
   (A) define and describe anorexia nervosa
   (B) tell what caused Joan's starvation
   (C) give Joan's past and present weight
   (D) suggest a cure for anorexia nervosa

2. The main idea of paragraph 2 is
   (A) an anorexic is most likely to be an adolescent
   (B) an anorexic is in rebellion against pressures in her environment
   (C) Joan regressed to childhood
   (D) Joan's parents wanted her to succeed

3. The main idea of paragraph 3 is
   (A) an anorexic can cure herself
   (B) the family of an anorexic must agree to see a psychiatrist
   (C) the cure of anorexia involves time, discussion, and professional help
   (D) anorexia is now considered a disease

4. List the details in paragraph 2 that support the main idea.

   (A) _____

   (B) _____

   (C) _____

   (D) _____

   (E) _____

5. Describe Joan before and after she developed anorexia nervosa.

   _____

   _____

6. Anorexia nervosa is currently recognized as a

   (A) mystery

   (B) cure

   (C) disease

   (D) regression

7. The cure for anorexia nervosa is

   (A) forced feeding

   (B) psychiatric treatment

   (C) intense discussion

   (D) dependence upon the family

Answers

1. **The correct answer is (A).**

2. **The correct answer is (B).**

3. **The correct answer is (C).**

4. **(A)** Joan refuses to eat to rebel against the pressures imposed upon her by her environment.

   (B) Family members require her to achieve more than they have.

   (C) School unites with her family to push her forward.

   (D) She holds back her physical growth by self-imposed starvation.

   (E) She regresses to childhood when no one expected much from her and she was dependent upon adults who gave her love without demanding anything from her in return.

5. Before Joan developed anorexia nervosa, she weighed 110 pounds; now she weighs 81 pounds and is in the hospital, where she is undergoing psychiatric treatment and being fed intravenously.

6. **The correct answer is (C).**

7. **The correct answer is (B).**

Sample Reading Passage 18

Fortunately there are still a few tasty things for us gourmands to enjoy in relative security. Their numbers, however, are depleted almost daily, it seems, by ruthless proclamations from the ever-vigilant Food and Drug Administration and its allies, our doctors. The latest felon to face prosecution is the salt of life, sodium chloride.

(5) Ostensibly, overuse of salt causes high blood pressure and hypertension. A few years ago the antisalt campaigners raised such a rumpus that salt was banned from baby food. Pressure was being applied to food manufacturers to oblige them to label their products to show sodium content. Because doing so would cost manufacturers money, they argued that they had no idea how much salt remains

(10) on such things as potato chips and how much sticks to the bag. Furthermore, salt isn't the only harmful ingredient in food. The debate at the time was if the manufacturer has to provide sodium content, why not require him to list every ingredient and specify which are detrimental to our health? Cigarettes have a warning printed on them. Shouldn't the same type of warning appear on canned

(15) foods that are notoriously oversalted?

There are endless ifs and buts in the controversy, but the most telling of these is the questionable proof of salt's diabolic effect upon the blood pressure. True, people who cut their salt intake lowered their blood pressure, but where is the scientific proof that something other than salt didn't do the trick? The most common means

(20) of providing dubious proof that salt causes hypertension is to compare societies that use little salt with those that use mountains of salt in their daily diets. Which group has the higher rate of hypertension? Whose blood pressure is lower? What happens when salt is introduced into a group where salt is a novelty? Does the blood pressure rise significantly? Studies of Japanese salt-intake indicated that as

(25) the world's greatest salters, they suffer the most from hypertension. On the other hand, the simple, salt-free cuisine of several tribes in the Solomon Islands has kept older members of the tribe from developing hypertension and high blood pressure. No account is taken of the effects of inflation, recession, pollution, crime, and sundry other ills to which Americans, unlike people on underdeveloped islands,

(30) are exposed.

To salt or not to salt? That is the question. Now that the question has arisen, it must not be treated with levity but, rather, with searching scientific investigation so that those of us who are preoccupied with both savory food and longevity may decide which of the two is worth its salt.

1. The attitude of the author of this passage toward the salt controversy is that

    (A) we must stop eating salt immediately

    (B) she is still not convinced that salt is harmful

    (C) the Food and Drug Administration works well with doctors

    (D) soon there won't be anything tasty left to eat

2. The author's approach to the topic is

    (A) angry

    (B) humorous

    (C) scientific

    (D) sympathetic

3. Presumably a gourmand is a
    (A) person
    (B) theory
    (C) food
    (D) protest

4. Some food manufacturers did not want to label packages with sodium content because
    (A) they disagree with the FDA
    (B) salt doesn't stick to potato chips
    (C) they would have to spend more money
    (D) it isn't important to single out salt

5. True or false? At present baby food contains salt. _____

6. Canned goods should have the same type of warning as cigarettes because
    (A) both contain salt
    (B) the author likes to smoke and eat
    (C) the cigarette warning reduces smoking
    (D) both are harmful to your health

7. True or false? Comparing societies is a scientific means of determining the dangers of salt consumption. _____

8. According to the passage, the Japanese use a lot of salt
    (A) but they suffer from hypertension
    (B) and they suffer from hypertension
    (C) because they suffer from hypertension
    (D) when they suffer from hypertension

9. True, false, or information not given? People in societies that use little salt never have high blood pressure. _____

10. The author suggests that Americans suffer from hypertension as a result of
    (A) too much salt
    (B) emotional stress
    (C) salt-free cuisine
    (D) ailments

Answers

1. **The correct answer is (B).**

2. **The correct answer is (B).**

3. **The correct answer is (A).**

4. The correct answer is (C).

5. The correct answer is false.

6. The correct answer is (D).

7. The correct answer is false.

8. The correct answer is (B).

9. The correct answer is information not given.

10. The correct answer is (B).

Sample Reading Passage 19

Most people are unaware of the fact that an ailment has developed among subway users. Called "subway syndrome," it causes people to turn pale and cold and even to faint. Commuters misdiagnose the symptoms—acute chest pains and nausea—and rush to hospital emergency rooms in the belief that they are about to succumb (5) to a heart attack. Hearing that their heart attack is only a case of nerves makes them feel better.

What makes people get sick on subways? Various and sundry things. One is that they rush off to work in the morning without having eaten a proper breakfast. Sudden dizziness attacks them. A second cause is the overcrowding and ensuing (10) feeling of claustrophobia, which brings on stress and anxiety. In addition, they are so afraid of mechanical failure, fire, and/or crime that they show signs of panic— men by having chest pains and women by becoming hysterical. Contributing especially to their stress are other factors: overcrowding of both sexes, continual increase in the numbers of passengers, and people's inability to avoid interacting (15) with strangers.

Noise, lack of space, summer heat, fear of entrapment underground—it is a wonder that more people don't have subway syndrome. What therapeutic measures can a commuter take to inoculate himself or herself from the disease? Eat a good breakfast, concentrate on pleasant thoughts as you stand surrounded, bounce a bit (20) on your toes, and roll your head. Thus, mind and body will be restored to a semblance of normality despite the adverse conditions of subway transportation.

1. What is the main idea of paragraph 1? Is it stated in a specific sentence or is it implied? _____

_____

2. List the supporting details of the main idea in paragraph 1.

    (A) _____

    (B) _____

    (C) _____

3. What is the main idea of paragraph 2? Is it stated or implied?

_____

_____

4. List the supporting details in paragraph 2.

    (A) _____

    (B) _____

    (C) _____

    (D) _____

    (E) _____

5. What is the main idea of paragraph 3? _____

    _____

6. List the supporting details in paragraph 3.

    (A) _____

    (B) _____

    (C) _____

    (D) _____

7. Why do subway riders think they might be having a heart attack?

    (A) They are overcrowded.

    (B) They are afraid.

    (C) They suffer from chest pains.

    (D) They don't eat breakfast.

8. According to the passage, if you don't have a good breakfast, you might get

    (A) cold

    (B) pale

    (C) afraid

    (D) dizzy

9. The author suggests that subway riders will feel better if they

    (A) exercise a little

    (B) think about pleasant things

    (C) eat breakfast

    (D) All of the above.

10. A good title for this passage might be

    (A) How to Ride the Subway

    (B) A Case of Nerves

    (C) The Subway Syndrome

    (D) Overcrowding on the Subways

Answers

1. A new ailment has developed among subway users. It is stated in the first sentence.

2. **(A)** New ailment called subway syndrome.

   (B) Causes people to turn pale and cold and even to faint.

   (C) Commuters rush to the hospital, thinking they are having a heart attack.

3. Various and sundry things make people sick on subways. It is stated.

4. **(A)** Dizziness is caused by not having eaten a proper breakfast.

   (B) The overcrowding causes claustrophobia, which brings on stress and anxiety.

   (C) People are afraid of mechanical failure, fire, and/or crime, so they panic.

   (D) Men show panic by having chest pains, women by becoming hysterical.

   (E) Overcrowding of both sexes, continual increase in the number of passengers, and people's inability to avoid interacting with strangers contribute to stress.

5. There are measures commuters can take to protect themselves from subway syndrome.

6. **(A)** Eat a good breakfast.

   (B) Concentrate on pleasant thoughts.

   (C) Bounce a bit on your toes.

   (D) Roll your head.

7. **The correct answer is (C).**

8. **The correct answer is (D).**

9. **The correct answer is (D).**

10. **The correct answer is (C).**

EXERCISES: UNDERSTANDING CONTEMPORARY READING PASSAGES

> **Directions:** The passages below are followed by questions based on their content. Answer the questions on the basis of what is stated or implied in the passages.

QUESTIONS 1–5 ARE BASED ON THE FOLLOWING PASSAGE.

Not since Americans crossed the continent in covered wagons have they exercised and dieted as strenuously as they are doing today. Consequently, they do
(5) not only look younger and slimmer, but feel better. Because of increased physical fitness, life expectancy in the nation has risen to seventy-three years, with fewer people suffering from heart dis-
(10) ease, the nation's number one killer.

Jogging, the easiest and cheapest way of improving the body, keeps more than 30 million people of all ages on the run. For the price of a good pair of run-
(15) ning shoes, anyone anywhere can join the race.

Dieting, too, has become a national pastime. Promoters of fad diets that eliminate eating one thing or another,
(20) such as fats or carbohydrates, promise as much as 20-pound weight losses within two weeks. Books describing such miraculous diets consistently head up the best-seller lists because
(25) everybody wants to lose weight quickly and easily.

Nevertheless, both jogging and dieting, carried to extremes, can be hazardous. Many confused joggers overdo and
(30) ultimately suffer from ankle and foot damage. Fad dieting, fortunately, becomes only a temporary means for shedding a few pounds while the body is deprived of the balanced nutrition it
(35) requires, so most dieters cannot persevere on fad diets. Above all, common sense should be the keystone for any dieting and exercise scheme.

1. The main idea of paragraph 1 is

   (A) Americans got exercise when they crossed the continent in covered wagons

   (B) exercise and diet are more widespread in America than ever before

   (C) heart disease is the number one killer among Americans

   (D) Americans live longer than they did before

2. The main idea of paragraph 2 is

   (A) jogging as an exercise appeals to a large number of Americans

   (B) joggers have to buy special shoes

   (C) joggers must be a certain age

   (D) jogging is inexpensive

3. The main idea of paragraph 3 is

   (A) people are so eager to lose weight that they will try any kind of diet

   (B) fad diets are so popular because they are on the best-seller lists

   (C) eliminating fats or carbohydrates will cause drastic weight loss

   (D) diet books guarantee 20-pound weight losses

4. The main idea of paragraph 4 is

   (A) it's good for you to jog and restrict your eating

   (B) improperly controlled, diet and exercise harm rather than benefit your health

   (C) jogging can damage the body because it is too strenuous an exercise

   (D) in the long run, dieting doesn't help people reduce because they don't stay on a diet

5. You can infer from this passage that

(A) a person's life expectancy depends upon diet

(B) inactive and corpulent people are prone to heart disease

(C) more people succumb to heart disease than to any other ailment

(D) All of the above.

Directions: Scan the passage as quickly as possible to get the information required to fill in the blanks in the following sentences.

QUESTIONS 6–10 REFER TO THE FOLLOWING PASSAGE, WRITTEN IN 1983.

The statistics relating to the skyrocketing costs of treating the sick indicate that there is no easy cure for inflation in America. Health costs rose 15.1% in
(5) 1981, whereas the inflation rate was only 8.9%. The entire nation spent approximately $287 billion on health care, an average of $1,225 per person. Since 85% of all Americans are covered by
(10) health insurance and get reimbursements of up to 75%, there are no incentives for reducing costs. Medicare and Medicaid, programs for the poor and the elderly, paid out $73 billion in 1981,
(15) an increase of $30 billion over the cost in 1976.

Between 1972 and 1982, hospital care costs quadrupled to $118 billion; doctors' services tripled to $54.8 billion; and
(20) nursing home costs quadrupled to $24.2 billion. A day in a hospital cost $133 in 1975; in 1982, the price was $250. There are multiple causes for soaring medical costs. New construction, particularly
(25) when special highly technical areas like burn centers are required, has escalated in cost. To keep a patient alive with modern mechanisms like the kidney dialysis machine costs an added $9 million
(30) a year nationwide. The more highly technical treatment becomes, for example for heart and other organ transplants, the more impossible it becomes to halt the inflationary rise of medical costs.

(35) The cost of medical services has a direct influence upon the cost of other things Americans purchase. Large companies provide health plans for their employees, and, as the premiums rise
(40) for those plans, the manufacturers must cover their expenses by increasing the sales price of their products. One automobile manufacturer, for example, estimates that the soaring costs of health
(45) insurance have added $350 to the cost of a car. Health costs are not isolated but, rather, have had an increasingly appalling effect upon the rate of inflation.

6. _____ of all Americans have health insurance.

7. The rate of inflation in 1981 was _____.

8. Medical costs in 1981 rose _____.

9. The average cost per person in the United States for medical care was _____.

10. Medical plans pay up to _____ in reimbursements to participants.

ANSWER KEY

1.	B	6.	85%
2.	A	7.	8.9%
3.	A	8.	15.1%
4.	B	9.	$1,225
5.	D	10.	$287 billion

READING HISTORY TEXTBOOKS

When reading historical material, it is crucial to understand cause and effect relations, chronological sequence, and comparison/contrast. As you work through these passages and accompanying exercises, keep in mind that it is not necessary to remember the specific information given here. Your purpose should be to develop the skills and strategies necessary for effective study reading.

Sample Reading Passage 20

The Olympic Games originated in 776 B.C. in Olympia, a small town in Greece. Participants in the first Olympiad are said to have run a 200-yard race, but as the Games were held every four years, they expanded in scope. Only Greek amateurs were allowed to participate in this festival in honor of the god Zeus. The event
(5) became a religious, patriotic, and athletic occasion where winners were honored with wreaths and special privileges. There was a profound change in the nature of the Games under the Roman emperors. After they became professional circuses and carnivals, they were banned in 394 A.D. by Emperor Theodosius.

The modern Olympic Games began in Athens in 1896 as a result of the initiative
(10) of Baron Pierre de Coubertin, a French educator whose desire was to promote international understanding through athletics. Nine nations participated in the first Games; over 100 nations currently compete.

The taint of politics and racial controversy, however, has impinged upon the Olympic Games in our epoch. In 1936, Hitler, whose country hosted the Games,
(15) affronted Jesse Owens, an African American runner, by refusing to congratulate Owens for the feat of having won four gold medals. In the 1972 Munich Games, the world was appalled by the deplorable murder of eleven Israeli athletes by Arab terrorists. The next Olympic Games in Montreal were boycotted by African nations; in addition, Taiwan withdrew. In 1980, following the Soviet invasion of
(20) Afghanistan, sixty-two nations caused great consternation to their athletes by refusing to participate in the Games. The consensus among those nations was that their refusal would admonish the Soviets.

1. The first Olympic Games were held
    (A) for political reasons
    (B) as an international competition
    (C) as a religious festival
    (D) as a professional athletes' competition

2. Why were the Games discontinued?
    (A) They had ceased to be sports events.
    (B) The Romans did not enjoy them.
    (C) The emperors hated athletes.
    (D) Winners were getting special privileges.

3. Olympic Games are held
   (A) every decade
   (B) biannually
   (C) every four years
   (D) perennially

4. The Greek Olympic Games were _____ in nature.
   (A) religious
   (B) national
   (C) athletic
   (D) All of the above.

5. The Games were resumed in modern times for the purpose of
   (A) giving amateur athletes a chance to participate
   (B) promoting goodwill among nations
   (C) creating an apolitical arena
   (D) None of the above.

6. You can infer that the athletes in sixty-two nations in 1980 were
   (A) terribly disappointed
   (B) very happy
   (C) participants
   (D) boycotted

7. The last three Olympic Games mentioned in the passage were notorious for their
   (A) racial discrimination
   (B) triumphant victories
   (C) fidelity to the goals of the Olympic Games
   (D) political controversy

Answers

1. **The correct answer is (C).**

2. **The correct answer is (A).**

3. **The correct answer is (C).**

4. **The correct answer is (D).**

5. **The correct answer is (B).**

6. **The correct answer is (A).**

7. **The correct answer is (D).**

Sample Reading Passage 21

When Christopher Columbus landed on America's shores, he encountered copper-skinned people whom he promptly called "Indians." Mistaken in his geography, he believed he had reached India. Current estimates indicate that there were over a million Native Americans inhabiting North America then. There
(5) are approximately 800,000 Native Americans today, of whom about 250,000 live on reservations.

The early settlers had an amicable relationship with Native Americans, who shared their knowledge of hunting, fishing, and farming with their uninvited guests.

Antipathy developed between the Native Americans and the settlers, whose
(10) encroachment on Native American lands provoked an era of turbulence. As early as 1745, Native American tribes coalesced to drive the French off their land. The French and Indian War did not end until 1763. The Native Americans had succeeded in destroying many of the Western settlements. The British, superficially submissive to the Native Americans, promised that further migrations west
(15) would not extend beyond a specified boundary. However, there was no holding back ardent adventurers like Daniel Boone, who ignored the British covenant with the Native Americans and blazed a trail westward.

Evicted from their lands or, worse still, ingenuously ceding their property to the whites for a few baubles, Native Americans were ruthlessly pushed west. Tempes-
(20) tuous wars broke out, but lacking their former stamina and large numbers, the Native Americans were doomed to capitulation. The battle in 1876 at Little Big Horn River in Montana, in which Sitting Bull and the Sioux tribes massacred General Custer's cavalry, caused the whites to intensify their campaign against the Native Americans. The battle at Wounded Knee, South Dakota, in 1890
(25) rescinded the last vestige of hope for amity between Indians and whites. Thenceforth Native Americans were relegated to their own reservations, lands allotted to them by the federal government.

Although the Bureau of Indian Affairs has operated since 1824, presumably for the purpose of guarding Native Americans' interests, Native Americans on reservations
(30) lead notoriously deprived lives. Poverty, unemployment, high infant mortality, and deficient medical care have maimed a once proud race. In recent times, irate Native Americans have taken a militant stand and have appealed to the courts and the American people to ameliorate their substandard living conditions.

1. You can infer that the author of this passage
   (A) works for the Bureau of Indian Affairs
   (B) thinks Native Americans are satisfied living on reservations.
   (C) admires the settlers for their endurance
   (D) sympathizes with Native Americans

2. The early settlers in America
   (A) had to fight Native Americans
   (B) found the Native Americans very helpful
   (C) went hunting and fishing
   (D) were indifferent to the Native Americans

3. The French and Indian War

    (A) was quickly terminated

    (B) caused great destruction among the French forces

    (C) lasted eighteen years

    (D) led to westward migration

4. The British made an agreement with the Native Americans to

    (A) treat them fairly

    (B) get the Indians' land

    (C) stop westward migration

    (D) send Daniel Boone across the continent

5. The Indians sold their land

    (A) for huge profits

    (B) for a few trinkets

    (C) because they didn't understand the language

    (D) because they believed it was infertile

6. At Little Big Horn River the Indians were

    (A) defeated

    (B) the victors

    (C) forced to retreat

    (D) massacred

7. The battle at Wounded Knee

    (A) marks the end of the Indian wars

    (B) occurred on the Indian reservation

    (C) caused great hope among Native Americans

    (D) was won by the Native Americans

8. Apparently, the author feels that the Bureau of Indian Affairs

    (A) has been of great help to the Native Americans

    (B) was established in the nineteenth century

    (C) deprived the Native Americans

    (D) has never done much for Native Americans

Answers

1. **The correct answer is (D).**

2. **The correct answer is (B).**

3. **The correct answer is (C).**

4.   The correct answer is (C).

5.   The correct answer is (B).

6.   The correct answer is (B).

7.   The correct answer is (A).

8.   The correct answer is (D).

Sample Reading Passage 22

On July 4, 1776, a conclave of insurgent colonists in America passed the Declaration of Independence. War against the British had already been going on for over a year, so the Declaration came as the culmination of years of tempestuous events in America.

(5)   The impetus for the American Revolution was the Treaty of Paris in 1763, which ended the struggle between the British and the French for control over North America. Since the colonists no longer were intimidated by the French, they ceased to rely upon the British for protection and were not as submissive as they were formerly. On the other hand, the British regarded the colonies as a source of

(10)   revenue and began to impose inequitable taxes upon them. The Sugar Act in 1764 and the Stamp Act in 1765 were so vehemently opposed by disgruntled colonists that rioting broke out. The Stamp Act was repealed in 1766 as a result of the riots. The British continued their policy of taxation without collaboration with their once docile subjects. The Townshend Acts (a series of taxes on glass, lead, paper, and

(15)   tea) created such antipathy that the citizens of Boston attacked British soldiers who fired upon them. That was the Boston Massacre of 1770. After the repeal of the Townshend Acts, a new tea tax in 1773 again consolidated Boston residents' dissension. About fifty men disguised as Indians boarded British ships and jettisoned their cargo of tea in protest against the tea tax. That was the famous

(20)   Boston Tea Party. In reprisal, the British abolished the Bostonians' right to self-rule, and by passing what were referred to as Intolerable Acts in Boston, they infuriated all of the colonies and caused them to unite in protest.

Representatives from twelve colonies gathered in Philadelphia in 1774 to plan a stratagem to circumvent British interference in trade and to protest the infamy of

(25)   taxation without representation. The British responded that the colonies were in rebellion, and, since nothing would appease either side, both sides prepared for war.

1.   The author's intent in this passage is to

   (A)   tell about the American Revolution

   (B)   describe the temperament of the colonists

   (C)   give the causes of the American Revolution

   (D)   describe the effects of the American Revolution

2.   You may infer that the Treaty of Paris

   (A)   gave the French control of Canada

   (B)   gave the control of North America to the British

   (C)   made the colonists in America very angry

   (D)   had an immediate effect upon colonists' desire for independence

3. The colonists after the Treaty of Paris did not need the British because they
    (A) were independent
    (B) didn't like to pay taxes
    (C) didn't need protection from an enemy
    (D) made a treaty with the French

4. The Sugar Act and Stamp Act were
    (A) passed in 1765
    (B) taxes upon the colonists
    (C) repealed
    (D) equitable

5. The first violent protest against the British was made in
    (A) 1764
    (B) 1765
    (C) 1770
    (D) 1773

6. You can infer that in the Boston Massacre in 1770
    (A) Boston was a battlefield
    (B) Boston residents wanted independence
    (C) colonists were killed
    (D) British soldiers sided with Boston residents

7. The Boston Tea Party was
    (A) a celebration in Boston
    (B) an Indian rebellion
    (C) held on board a British ship
    (D) an act of aggression by the colonists

8. You can infer that the Intolerable Acts
    (A) were repealed
    (B) infringed upon colonists' rights
    (C) displeased the British
    (D) were entirely related to taxes

9. You can infer that the meeting in Philadelphia in 1774
    (A) was a very important social event
    (B) took place to discuss taxes
    (C) was a conclave of the British and the colonists
    (D) was the first time the colonists united to protest British injustice

10. The British and the colonists went to war because the
    (A) colonists wanted independence from their rulers
    (B) British fired at the Bostonians in the Boston Massacre
    (C) Bostonians dumped tea in the sea at the Boston Tea Party
    (D) colonists objected to taxation without representation

Answers

1. **The correct answer is (C).**

2. **The correct answer is (B).**

3. **The correct answer is (C).**

4. **The correct answer is (B).**

5. **The correct answer is (B).**

6. **The correct answer is (C).**

7. **The correct answer is (D).**

8. **The correct answer is (B).**

9. **The correct answer is (D).**

10. **The correct answer is (D).**

Sample Reading Passage 23

The *Titanic* was the last "unsinkable" ship ever to set sail. Built in 1912 for the British White Star Line, she was a colossal ship for the times—882 feet long, 46,328 tons, and capable of doing 25 knots an hour. Acclaimed as the zenith of luxury liners, the ship had been fitted out with palatial accoutrements. Her
(5) sixteen watertight compartments, her builders claimed, guaranteed that nothing could sink her.

April 10, 1912, was a glittering occasion as the *Titanic* began her maiden voyage from England to New York with 2,207 people on board, some of whom were American tycoons whose estimated worth was over $250 million.
(10) At 11:40 p.m. on April 14, many of the sleeping passengers were awakened by a slight jolt. The ship had struck an iceberg, incurred a 300-foot gash in her side, and five compartments were flooded. "Unsinkable," however, meant the ship could float if two, not five, compartments were inundated. Ten miles away from the *Titanic* was another ship, the *Californian*, which had stopped because of ice fields
(15) and which had wired six explicit warnings to nearby ships. Unfortunately, the *Titanic's* wireless, a new invention on shipboard, was being employed for frivolous messages to and from the passengers. The tired wireless operator had worked long hours and impatiently told the *Californian's* operator to shut up and stop annoying him.
(20) By 12:05 a.m. officers and crew fully comprehended that something was seriously amiss. Lifeboats were uncovered, and passengers and crew were mustered to the boat deck. Ten minutes later a "CQD" sent out to summon help was received by ships too distant to be of immediate help. The *Californian* might as well have been in the South Seas for all the assistance she ever gave. Her wireless operator,

(25) unfamiliar with the new equipment, had failed to wind up the mechanism that kept the set running. At about 11:40 he tuned in, heard nothing from his dead set, and went to bed.

Secure in the knowledge that their ship was unsinkable, the White Star Line had provided enough lifeboat space for only 1,178 people. There were sixteen wooden (30) lifeboats and four collapsible canvas boats on board for 2,207 people. The crew's efforts to load the lifeboats in the midst of chaos and bitterly cold weather were heroic but disorganized. Women and children were supposed to be first in the lifeboats, but no matter how chivalrous the men, the women were querulous about leaving the ship for a cold, open boat and had to be cajoled into the boats. At 12:45 (35) the *Californian* crew watched the *Titanic*'s rockets overhead and regarded them as "strange." The first boat was being lowered into the icy sea at the same moment; with a capacity for forty, it contained twelve. Throughout the fiasco of lifeboat loading, the ship's orchestra played ragtime, the lights blazed, and the *Titanic* continued to slip downward at the bow.

(40) Meanwhile, three ships had received an SOS, the first time that signal had ever been used, and they were confused. All had been advised that the *Titanic* was sinking. The *Carpathia* was fifty-eight miles away. The *Californian* watched the last rocket go off at 1:40. At 2:05 the last boat was lowered as the band played an Episcopal hymn, "Autumn," not "Abide with Me," as is usually believed. With the (45) ship standing at a 90° angle, perpendicular in the water, at 2:10 the last SOS was sent out. At 2:20 A.M. on April 15, 1912, the *Titanic* sank. The crew of the *Californian* believed that the disappearing lights indicated that the ship was leaving the area.

At 4:10 the *Carpathia* was the first ship to reach the scene. The *Californian* (50) arrived at 5:40, too late to rescue any survivors. From eighteen boats 705 people were rescued. Following inquiries regarding the disaster, it was revealed that very few of the third-class passengers had been saved. Of 143 women in first class, 4 were lost; of 93 women in second class, 15 were lost; of 179 women in third class, 81 were lost. All but one child in first and second class were saved, but of the 76 (55) children in third class, only 23 survived.

1. You can infer that "the *Titanic* was the last 'unsinkable' ship" means that

   (A) the *Titanic* was not unsinkable

   (B) the *Titanic* would not have sunk if only two compartments had been flooded

   (C) nobody ever believed in an "unsinkable" ship after the *Titanic* disaster

   (D) nobody ever built a ship like the *Titanic* again

2. You can infer from the statistics regarding the number of third-class passengers who survived that

   (A) they did not know the ship was sinking

   (B) they ignored the crew's calls to the lifeboats

   (C) they courteously allowed the first- and second-class passengers to leave the ship first

   (D) there was class distinction in the filling of the lifeboats

3. You can infer that the *Californian* crew
   (A) callously ignored the *Titanic*'s plight
   (B) could have saved many if it had heeded the rockets
   (C) didn't want to lose any sleep
   (D) did its best to aid the *Titanic*

4. You can infer that many of the *Titanic*'s male passengers
   (A) succumbed quickly in the icy sea
   (B) were frivolous
   (C) saved themselves instead of the women and children
   (D) were very rich

5. The first SOS signal was called
   (A) a wireless
   (B) a warning
   (C) CQD
   (D) a message

Answers

1. **The correct answer is (C).**

2. **The correct answer is (B).**

3. **The correct answer is (D).**

4. **The correct answer is (A).**

5. **The correct answer is (C).**

EXERCISES: READING HISTORY TEXTBOOKS

> **Directions:** The passages below are followed by questions based on their content. Answer the questions on the basis of what is *stated* or *implied* in the passages.

QUESTIONS 1–7 ARE BASED ON THE FOLLOWING PASSAGE.

When Franklin D. Roosevelt was elected President of the United States in 1932, not only the United States but also the rest of the world was in the throes of
(5) an economic depression. Following the termination of World War I, Britain and the United States at first experienced a boom in industry. Called the Roaring Twenties, the 1920s ushered in a num-
(10) ber of things—prosperity, greater equality for women in the work world, rising consumption, and easy credit. The outlook for American business was rosy.

October 1929 was a month that had
(15) catastrophic economic reverberations worldwide. The American stock market witnessed the "Great Crash," as it is called, and the temporary boom in the American economy came to a standstill.
(20) Stock prices sank, and panic spread. The ensuing unemployment figure soared to 12 million by 1932.

Germany in the postwar years suffered from extreme deprivation because
(25) of onerous reparations it was obliged to pay to the Allies. The country's industrial capacity had been greatly diminished by the war. Inflation, political instability, and high unemployment
(30) were factors conducive to the growth of the embryonic Nazi party. Germans had lost confidence in their old leaders and heralded the arrival of a figure who would lead them out of their economic
(35) wilderness.

Roosevelt was elected because he promised a "New Deal" to lift the United States out of the doldrums of the depression. Following the principles advocated
(40) by Keynes, a British economist, Roosevelt mustered the spending capacities of the federal government to provide welfare, work, and agricultural aid to the millions of down-and-out
(45) Americans. Elected President for four terms because of his innovative policies, Roosevelt succeeded in dragging the nation out of the Depression before the outbreak of World War II.

1. A good title for this selection would be
   (A) The Twenties
   (B) The End of World War I
   (C) The Great Crash
   (D) The Depression

2. The 1920s were called the Roaring Twenties because
   (A) social and economic affairs were prospering
   (B) women were advancing in the fight for equal rights
   (C) there was little unemployment
   (D) people were celebrating the end of World War I

3. When Roosevelt was elected,
   (A) the nation was in a deep depression
   (B) there were 12 million unemployed workers
   (C) the nation needed help from the federal government
   (D) All of the above.

4. The "Great Crash" refers to
   (A) the end of World War I
   (B) the Great Depression
   (C) a slump in the stock market
   (D) high unemployment figures

5. In the postwar years, Germany

   (A) had a booming industrial program

   (B) had difficulty paying reparations

   (C) was optimistic about the future

   (D) None of the above.

6. Roosevelt's "New Deal" advocated

   (A) government spending to provide employment

   (B) providing support for the poor and unemployable

   (C) government aid to farmers

   (D) All of the above.

7. Four terms of office as President of the United States would mean

   (A) eight years in office

   (B) four years in office

   (C) sixteen years in office

   (D) until he dies in office

QUESTIONS 8–15 ARE BASED ON THE FOLLOWING PASSAGE.

On September 2, 1945, the Communist Viet Minh party took over Vietnam and declared the country autonomous. The French, however, backed by the British,
(5) returned to Vietnam and forced the Viet Minh to attend the Fountainebleau Conference in 1946. Ho Chi Minh, the Viet Minh leader, was inflexible in his demands for unification of his country.
(10) The French had divided it into three parts: Cochin China in the south, Tonkin in the middle, and Annam in the north. A French decree making Cochin China a separate republic closed the door on any
(15) possible negotiations at the conference. War broke out between the French and the Viet Minh.

In the conflict the United States supported the French, while the Chinese
(20) and the Soviets backed the Viet Minh. By 1954 public disapproval of the war and its financial burden forced the French to withdraw. At a peace confer-

ence in Geneva, Vietnam was divided
(25) with the proviso that reunification would take place by elections two years later.

The Communists in North Vietnam and the anti-Communists in South Vietnam refused to collaborate. Led by Ngo Dinh
(30) Diem, whose regime was backed by the United States, the South Vietnamese prevented unification elections and persecuted Communists in their region. In January 1959, militant Hanoi Commu-
(35) nists again declared war, this time against their own neighbors in the south.

The United States' involvement in Vietnam's internal affairs increased as President Kennedy sent military advis-
(40) ers in 1961 to assist the South Vietnamese. The war continued. President Johnson ordered American bombing of North Vietnam on February 8, 1965. Ground fighting intensified early in 1968.
(45) Neither side appeared to have gained ascendancy over the other, and the American people were fed up with human and financial losses in Vietnam. President Johnson ordered a cutback in
(50) the bombing. His successor, Richard Nixon, continued to support South Vietnam but ordered the withdrawal of American combat troops.

Peace negotiations between the United
(55) States and North Vietnam began in Paris in May 1968, but were not terminated until January 27, 1973. Fighting had reached a deadlock, and the Americans had renewed their bombing offensive in
(60) December 1972.

With Communist forces remaining in South Vietnam after the American withdrawal, the fighting was renewed immediately after the peace conference. South
(65) Vietnam was defeated on April 30, 1975. The following year Hanoi united North and South Vietnam. The conflict had lasted thirty chaotic years. The United States had supported the losing side with over
(70) half a million troops and billions of dollars.

8. You can infer from the fact that the United States supported South Vietnamese leader Ngo Dinh Diem that

   (A) he was a poor leader
   (B) he was anti-Communist
   (C) he was supportive of French colonization
   (D) the United States opposed the French

9. The author's final statement in this passage implies that

   (A) Americans ought to have stayed out of Vietnam
   (B) Americans should have put more effort into winning the war
   (C) Americans have a tendency to interfere in other nations' affairs
   (D) the cost to the Americans was worthwhile

10. The French withdrew from Vietnam because

   (A) they were weak
   (B) the people at home did not sanction fighting the war
   (C) they wanted to divide the country
   (D) the Vietnamese hated them

11. Negotiations at the Fontainebleau Conference broke down because the

   (A) Viet Minh attended it
   (B) French couldn't make up their minds
   (C) Americans interfered
   (D) French made Cochin China a separate state

12. The apparent cause of the entire Vietnam conflict was

   (A) French refusal to allow unification
   (B) Communists' demands for possession of North Vietnam
   (C) South Vietnam's withdrawal from the northern leaders
   (D) social upheaval throughout Vietnam

13. In 1959, the war in Vietnam was

   (A) an international struggle for power
   (B) expected to last a long time
   (C) almost over
   (D) an internal struggle

14. After seven years of conflict in Vietnam, the American people

   (A) favored increased efforts to win the war
   (B) paid little attention to the war
   (C) protested against the waste of the war
   (D) supported the South Vietnamese

15. You can infer that the renewed bombing of North Vietnam at the end of 1972

   (A) destroyed North Vietnam's forces
   (B) contributed to ending the conflict
   (C) made the Americans seek peace
   (D) caused very little damage

ANSWER KEY

1.	D	6.	D	11.	D
2.	A	7.	C	12.	A
3.	D	8.	B	13.	D
4.	C	9.	A	14.	C
5.	B	10.	B	15.	B

INTERPRETING SCIENTIFIC READING MATERIALS

As you read the following passages, you will notice that the writing is particularly clear and precise because of the many technical terms employed. This is characteristic of science materials. It is important for the author to present ideas in such a way that the reader can establish relationships between details and facts. As in the previous section, we will concentrate on some of the study skills taught earlier: scanning, understanding relationships, and locating specific information.

Sample Reading Passage 24

The moon goes around the earth in an average time of 27 days, 7 hours, and 43.2 minutes. This is called the sidereal period. The lunar month, the period from one new moon to the next, covers a span of 29 days, 12 hours, and 44.05 minutes. This is the moon's synodical period.

(5)   The moon is 238,857 miles from the earth. This is considered the mean distance because the moon's path is elliptical, not circular. The maximum distance the moon travels from earth is 252,710 miles, whereas the minimum is 221,463 miles. These distances are measured from the center of earth to the center of the moon.

The diameter of the moon is 2,160 miles. Deducting the radius of the moon, 1,080

(10)   miles, from the radius of the earth, a minimum of 3,963 miles, we get the closest figure of the bodies' surfaces, 216,420 miles.

The moon's rotation on its axis is exactly equal to its sidereal circuit around the earth—27.321666 days. Although the moon's circuit is irregular because of its elliptical course, its rotation is nevertheless regular. The regular rotation and the

(15)   irregular rotation create "libration in longitude," which makes it possible for us to see first farther around the east side and then farther around the west side of the moon. On the other hand, "libration in latitude" enables us to see farther over either the north or the south pole. These two librations allow us to see over 60% of the moon's surface at one time or another. The first time the other side of the

(20)   moon was photographed was in 1959, by the Soviet spaceship *Lunik III*. Since then, U.S. spaceships have taken many pictures of the moon's surface.

1.   What is the meaning of sidereal period? _____

     _____

2.   What is the meaning of synodical period? _____

     _____

3.   In line 5, what is the meaning of the word *mean*? _____

     _____

4.   True or false? The moon's path around the earth is circular. _____

5. In this passage, the word *rotation* presumably means
    (A) by rote
    (B) complete turn around a point
    (C) planting different crops
    (D) balance

6. Revolution of the moon refers to
    (A) the moon's elliptical path around the earth
    (B) the moon's turning on its axis
    (C) the turmoil in the composition of the moon
    (D) changes in the moon's surface

7. Librations of the moon cause
    (A) it to turn slowly
    (B) us to view it from different sides at various times
    (C) its irregular course
    (D) its distance from the earth

8. True or false? The Russians took the first pictures of the dark side of the moon.

    _____

9. True or false? Sixty percent of the moon's surface is hidden from us.

    _____

10. How do we determine the distances the moon travels? _____

    _____

11. Why are two different times given for the moon's circuit of the earth? _____

    _____

12. What has given us a clearer concept of the moon? _____

    _____

13. Why are two distances given for the moon's distance from earth? _____

    _____

14. What do latitude and longitude mean? _____

    _____

15. Libration in latitude means that

   (A) the moon's diameter is smaller than the earth's latitude

   (B) we see farther over the north and south poles

   (C) the moon's rotation is irregular

   (D) the moon's circuit is regular

Answers

1. Sidereal period is the time it takes for the moon to go around the earth.

2. Synodical period is the period from one new moon to the next.

3. **The correct answer is average.**

4. **The correct answer is false.**

5. **The correct answer is (B).**

6. **The correct answer is (A).**

7. **The correct answer is (B).**

8. **The correct answer is true.**

9. **The correct answer is true.**

10. We measure from the center of the earth to the center of the moon.

11. One time is the time the moon takes to go around the earth, and the other time is the period from one new moon to the other.

12. Photographs taken by Soviet and U.S. spaceships

13. The moon's path is elliptical, not circular.

14. Latitude is the distance north or south of the equator. Longitude is the position on the earth east or west of a meridian.

15. **The correct answer is (B).**

Sample Reading Passage 25

About a billion years after the earth had formed, the first signs of life appeared. Three billion years elapsed before creatures became complex enough to leave fossils their descendants could recognize and learn from. These were shelled creatures called trilobites, followed by jawless fish, the first vertebrates. During

(5)   the Devonian period, great upheavals occurred in the earth's crust, resulting in the formation of mountains and in the ebb and flow of oceans. In the aftermath, beds of mud rich in organic matter nourished vegetation, and insects, scorpions, and spiders appeared. Next developed the amphibians, descendants of fish that had crawled out of fresh water.

(10)   Between 225 and 65 million years ago, reptiles developed from which many new forms grew until finally evolved the mammal. Dinosaurs were overgrown reptiles. Although some were as small as chickens, others grew to be the largest animals on Earth, as long as 82 feet and as heavy as 50 tons, with long necks and a liking

for a vegetarian diet. Current theory suggests that dinosaurs were warm-blooded
(15) and behaved more like mammals than like reptiles.

The end of the Mesozoic Era (middle life) saw the inexplicable demise of
dinosaurs and large swimming and flying birds. Geological changes were convert-
ing the giant land mass into separate continents. The beginning of a new era,
called Cenozoic (recent life), saw the marked predominance of mammals that
(20) would ultimately become man's ancestors.

1. What would be a good title for this reading?

    (A) How Reptiles Became Dinosaurs

    (B) The Ages of Man

    (C) The Evolution of Life

    (D) The Formation of the Earth

2. What is required for vegetation?

    (A) Dinosaurs

    (B) Oceans

    (C) Organic matter

    (D) Mud

3. What must an amphibian be?

    (A) A spider

    (B) A person

    (C) A creature

    (D) A body of water

4. By inference, what would you say insects need?

    (A) Water

    (B) Vegetation

    (C) Mud

    (D) Organic matter

5. What does the prefix *Meso* mean in *Mesozoic*?

    (A) Mixed

    (B) Middle

    (C) Median

    (D) Mean

6. Presumably *over* in the word *overgrown* means

    (A) above

    (B) often

    (C) on top of

    (D) excessively

7. Why did the dinosaur disappear?

   (A) It was undernourished.

   (B) It was a reptile.

   (C) No one knows.

   (D) Large birds killed it.

8. What must *demise* mean?

   (A) Death

   (B) Appearance

   (C) Change

   (D) Evolution

Answers

1. The correct answer is (C).

2. The correct answer is (C).

3. The correct answer is (C).

4. The correct answer is (B).

5. The correct answer is (B).

6. The correct answer is (D).

7. The correct answer is (C).

8. The correct answer is (A).

Sample Reading Passage 26

Earthquakes are the most lethal of all natural disasters. What causes them? Geologists explain them in terms of a theory known as plate tectonics. Continents are floating apart from each other; this is referred to as the continental drift. About sixty miles below the surface of the sea, there is a semimolten bed of rock over
(5) which plates, or slabs, carry continents and sea floors at a rate of several inches a year. As the plates separate from each other, a new sea floor is formed by the molten matter that was formerly beneath. Volcanic islands and large mountain ranges are created by this type of movement. The collision of plates causes geological instability such as that in California called the San Andreas Fault,
(10) located between the Pacific and North American plates. The plates there are constantly pushing and pulling adjacent plates, thereby creating constant tremors and a potential for earthquakes in the area.

Geologists would like to be able to predict earthquakes accurately. Using laser beams, seismographs, gravity-measuring devices, and radio telescopes, they are
(15) presently studying the San Andreas Fault to determine the rate of strain and the amount of ground slippage. Calculations indicate that sometime in the future, California will be struck by a major earthquake.

In spite of the geologists' theory of plate tectonics, there are still gaps in man's understanding and knowledge of the causes of earthquakes. Powerful earth-

(20) quakes have occurred in places where plate boundaries are hundreds of miles away. In the 1800s New Madrid, Missouri, and Charleston, South Carolina, were shaken by earthquakes that no one had foreseen.

Certain areas of the world are quake prone. Italy, Yugoslavia, and Algeria have experienced many quakes. In November 1980, Naples was struck by an especially *(25)* devastating quake. China and Japan have also been hit by horrendous quakes. In 1923, Tokyo and Yokohama were reduced to rubble by gigantic tremors that were followed by fires, tornadoes, and finally a thirty-four-foot *tsunami*, or tidal wave, which was caused by the earth's drop into the waters of Tokyo Bay.

What effects have geologists' predictions of earthquakes had? The Chinese in *(30)* Haicheng in 1974 were warned that an earthquake might occur within the next year or two. With the help of amateur seismologists' observations of animal behavior and the rise and fall of water in wells and measurements of quantities of radioactive gas in water, professional geologists were able, in January 1975, to predict an earthquake within the next six months. On February 4, Haicheng was *(35)* destroyed, but because its residents had been evacuated, very few people were killed. In California, where earthquake is an ever-present menace, building codes now require quakeproof structures, and Civil Defense units have intensified their training in how to deal with disaster should it strike or, perhaps more accurately, when it strikes.

1. Continental drift is the concept that
   (A) continents are drawing nearer to each other
   (B) continents are separating
   (C) continents are 60 miles apart from each other
   (D) new continents are developing beneath the sea

2. Geologists are using modern technology to
   (A) help predict earthquakes
   (B) enhance their reputations
   (C) measure the accuracy of earthquakes
   (D) control ground slippage

3. An earthquake may be followed by
   (A) wind, fire, and tidal waves
   (B) predictions
   (C) radioactive gas
   (D) strange behavior by animals

4. The Chinese predicted an earthquake by
   (A) employing amateur seismologists
   (B) observing professional geologists
   (C) watching animals, wells, and radioactive gas
   (D) evacuating the population

5. Californians are preparing for an earthquake by
   (A) saving their property
   (B) building stronger houses and practicing techniques to handle emergencies
   (C) ignoring the San Andreas Fault
   (D) moving to another state

6. No one had foreseen quakes in Missouri because
   (A) the area is not quake prone
   (B) geologists do not understand the area
   (C) there are gaps in the area
   (D) the theory of plate tectonics is incorrect

7. Geologists have been able to predict an earthquake
   (A) with unerring accuracy
   (B) within months
   (C) by measuring tremors
   (D) by knowing about continental drift

8. Volcanic islands are formed by
   (A) the separation of plates and the consequent uncovering of the molten sea floor beneath them
   (B) the constant pushing and pulling of adjacent plates
   (C) constant tremors
   (D) huge mountain ranges

Answers

1. The correct answer is (B).

2. The correct answer is (A).

3. The correct answer is (A).

4. The correct answer is (C).

5. The correct answer is (B).

6. The correct answer is (A).

7. The correct answer is (B).

8. The correct answer is (A).

EXERCISES: INTERPRETING SCIENTIFIC READING MATERIALS

Directions: The passages below are followed by questions based on their content. Answer the questions on the basis of what is *stated* or *implied* in the passages.

QUESTIONS 1–6 ARE BASED ON THE FOLLOWING PASSAGE.

The Federal Surface Mining Act was passed in 1977 for the laudable purpose of protecting the environment from the ravages of strip-mining of coal. For many (5) years environmentalists had fought to get the bill passed. Strip-mining menaces the habitat of wildlife and causes incalculable damage to the environment. The law is explicit on such matters as (10) where strip-mining is prohibited, the disposal of toxic waste, the placement of power lines, and the rights of the public to take part in the control of strip-mining. However, the Secretary of the Interior has recently incurred the wrath of (15) rior has recently incurred the wrath of environmentalists by advocating numerous proposals that repudiate the existing law.

According to the law, strip-mining is (20) prohibited in national forests, national wildlife refuges, public parks, historic places, and within a specified number of feet from roads, cemeteries, parks, houses, and schools. The exception to (25) this prohibition is stated in the words *valid existing rights*, referring to those miners who had rights in protected lands before the law was passed. By redefining "valid existing rights," the local gov- (30) ernment could infringe upon the law by opening over a million acres of national forest and wildlife refuges to strip-mining. Naturally, the National Wildlife Federation is appalled. This proposal does (35) not augur well for wildlife, which will be destroyed by such latent killers as power lines and tainted ponds near strip-mines.

It doesn't require a sage to foresee the wrangle that is forthcoming between (40) proponents of conservation and the government. The consensus among environmentalists is that unless they obstruct the regulations, this land will be ravaged and our wildlife severely (45) maimed by strip-mining companies for the sake of a few pennies' profit.

1. From the context of the passage, the meaning of strip-mining is

   (A) the mining of coal on public lands
   (B) surface mining
   (C) shaft mining
   (D) illegal mining

2. The Federal Surface Mining Act

   (A) limits coal production
   (B) prohibits strip-mining
   (C) restricts strip-mining to specific locations
   (D) menaces wildlife

3. The expression *existing valid rights* refers to

   (A) mining rights in existence before 1977
   (B) miners' rights that cannot be violated
   (C) the right to mine coal any place in the United States
   (D) the right to mine on protected land

4. Wildlife is endangered by

   (A) coal mining
   (B) the Secretary of the Interior
   (C) toxic waste in bodies of water
   (D) migration paths

5. The proposed regulations will

   (A) curtail the rights of environmentalists
   (B) increase the area of strip-mining
   (C) help clean up the environment
   (D) cost miners a lot of money

6. The main idea of this passage is that

(A) changes in the present law would be detrimental to the environment

(B) a powerful government official can change laws

(C) environmentalists protect our land

(D) laws are made to be broken

QUESTIONS 7–11 ARE BASED ON THE FOLLOWING PASSAGE.

The nuclear industry is beset by controversy and mischance. Partially constructed plants have been closed down for several reasons. Construction costs
(5) have escalated, the demand for power has decreased, and the number of antagonists to nuclear plants has increased tremendously. Nuclear energy, once hailed with hope for a future with cheap,
(10) plentiful power, has reached an impasse.

The major cause of the deterioration in the nuclear industry is the fiasco at Three Mile Island in 1979. Ordinary machines break down, and humans are
(15) prone to error, but a nuclear power plant accident can cause widespread catastrophe. The most significant factor about the accident is, however, that it has jeopardized the whole future of nuclear
(20) energy. Public dissent, present though dormant when the first nuclear plants were constructed, has solidified after the deplorable chaos at Three Mile Island.

(25) Nevertheless, the nuclear plants built earlier continue to operate safely and economically. Smaller than more recently built plants, they have produced power that is consistently less expen-
(30) sive than power from coal or oil.

The investigaton of the Three Mile Island accident revealed that supervisors and management alike were inadequately trained to cope with a crucial
(35) mechanical failure in the nuclear system. Training programs today are developed more precisely. Now, prospective operators take years of classroom work and spend months under supervision in
(40) a control room and more months at the simulator, a computer programmed to recreate the Three Mile Island disaster, before returning to additional months in the classroom. The Nuclear Regulatory
(45) Commission administers oral and written exams before licensing new operators. Every six weeks compulsory refresher courses are given. Presumably, more scrupulous training requi-
(50) sites will reduce the chances of another Three Mile Island debacle.

7. What is the public's biggest objection to nuclear plants?

(A) Their cost

(B) The length of time it takes to construct them

(C) The amount of electricity they generate

(D) Their danger

8. Why has construction on new nuclear plants been stopped?

(A) They cost too much to build.

(B) People are using less electricity.

(C) The plants are potentially unsafe.

(D) All of the above.

9. Why has the Three Mile Island accident jeopardized the future of nuclear energy?

(A) The public saw the potential danger of nuclear plants and has united to protest their use.

(B) It cost more than a billion dollars to clean up the debris.

(C) It took twenty years to get the plant running again.

(D) Nuclear energy is too expensive.

10. Why are the older plants still in operation?

    (A) They were built twenty years ago.

    (B) They have better supervision than the new plants.

    (C) They are cheap to operate.

    (D) They are relatively safe, produce cheap electricity, and have efficient personnel.

11. What must the United States do before nuclear plants can be considered acceptable to their antagonists?

    (A) Nuclear plants must be nationalized.

    (B) Nuclear plants must be less expensive to build.

    (C) Waste disposal and safety must be assured.

    (D) Antinuclear groups must conceal their fears.

ANSWER KEY

1.	B	5.	B	9.	A
2.	C	6.	A	10.	D
3.	A	7.	D	11.	C
4.	C	8.	D		

SUMMING IT UP

- The reading passages progress from relatively simple to relatively difficult.

- You may need to refer back to the passage to know exactly what is said about the subject of the question.

- Inference questions are designed to measure whether you comprehend an argument or idea that is implied, but not stated in the passage.

- It is important to be able to recognize and understand signal words or connectives, which introduce, connect, order, and relate individual ideas to more general concepts.

PART IV
TWO PRACTICE TESTS

ANSWER SHEET PRACTICE TEST 2

1. Ⓐ Ⓑ Ⓒ Ⓓ   11. Ⓐ Ⓑ Ⓒ Ⓓ   21. Ⓐ Ⓑ Ⓒ Ⓓ   31. Ⓐ Ⓑ Ⓒ Ⓓ   41. Ⓐ Ⓑ Ⓒ Ⓓ

2. Ⓐ Ⓑ Ⓒ Ⓓ   12. Ⓐ Ⓑ Ⓒ Ⓓ   22. Ⓐ Ⓑ Ⓒ Ⓓ   32. Ⓐ Ⓑ Ⓒ Ⓓ   42. Ⓐ Ⓑ Ⓒ Ⓓ

3. Ⓐ Ⓑ Ⓒ Ⓓ   13. Ⓐ Ⓑ Ⓒ Ⓓ   23. Ⓐ Ⓑ Ⓒ Ⓓ   33. Ⓐ Ⓑ Ⓒ Ⓓ   43. Ⓐ Ⓑ Ⓒ Ⓓ

4. Ⓐ Ⓑ Ⓒ Ⓓ   14. Ⓐ Ⓑ Ⓒ Ⓓ   24. Ⓐ Ⓑ Ⓒ Ⓓ   34. Ⓐ Ⓑ Ⓒ Ⓓ   44. Ⓐ Ⓑ Ⓒ Ⓓ

5. Ⓐ Ⓑ Ⓒ Ⓓ   15. Ⓐ Ⓑ Ⓒ Ⓓ   25. Ⓐ Ⓑ Ⓒ Ⓓ   35. Ⓐ Ⓑ Ⓒ Ⓓ   45. Ⓐ Ⓑ Ⓒ Ⓓ

6. Ⓐ Ⓑ Ⓒ Ⓓ   16. Ⓐ Ⓑ Ⓒ Ⓓ   26. Ⓐ Ⓑ Ⓒ Ⓓ   36. Ⓐ Ⓑ Ⓒ Ⓓ   46. Ⓐ Ⓑ Ⓒ Ⓓ

7. Ⓐ Ⓑ Ⓒ Ⓓ   17. Ⓐ Ⓑ Ⓒ Ⓓ   27. Ⓐ Ⓑ Ⓒ Ⓓ   37. Ⓐ Ⓑ Ⓒ Ⓓ   47. Ⓐ Ⓑ Ⓒ Ⓓ

8. Ⓐ Ⓑ Ⓒ Ⓓ   18. Ⓐ Ⓑ Ⓒ Ⓓ   28. Ⓐ Ⓑ Ⓒ Ⓓ   38. Ⓐ Ⓑ Ⓒ Ⓓ   48. Ⓐ Ⓑ Ⓒ Ⓓ

9. Ⓐ Ⓑ Ⓒ Ⓓ   19. Ⓐ Ⓑ Ⓒ Ⓓ   29. Ⓐ Ⓑ Ⓒ Ⓓ   39. Ⓐ Ⓑ Ⓒ Ⓓ   49. Ⓐ Ⓑ Ⓒ Ⓓ

10. Ⓐ Ⓑ Ⓒ Ⓓ   20. Ⓐ Ⓑ Ⓒ Ⓓ   30. Ⓐ Ⓑ Ⓒ Ⓓ   40. Ⓐ Ⓑ Ⓒ Ⓓ   50. Ⓐ Ⓑ Ⓒ Ⓓ

answer sheet

Practice Test 2

QUESTIONS 1–10 REFER TO THE FOLLOWING PASSAGE.

People have been donating blood since the early twentieth century to help accident victims and patients undergoing surgical procedures. Usually a pint of
(5) whole blood is donated, and it is then divided into platelets, white blood cells, and red blood cells. People can donate blood (for red blood cells) about once every two months.

(10) Transfusing the blood from the donor to the recipient is straightforward. It involves taking the blood from a donor's arm vein by means of a hypodermic syringe. The blood flows through a plas-
(15) tic tube to a collection bag or bottle that contains sodium citrate, which prevents the blood from clotting.

When the blood is given to a patient, a plastic tube and hypodermic needle are
(20) connected to the recipient's arm. The blood flows down from the container by gravity. This is a slow process and may last as long as 2 hours to complete the infusion of blood into the recipient. The
(25) patient is protected from being infected during the transfusion. Only sterile containers, tubing, and needles are used, and this helps ensure that transfused or stored blood is not exposed to disease-
(30) causing bacteria.

Negative reactions to transfusions are not unusual. The recipient may suffer an allergic reaction or be sensitive to donor leukocytes. Some may suffer from
(35) an undetected red-cell incompatibility. Unexplained reactions are also fairly common. Although they are rare, other causes of such negative reactions include contaminated blood, air bubbles in
(40) the blood, overloading of the circulatory system through administration of excess blood, or sensitivity to donor plasma or platelets.

Today, hospitals and blood banks go to
(45) great lengths to screen all blood donors and their blood. All donated blood is routinely and rigorously tested for diseases, such as HIV (which causes AIDS), hepatitis B, and syphilis. When the re-
(50) cipient is a newborn or an infant, the blood is usually irradiated to eliminate harmful elements. Donated blood is washed, and the white blood cells and platelets are removed.

(55) Storing the blood sometimes requires a freezing process. To freeze the red blood cells, a glycerol solution is added. To unfreeze, the glycerol is removed. The ability to store blood for long periods has
(60) been a boon to human health.

1. Which of the following words is closest in meaning to the word "donating" in line 1?

   (A) Adorning
   (B) Giving
   (C) Taking
   (D) Distributing

2. In line 5, the word "it" refers to
   (A) accident victims
   (B) surgical procedures
   (C) a pint of whole blood
   (D) surgery patients

3. According to the passage, how often can people donate blood for red blood cells?
   (A) Every four months
   (B) Every three months
   (C) Every two months
   (D) Every month

4. Where in the passage is the best place for the following sentence?

   Inserting the needle into the recipient's arm causes little pain.

   (A) After the last sentence in the first paragraph
   (B) After the word "syringe" in paragraph 2
   (C) After the word "arm" in paragraph 3
   (D) After the word "transfusion" in paragraph 3

5. Which sentence in paragraph 2 explains how clotting is prevented in the blood container?
   (A) The first sentence
   (B) The second sentence
   (C) The third sentence
   (D) None of the above.

6. All of the following are mentioned as potential negative reactions to transfusions EXCEPT:
   (A) allergies
   (B) red-cell incompatibility
   (C) air bubbles in the blood
   (D) sensitivity to donor leukocytes

7. What answer choice is closest in meaning to the word "undetected" in line 35?
   (A) Not wanted
   (B) Not captured
   (C) Not found
   (D) Not illustrated

8. Look at the phrase "go to great lengths to screen" in paragraph 5, lines 44–45. Choose the word that has the same meaning.
   (A) Routinely
   (B) Rigorously
   (C) Irradiated
   (D) Removed

9. Based on the information in the passage, what can be inferred about blood transfused to infants and newborns?
   (A) It is as rigorously tested as blood for adults.
   (B) It is treated with radiant energy.
   (C) It is not treated differently from adults.
   (D) It is not dangerous for children.

10. What does the author imply in the passage?
    (A) Transfusing blood is a dangerous process.
    (B) Storing blood benefits mankind.
    (C) Clotting cannot be prevented.
    (D) Freezing blood destroys platelets.

QUESTIONS 11–20 REFER TO THE FOLLOWING PASSAGE.

Duncan Phyfe made some of the most beautiful furniture found in America. His family name was originally Fife, and he was born in Scotland in 1768. In 1784,
(5) the Fife family immigrated to Albany, New York where Duncan's father opened a cabinetmaking shop. Duncan followed in his father's footsteps and was apprenticed to a cabinetmaker. After complet-
(10) ing his training, Duncan moved to New York City.

Duncan Fife was first mentioned in the 1792 NYC Directory as a furniture "joiner" in business at 2 Broad Street.
(15) Two years later, he moved, expanded his business, and changed his name to Phyfe. He was a quiet-living, God-fearing young man who felt his new name would probably appeal to potential customers who
(20) were definitely anti-British in this post–Revolutionary War period.

Duncan Phyfe's name distinguished him from his contemporaries. Although the new spelling helped him better com-
(25) pete with French émigré craftsmen, his new name had more to do with hanging it on a sign over his door stoop.

The artisans and merchants who came to America discovered a unique kind of
(30) freedom. They were no longer restricted by class and guild traditions of Europe. For the first time in history, a man learned that by working hard, he could build his business based on his own
(35) name and reputation and quality of work.

Phyfe's workshop apparently took off immediately. At the peak of his success, Phyfe employed 100 craftsmen. Some economic historians point to Phyfe as
(40) having employed division of labor and an assembly line. What his workshop produced shows Phyfe's absolute dedication to quality in workmanship. Each piece of furniture was made of the best
(45) available materials. He was reported to have paid $1,000 for a single Santo Domingo mahogany log.

Phyfe did not create new designs. Rather, he borrowed from a broad range
(50) of the period's classical styles, Empire, Sheraton, Regency, and French Classical among them. Nevertheless, Phyfe's highquality craftsmanship established him as America's patriotic interpreter of
(55) European design in the late eighteenth and early nineteenth centuries.

Although the number of pieces produced by Duncan Phyfe's workshop is enormous, comparatively few marked
(60) or labeled pieces have been found extant. In antiques shops and auctions, collectors have paid $11,000 for a card table, $24,200 for a tea table, and $93,500 for a sewing table.

11. Based on the information in the passage, what can be inferred about Duncan Phyfe?

(A) He was an excellent businessman with a good sense of craftsmanship and design.

(B) He regretted that Great Britain no longer governed New York City.

(C) He built all his furniture by himself in a workshop in Santo Domingo.

(D) He joined the cabinetmakers' guild after he moved to Scotland in 1792.

12. According to the passage, which of the following does the author imply?

(A) Duncan Fife and his father had the same first name.

(B) Duncan Fife worked for his father in Scotland.

(C) Duncan Fife and his father were in the same business.

(D) Duncan Phyfe made over 100 different kinds of tables.

13. Which sentence in paragraph 2 explains Duncan's name change?

(A) The first sentence

(B) The second sentence

(C) The third sentence

(D) None of the above.

14. Which choice does the word "it" refer to in line 27?

    (A) His spelling

    (B) His chair

    (C) His French

    (D) His name

15. Which choice is closest in meaning to the word "guild" in line 31?

    (A) Verdict of a jury

    (B) Organization of craftsmen

    (C) Political party of émigrés

    (D) Immigrant's club

16. Which of the following does the word "freedom" in line 30 refer to?

    (A) No longer restricted

    (B) Restricted

    (C) By working hard

    (D) Took off

17. Where in the passage could the following sentence be added to the passage?

    Every joint was tight, and the carved elements were beautifully executed.

    (A) After the word "workmanship" in paragraph 5

    (B) After the word "cabinetmaker" in paragraph 1

    (C) After the word "stoop" in paragraph 3

    (D) After the word "table" in the last paragraph

18. In his business, Duncan Phyfe used all of the following EXCEPT:

    (A) division of labor

    (B) an assembly line

    (C) continental designs

    (D) the least expensive materials

19. Based on information in the passage, what can be inferred about Duncan Phyfe's death?

    (A) He died in the eighteenth century.

    (B) He died in Albany.

    (C) He died in the nineteenth century.

    (D) He died in Scotland.

20. The author implies that

    (A) furniture from Duncan Phyfe's workshop no longer exists

    (B) furniture from Duncan Phyfe's workshop costs a lot of money today

    (C) furniture from Duncan Phyfe's workshop was ignored by New Yorkers

    (D) furniture from Duncan Phyfe's workshop was made by his father

QUESTIONS 21–30 REFER TO THE FOLLOWING PASSAGE.

Roman gladiators are intriguing figures in history. We get "gladiator" from the Latin word *gladius*, which means sword. Gladiators were professional com-
(5) batants who originally performed, to the death, at Etruscan funerals. The losers became armed attendants in the next world to the person whose funeral was being held.
(10) In Rome, these exhibitions became very popular and increased in size from 3 pairs at the first known exhibition in 264 B.C. to 300 pairs in the middle of the first century B.C. These spectacles in-
(15) creased to as many as 100 pairs under the emperor Titus, while the emperor Trajan in 107 A.D. had 5,000 pairs of gladiators for his triumph.

There were various classes of gladia-
(20) tors, distinguished by their arms or modes of fighting. The Samnites fought with the national weapons—a large oblong shield, a visor, a plumed helmet, and a short sword. Thracians had a
(25) small round shield, called a buckler, and a dagger curved like a scythe. They usually fought the Mirmillones, who were armed in Gallic fashion with helmet, sword, and shield. Similarly, a Retiarius,

(30) or net man, was often matched with a Secutor, or pursuer. The netman wore nothing but a short tunic or apron and tried to entangle the fully armed pursuer with the cast net he carried in his

(35) right hand. If successful, the netman dispatched the pursuer with a large, threepronged weapon called a trident, which the netman carried in his left. Others fought on horseback, and some

(40) carried a short sword in each hand. There were also gladiators who fought from chariots and others who tried to lasso their antagonists.

Gladiators came from a variety of so-

(45) cial classes. Though they were usually slaves and criminals, a ruined man of high social position might hire himself out as a gladiator. Emperor Domitian had unusual gladiators, dwarfs and

(50) women, and the half-mad emperor Commodus fought in the arena, where he won his bouts with the aid of his Praetorian Guard.

To a victorious gladiator was given

(55) branches of palm and sometimes money. If they survived a number of combats, they were often freed from gladiatorial service. However, many gladiators reentered after discharge. Some became

(60) politically important bodyguards to controversial politicians.

21. What is the main topic of the passage?

(A) The life of Roman gladiators

(B) The emperors of Rome

(C) The weapons used in the Roman arena

(D) The social status of gladiators

22. According to the passage, where did gladiators originally perform?

(A) In Roman arenas

(B) At Thracian cities

(C) At Etruscan funerals

(D) In Trajan's triumph

23. According to the passage, when did the first known gladiatorial exhibition take place in Rome?

(A) In 50 B.C.

(B) In 264 B.C.

(C) In 107 A.D.

(D) In 157 B.C.

24. Which of the words below is closest in meaning to the word "spectacles" as used in line 14?

(A) Eyeglasses

(B) Displays

(C) Prospects

(D) Corpses

25. The word "they" in line 26 refers to which of the following?

(A) Samnites

(B) Gladiators

(C) Thracians

(D) Daggers

26. All of the following were used as weapons by gladiators EXCEPT:

(A) a buckler

(B) a cast net

(C) a tunic

(D) a trident

27. Where would the following sentence fit best in the passage?

In the 2000 film *Gladiator*, Joaquin Phoenix played the role of Commodus and fought Maximus, the gladiator.

(A) At the end of paragraph 1

(B) At the end of paragraph 2

(C) At the end of paragraph 3

(D) At the end of paragraph 4

28. Which word is closest in meaning to the word "antagonists" as used in line 43?

(A) Enemies

(B) Injured soldiers

(C) Horsemen

(D) Fighters

29. From the passage, it can be inferred that

(A) gladiators could become Emperor

(B) emperors enjoyed fighting gladiators

(C) gladiators sometimes gained their freedom

(D) emperors fought on horseback

30. Where could the following sentence best be added to the passage?

Some, in turn, became trainers of new gladiators.

(A) After the word "history" in paragraph 1

(B) After the word "shield" in paragraph 3

(C) After the word "classes" in paragraph 4

(D) After the word "service" in paragraph 5

QUESTIONS 31–40 REFER TO THE FOLLOWING PASSAGE.

The Forbidden City is the former imperial palace in the center of Beijing, China. Construction began in 1406, and the emperor's court officially moved in by
(5) 1420. The Forbidden City got its name because most people were barred from entering the 72-hectare site, surrounded by walls. Even government officials and the imperial family were permitted only
(10) limited access. Only the emperor could enter any section at will.

The architecture of the Forbidden City conforms rigidly to traditional Chinese principles. All buildings within the walls
(15) follow a north-south line, and the most important ones face south to honor the sun. The designers arranged the other buildings, and the ceremonial spaces between them, to impress all visitors
(20) with the great power of the Emperor, while reinforcing the insignificance of the individual. This architectural con-

cept was carried out to the smallest detail. For example, the importance of a
(25) building was determined not only by its height or width but also by the style of its roof and the quantity of statuettes placed on the roof's ridges.

In recognition of the importance of its
(30) unparalleled architecture, UNESCO added the palace to its World Heritage List in 1987. Today, visitors from all over the world do not wait for an imperial invitation to walk about this palace,
(35) now a museum of imperial art.

One of the most impressive landmarks of the Forbidden City is the Meridian Gate, the formal entrance to the southern side of the Forbidden City. The gate,
(40) with its auxiliary wings on either side of the entryway, is 38 meters high at its roof ridge. When you stand in front of this majestic structure, you understand how awed people felt when they stood
(45) there listening to imperial proclamations.

As you walk through the gate, you come into a large courtyard, 140 meters long and 210 meters wide. Running
(50) through the courtyard is the Golden River, which is crossed by five parallel white marble bridges. These bridges lead to the Gate of Supreme Harmony, which, in turn, leads to the heart of the Forbid-
(55) den City. Its three main halls stand atop a three-tiered marble terrace overlooking an immense plaza. The plaza has enough space to hold tens of thousands of subjects paying homage to the em-
(60) peror.

At the northernmost end of the Forbidden City is the Imperial Garden, which is totally different from the rest of the compound. Instead of rigid formality, you see
(65) a seemingly spontaneous arrangement of trees, fishponds, flowerbeds, and sculpture. Here is the place of relaxation for the emperor. The motion picture *The Last Emperor* (1987), which portrays the
(70) life of Hsüan-t'ung P'u-i, was filmed partly within the Forbidden City.

31. Which sentence in paragraph 1 explains who could go anywhere in the Forbidden City at any time?

(A) Sentence 2

(B) Sentence 3

(C) Sentence 4

(D) Sentence 5

32. How long did it take to build the Forbidden City?

(A) About five years

(B) About seven years

(C) About ten years

(D) About fourteen years

33. From the passage, it can be inferred that

(A) Chinese architects borrowed ideas from many different countries

(B) the design of the Forbidden City is dull and colorless

(C) the architecture of the Forbidden City exemplifies traditional Chinese values

(D) the garden of the Forbidden City was laid out in a strict, rectangular pattern

34. Which phrase is closest in meaning to the word "unparalleled" as used in line 30?

(A) At an angle from the main line

(B) A high quality found nowhere else

(C) Partially designed in a foreign country

(D) Careless of small details in design

35. Which word(s) does the word "its" refer to in line 31?

(A) UNESCO

(B) Architecture

(C) Palace

(D) World Heritage List

36. From the passage, it is implied that the main entrance area to the Forbidden City is

(A) surrounded by three tall walls

(B) painted gold and green

(C) decorated with statuettes

(D) not very impressive

37. Which phrase is closest in meaning to the word "proclamations" as used in lines 45–46?

(A) Music composed for public ceremonies

(B) Speeches encouraging soldiers to fight

(C) Official public announcements

(D) Poetry written for the emperor

38. All of the following are found in the Imperial Garden EXCEPT:

(A) fishponds

(B) sculpture

(C) white marble bridges

(D) flowerbeds

39. According to the passage, what do the bridges over the Golden River lead to?

(A) The Meridian gate

(B) The center of Beijing

(C) The Gate of Supreme Harmony

(D) The Imperial Gardens

40. Which phrase is closest in meaning to the word "spontaneous" as used in line 65?

(A) Without meaning

(B) Without thinking

(C) Without planning

(D) Without drawing

QUESTIONS 41–50 REFER TO THE FOLLOWING PASSAGE.

Early mariners gradually developed ways of observing and recording in their journals their position, the distances and directions they traveled, the cur-
(5) rents of wind and water, and the hazards and havens they encountered. The information in these journals enabled them to find their way home and, for them or their successors, to repeat and
(10) extend the recorded voyages. Each new observation could be added to an ever-increasing body of reliable information.

Ship captains and navigators were not concerned about running into other ves-
(15) sels, but as heavy traffic developed along shipping routes, avoiding such collisions became a serious matter. In all fields of navigation, keeping a safe distance between ships moving in different direc-
(20) tions at different speeds became as important as knowing how to reach one's destination.

The larger the ship, the easier it is to see, but the larger a ship, the more time
(25) it requires to change its speed or direction. When many ships are in a small area, an action taken by one ship to avoid colliding with another might endanger a third. In busy seaports, such as
(30) Hamburg and New York, this problem has been solved by assigning incoming and outgoing ships to separate lanes, which are clearly marked and divided by the greatest practical distance.

(35) The speed of jet airplanes makes collision a deadly possibility. Even if two pilots see one another in time to begin evasive action, their maneuvers may be useless if either pilot incorrectly pre-
(40) dicts the other's move. Ground-based air traffic controllers assign aircraft to flight paths that keep airplanes a safe distance from one another.

When steam engines began to replace
(45) sails during the first half of the nineteenth century, a ship's navigator had to compute fuel consumption as well as course and location. Today, in airplanes as well as in ships, large amounts of fuel,
(50) needed for long trips, reduce the cargo capacity, and economy requires that its consumption be kept to a minimum.

In modern air and sea navigation, a schedule has to be met. A single voyage
(55) or flight is only one link in a complicated and coordinated transportation network that carries goods and people from any starting place to any chosen destination. Modern navigation selects a ship's
(60) course, avoids collision with other moving ships, minimizes fuel consumption, and follows an established timetable.

41. What is the main topic of the passage?

(A) Historical records of navigation

(B) Airplane navigation in Europe

(C) Schedules and shipping long distances

(D) The growing importance of navigation

42. Which of the choices is closest in meaning to the word "hazards" as used in lines 5–6?

(A) Dangerous obstacles

(B) Safe seaports

(C) Whales and large fish

(D) Inaccurate navigation

43. Which of the following has the same meaning as the word "collisions" as used in line 16?

(A) Other vessels

(B) Running into

(C) Avoiding such

(D) Serious matter

44. Which of the following does the word "it" in line 23 refer to?

(A) Ship

(B) Time

(C) Speed

(D) Larger

45. Where can the following sentence be added to the passage?

In fact, many harbors were burned down from fires begun as a result of ships' colliding in port.

(A) After the word "encountered" in paragraph 1

(B) At the end of paragraph 2

(C) After the word "third" in paragraph 3

(D) After the word "possibility" in paragraph 4

46. How are ships kept apart in the ports of Hamburg and New York?

(A) The port controllers guide ship captains by radio.

(B) Incoming and outgoing ships are assigned to clearly marked lanes.

(C) Ships are not allowed to change their course or their speed while in port.

(D) Captains use their journals to determine the hazards in port.

47. What does the author imply about the speed of jet airplanes?

(A) Air traffic is now safer than it was with planes with piston-driven engines.

(B) Radio communication between ships and planes help schedules.

(C) Collisions of jet airplanes almost always result in the deaths of passengers and crew.

(D) Pilots are now able to predict evasive maneuvers that others will take.

48. What can be inferred about fuel consumption in the nineteenth century?

(A) A ship's captain had to decide how many sails would be used on a ship.

(B) A navigator had to determine how much fuel a ship needed for a voyage.

(C) A large amount of fuel made room for extra cargo space.

(D) A journal was kept about the amount of coal a steam engine used during a voyage.

49. Look at the word "timetable" in the last sentence of the passage. Which of the following words has the same meaning?

(A) Schedule

(B) Network

(C) Navigation

(D) Established

50. Which of the following statements is supported by the passage?

(A) Information in mariners' journals is better than modern navigation techniques.

(B) Collisions in the air are more dangerous than those at sea.

(C) Mariners today have to compute more things than those in the past did.

(D) Air traffic controllers use the same navigation techniques as sea captains.

ANSWER KEY AND EXPLANATIONS

1.	B	11.	A	21.	A	31.	D	41.	D
2.	C	12.	C	22.	C	32.	D	42.	A
3.	C	13.	C	23.	B	33.	C	43.	B
4.	C	14.	D	24.	B	34.	B	44.	A
5.	C	15.	B	25.	C	35.	A	45.	C
6.	C	16.	A	26.	C	36.	A	46.	B
7.	C	17.	A	27.	D	37.	C	47.	C
8.	B	18.	D	28.	A	38.	C	48.	B
9.	B	19.	C	29.	C	39.	C	49.	A
10.	B	20.	B	30.	D	40.	C	50.	C

1. **The correct answer is (B).** *Adorning* means "making beautiful" or "adding decorations to." *Taking* is the opposite of *donating*. *Distributing* is similar to *donating* but means "giving the same amount to more than two people."

2. **The correct answer is (C).** *It* refers to "a pint of whole blood." The whole phrase is necessary for the rest of the sentence to be understood. All other answer choices are plural; *it* is singular.

3. **The correct answer is (C).** The last sentence of paragraph 1 is, "People can donate blood [for red blood cells] about once every two months."

4. **The correct answer is (C).** The sentence fits best in the third paragraph, after the first sentence. The paragraph is about what happens to the person who receives the blood. That person is a recipient or a patient.

5. **The correct answer is (C).** The sentence is as follows: "The blood flows through a plastic tube to a collection bag or bottle that contains sodium citrate, which prevents the blood from clotting."

6. **The correct answer is (C).** "Air bubbles in the blood" is not a reaction to a transfusion. It is a *cause* of a negative reaction.

7. **The correct answer is (C).** *Undetected* means "not discovered" or "not realized." In the sentence, the other answer choices are incorrect.

8. **The correct answer is (B).** The correct word is *rigorously.*

9. **The correct answer is (B).** In the fifth paragraph, it is stated that blood is irradiated when the recipient is a newborn or an infant. To radiate means to treat with radiant energy.

10. **The correct answer is (B).** None of the other answer choices are stated or implied in the passage.

11. **The correct answer is (A).** The other answer choices use countries and dates mentioned in the passage but in an incorrect way.

12. **The correct answer is (C).** The first name of Duncan's father is neither mentioned nor implied. Duncan did not work in Scotland. He worked after he came to America. Duncan Phyfe employed 100 craftsmen, but the passage does not say how many kinds of tables his workshop made.

13. **The correct answer is (C).** "He was a quiet-living, God-fearing young man who felt his new name would probably appeal to potential customers who were definitely anti-British in this post–Revolutionary War period." In paragraph 2, this is the only sentence about his name change.

14. **The correct answer is (D).** Phyfe did not put *his spelling, his chair,* or *his French* on a sign over his door stoop.

15. **The correct answer is (B).** As the word was used in the fourth paragraph, it refers to the organizations that trained craftsmen for a variety of work. Guilds also controlled who could work in a particular craft and stood for high standards. As the word was used in the

fourth paragraph, trials are not mentioned. The verdict of a jury may be "Guilty" but never "guild." As the word was used in the fourth paragraph, it does not refer to émigrés, political parties, or clubs.

16. **The correct answer is (A).** *No longer restricted* is the correct phrase.

17. **The correct answer is (A).** The sentence best fits in the fifth paragraph after the following sentence: "What his workshop produced shows Phyfe's absolute dedication to quality in workmanship." The inserted sentence tells the reader about the results of Phyfe's dedication to quality in workmanship.

18. **The correct answer is (D).** In paragraph 5, the last sentence reports that Phyfe spent a lot of money on materials.

19. **The correct answer is (C).** Paragraph 2 tells the reader that Phyfe began his work as a joiner in 1792, in the late eighteenth century. Paragraph 6 tells us he interpreted European design in the late eighteenth and early nineteenth centuries.

20. **The correct answer is (B).** The last paragraph says that few pieces of Phyfe's work have been found, but they do exist ("are extant"). His furniture was not ignored; it was popular. His father did not work for him.

21. **The correct answer is (A).** The emperors, weapons, and social status are mentioned in the passage, but they are only part of the main topic, not the main topic itself.

22. **The correct answer is (C).** See the third sentence of the first paragraph.

23. **The correct answer is (B).** See paragraph 2, first sentence.

24. **The correct answer is (B).** *Spectacles* sometimes means the same thing as eyeglasses but not in this passage. The other two words are distractors that have no connection to the meaning of the word *spectacle*.

25. **The correct answer is (C).** *They* is a plural pronoun, which has to refer to a plural noun. The plural noun in the preceding sentence is *Thracians*.

26. **The correct answer is (C).** A *tunic* is an article of clothing, not a weapon.

27. **The correct answer is (D).** This sentence would best fit the passage at the end of paragraph 4. It adds information about the previous sentence that mentions the emperor Commodus.

28. **The correct answer is (A).** The other answer choices are not related to the meaning of the word as it is used in the last sentence of paragraph 3.

29. **The correct answer is (C).** See the second sentence of paragraph 5. Gladiators could not become emperors. Although Commodus fought gladiators, no other emperor did so. The passage does not mention whether emperors fought on horseback.

30. **The correct answer is (D).** The sentence best fits in paragraph 5, after the second sentence. *Some* refers to gladiators who had been freed from gladiatorial service.

31. **The correct answer is (D).** Only the emperor could enter any section at will. See the last sentence of paragraph 1.

32. **The correct answer is (D).** See sentence 2 in paragraph 1.

33. **The correct answer is (C).** The first sentence of the second paragraph tells the reader that Chinese architects did not borrow ideas from any other country. The first sentence of the third paragraph tells the reader how important the design was. Paragraph 4 tells the reader to enter through the Meridian Gate.

34. **The correct answer is (B).** *Unparalleled* is not related in meaning to *parallel*. The last two answer choices are distractors that contain words, but incorrect ideas, from the passage.

35. **The correct answer is (A).** *Its* refers to UNESCO.

36. **The correct answer is (A).** The fourth paragraph tells the reader about the gate and its two auxiliary walls.

37. **The correct answer is (C).** All other choices are distracters that incorrectly define the word *proclamations*.

38. **The correct answer is (C).** White marble bridges are found in the courtyard behind the Meridian gate. See the second sentence of paragraph 5.

39. **The correct answer is (C).** See the fifth paragraph of the passage.

40. **The correct answer is (C).** The other three choices are distracters that are not related in meaning to the correct answer.

41. **The correct answer is (D).** The three other choices are mentioned or implied in the passage, but the main topic includes these ideas.

42. **The correct answer is (A).** *Safe seaports* are not hazards. *Whales and large fish* could be a hazard but are not as close in meaning to *hazards* as *dangerous obstacles*. *Inaccurate* is a distractor that is not related to the meaning of the word in context.

43. **The correct answer is (B).** The correct phrase is *running into other vessels*.

44. **The correct answer is (A).** The correct word is *ship*.

45. **The correct answer is (C).** The sentence best fits in paragraph 3, after the second sentence. This sentence reports the results of two ships colliding in a harbor.

46. **The correct answer is (B).** See the third sentence in paragraph 3.

47. **The correct answer is (C).** See the first sentence of paragraph 4.

48. **The correct answer is (B).** See the first sentence of paragraph 5.

49. **The correct answer is (A).**

50. **The correct answer is (C).** The passage reports how navigation became more complex over time.

ANSWER SHEET PRACTICE TEST 3

1. Ⓐ Ⓑ Ⓒ Ⓓ	11. Ⓐ Ⓑ Ⓒ Ⓓ	21. Ⓐ Ⓑ Ⓒ Ⓓ	31. Ⓐ Ⓑ Ⓒ Ⓓ	41. Ⓐ Ⓑ Ⓒ Ⓓ
2. Ⓐ Ⓑ Ⓒ Ⓓ	12. Ⓐ Ⓑ Ⓒ Ⓓ	22. Ⓐ Ⓑ Ⓒ Ⓓ	32. Ⓐ Ⓑ Ⓒ Ⓓ	42. Ⓐ Ⓑ Ⓒ Ⓓ
3. Ⓐ Ⓑ Ⓒ Ⓓ	13. Ⓐ Ⓑ Ⓒ Ⓓ	23. Ⓐ Ⓑ Ⓒ Ⓓ	33. Ⓐ Ⓑ Ⓒ Ⓓ	43. Ⓐ Ⓑ Ⓒ Ⓓ
4. Ⓐ Ⓑ Ⓒ Ⓓ	14. Ⓐ Ⓑ Ⓒ Ⓓ	24. Ⓐ Ⓑ Ⓒ Ⓓ	34. Ⓐ Ⓑ Ⓒ Ⓓ	44. Ⓐ Ⓑ Ⓒ Ⓓ
5. Ⓐ Ⓑ Ⓒ Ⓓ	15. Ⓐ Ⓑ Ⓒ Ⓓ	25. Ⓐ Ⓑ Ⓒ Ⓓ	35. Ⓐ Ⓑ Ⓒ Ⓓ	45. Ⓐ Ⓑ Ⓒ Ⓓ
6. Ⓐ Ⓑ Ⓒ Ⓓ	16. Ⓐ Ⓑ Ⓒ Ⓓ	26. Ⓐ Ⓑ Ⓒ Ⓓ	36. Ⓐ Ⓑ Ⓒ Ⓓ	46. Ⓐ Ⓑ Ⓒ Ⓓ
7. Ⓐ Ⓑ Ⓒ Ⓓ	17. Ⓐ Ⓑ Ⓒ Ⓓ	27. Ⓐ Ⓑ Ⓒ Ⓓ	37. Ⓐ Ⓑ Ⓒ Ⓓ	47. Ⓐ Ⓑ Ⓒ Ⓓ
8. Ⓐ Ⓑ Ⓒ Ⓓ	18. Ⓐ Ⓑ Ⓒ Ⓓ	28. Ⓐ Ⓑ Ⓒ Ⓓ	38. Ⓐ Ⓑ Ⓒ Ⓓ	48. Ⓐ Ⓑ Ⓒ Ⓓ
9. Ⓐ Ⓑ Ⓒ Ⓓ	19. Ⓐ Ⓑ Ⓒ Ⓓ	29. Ⓐ Ⓑ Ⓒ Ⓓ	39. Ⓐ Ⓑ Ⓒ Ⓓ	49. Ⓐ Ⓑ Ⓒ Ⓓ
10. Ⓐ Ⓑ Ⓒ Ⓓ	20. Ⓐ Ⓑ Ⓒ Ⓓ	30. Ⓐ Ⓑ Ⓒ Ⓓ	40. Ⓐ Ⓑ Ⓒ Ⓓ	50. Ⓐ Ⓑ Ⓒ Ⓓ

answer sheet

Practice Test 3

QUESTIONS 1–10 REFER TO THE FOLLOWING PASSAGE.

Jonas Salk is the American physician and medical researcher who developed the first safe and effective vaccine for poliomyelitis. Salk received his M.D. in
(5) 1939 from New York University College of Medicine, where he worked with Thomas Francis Jr., who was studying how to develop vaccines from killed viruses. Salk joined Francis in 1942 at the Uni-
(10) versity of Michigan School of Public Health and became part of a group that was working to develop a vaccine against influenza.

In 1947, Salk became associate profes-
(15) sor of bacteriology and head of the Virus Research Laboratory at the University of Pittsburgh School of Medicine, where he began research on poliomyelitis. Working with scientists from other uni-
(20) versities in a program to classify the various strains of the polio virus, Salk corroborated other studies in identifying three separate strains. He then demonstrated that killed virus of each of the
(25) three, although incapable of producing the disease, could induce antibody formation in monkeys.

In 1952, he conducted field tests of his killed-virus vaccine, first on children
(30) who had recovered from polio and then on subjects who had not had the disease. The results of both tests showed that the children's antibody levels rose signifi-

cantly and no subjects contracted polio
(35) from the vaccine. His findings were published the following year in the *Journal of the American Medical Association*. In 1954, a mass field trial was held, and the vaccine, injected by needle, was found to
(40) safely reduce the incidence of polio. On April 12, 1955, the vaccine was released for use in the United States.

Salk served successively as professor of bacteriology, preventive medicine, and
(45) experimental medicine at Pittsburgh, and in 1963, he became fellow and director of the Institute for Biological Studies in San Diego, California, later called the Salk Institute. Among many other hon-
(50) ors, he was awarded the Presidential Medal of Freedom in 1977.

1. What is the main idea of the passage?

    (A) How Jonas Salk trained to be a physician and medical researcher

    (B) How the medical research of Jonas Salk led to the development of the polio vaccine

    (C) How Salk and his colleagues learned to kill viruses

    (D) How Salk was promoted to important positions at the University of Pennsylvania

2. Which of the following is the closest in meaning to the word "vaccine" as used in line 3 of the passage?

   (A) Medicine designed to cure a disease temporarily

   (B) Medicine that cures a disease after the patient gets sick

   (C) Medicine designed to kill viruses that are fatal to children

   (D) Medicine that creates immunity against a disease

3. In the first paragraph, what was Thomas Francis Jr. studying?

   (A) How to prevent the spread of influenza in Michigan

   (B) How to work with physicians from Manhattan

   (C) How to develop vaccines from killed viruses

   (D) How to get a degree in medicine from New York University

4. Which sentence in the second paragraph describes Salk's first work at the University of Pittsburgh?

   (A) The first sentence

   (B) The second sentence

   (C) The third sentence

   (D) None of the above.

5. Which word is closest in meaning to the word "corroborated" as used in line 22 of the passage?

   (A) Rejected

   (B) Published

   (C) Examined

   (D) Confirmed

6. All of the following statements about the killed virus vaccine are true EXCEPT:

   (A) it did not induce antibody formation in monkeys

   (B) it had three strains that scientists worked with

   (C) it was incapable of producing the disease

   (D) it helped monkeys form antibodies

7. Look at the word "findings" in line 35. Which of the following words or phrases from the previous sentence does the word "findings" refer to?

   (A) Results

   (B) Antibody levels

   (C) Vaccine

   (D) Polio

8. From the passage, it can be inferred that the experimental polio vaccine was given to people by

   (A) pill

   (B) injection

   (C) surgery

   (D) liquid

9. In the passage, it is implied that the Salk Institute was

   (A) originally called the Institute for Biological Studies

   (B) originally the University of Michigan School of Public Health

   (C) originally the Virus Research Laboratory at the University of Pittsburgh

   (D) originally the medical school at New York University

10. Where in the passage could the following sentence best fit?

    Thousands of children and adults were free from the fears of contracting this terrible disease.

    (A) At the end of paragraph 1

    (B) At the end of paragraph 2

    (C) At the end of paragraph 3

    (D) At the end of paragraph 4

QUESTIONS 11–20 REFER TO THE FOLLOWING PASSAGE.

The word *synthesize* means to produce by combining separate elements. Thus, synthesized sound is sound that a musician builds from component elements.
(5) A synthesized sound may resemble a traditional acoustic musical timbre, or it may be completely novel and original. One characteristic is common to all synthesized music, however. The sound
(10) qualities themselves, as well as the relationships among the sounds, have been "designed," or "composed," by a musician.

Many people believe that synthesized
(15) music imitates traditional musical instruments and ensembles. They believe that synthesized music is created mechanically without control by a musician. These ideas are not true.
(20) A builder of a traditional musical instrument assembles a collection of acoustic elements whose interrelationships cannot change. For example, a violin has four strings positioned over a finger-
(25) board and coupled through the bridge to the violin's body. Violinists bring the strings into contact with the fingerboard and a bow to cause the strings to vibrate. The resultant sound is resonated by the
(30) hollow body of the violin. However, violinists do not change the relationship of the strings to the bridge, nor that of the bridge to the body. Nor, do they reconfigure its slightly hour-glass shape.
(35) Synthesists, on the other hand, view their instrument as a collection of parts that they configure to produce the sounds they want. They call this "programming," or "patching," and they may do this be-
(40) fore or during performance. The parts that synthesists work with depend on the design of the instruments that they are using. In general, synthesizers include elements that generate and com-
(45) bine waveforms and that shape loudness of the sounds. Other sound-producing and -processing elements, which can exist as electronic circuits or as built-in computer programs, may also be avail-
(50) able. To control these elements, a syn-

thesist may use a combination of a conventional keyboard and other manual control devices, such as wheels, sliders, and joysticks.

11. Which answer choice is closest in meaning to the word "resemble" as used in line 5?

   (A) Recreate

   (B) Put together

   (C) Sound like

   (D) Take apart

12. According to the passage, what do component elements of synthesizers include?

   (A) Computer programs and hollow bodies

   (B) Bridges and electronic circuits

   (C) Fingerboards and patchers

   (D) Computers and electronic keyboards

13. It can be inferred from the passage that many people

   (A) dislike synthesized music because it lacks harmony and beauty

   (B) enjoy imitating the sounds of musical instruments

   (C) build musical instruments in their home

   (D) believe that synthesized music is created by a machine, not by a musician

14. According to the passage, the interrelationships of acoustical elements in traditional musical instruments

   (A) comprise wood and horsehair

   (B) cannot be changed

   (C) resonate musical notes

   (D) resemble an hour glass

15. Which answer choice is the closest in meaning to the word "coupled" as used in line 25?

   (A) Connected

   (B) Performed

   (C) Folded

   (D) Vibrated

16. All of the following contribute to the sound of a violin EXCEPT:

   (A) a bridge

   (B) a fingerboard

   (C) a keyboard

   (D) a bow

17. Where in the passage would the following sentence best fit?

   This, in turn, vibrates the air and sends the sound to the listener's ears.

   (A) After the word "original" in the first paragraph

   (B) After the word "ensembles" in the second paragraph

   (C) After the phrase "hollow body of a violin" in the third paragraph

   (D) At the end of the fourth paragraph

18. The word "its" as used in line 34 refers to which of the following words or phrases from the preceding sentence?

   (A) Violinists

   (B) Strings

   (C) The body

   (D) The bridge

19. What is the main idea of the passage?

   (A) Synthesized music is loved by everyone who enjoys rock and popular music.

   (B) Synthesized music is used mostly in film and TV.

   (C) Synthesized music combines separate elements and changes the relationships of those elements.

   (D) Synthesized music cannot resemble traditional musical instruments.

20. According to the passage, what are wheels, sliders, and joysticks?

   (A) Relationships among elements

   (B) Parts of computer game boards

   (C) Manual control devices on sound synthesizers

   (D) Sound qualities designed by a synthesist

QUESTIONS 21–30 REFER TO THE FOLLOWING PASSAGE.

The *New York Times* is a daily newspaper published in New York City. For a long time, it has been the newspaper of record in the United States and one of
(5) the world's great newspapers. Its strength is in its editorial excellence; it has never been the largest newspaper in terms of circulation.

The *Times* was established in 1851 as
(10) a penny paper whose editors wanted to report the news in a restrained and objective fashion. It enjoyed early success as its editors set a pattern for the future by appealing to a cultured, intel-
(15) lectual readership instead of a mass audience. However, in the late nineteenth century, it came into competition with more popular, colorful, if not lurid, newspapers in New York City. Despite
(20) price increases, the *Times* was losing $1,000 a week when Adolph Simon Ochs bought it in 1896.

Ochs built the *Times* into an internationally respected daily. He hired Carr
(25) Van Anda as editor. Van Anda placed greater stress than ever on full reporting of the news of the day, and his reporters maintained and emphasized existing good coverage of international
(30) news. The management of the paper decided to eliminate fiction from the paper, added a Sunday magazine section, and reduced the paper's price back to a penny. In April 1912, the paper took
(35) many risks to report every aspect of the sinking of the *Titanic*. This greatly enhanced its prestige, and in its coverage of two world wars, the *Times* continued to enhance its reputation for excellence
(40) in world news.

In 1971, the *Times* was given a copy of the so-called "Pentagon Papers," a secret government study of U.S. involvement in the Vietnam War. When it
(45) published the report, it became involved in several lawsuits. The U.S. Supreme Court found that the publication was protected by the freedom-of-the-press clause in the First Amendment of the

(50) U.S. Constitution. Later in the 1970s, the paper, under Adolph Ochs's grandson, Arthur Ochs Sulzberger, introduced sweeping changes in the organization of the newspaper and its staff and brought
(55) out a national edition transmitted by satellite to regional printing plants.

21. What is the main idea of the passage?

    (A) The *New York Times* publishes the best fiction by American writers.

    (B) The *New York Times* became highly respected throughout the world.

    (C) The *New York Times* broadcasts its news to TV stations via satellite.

    (D) The *New York Times* lost its prestige after the Vietnam War.

22. It can be inferred from the passage that the circulation of the *Times* is

    (A) not the largest in the world.

    (B) not the best in the world.

    (C) the smallest in the world.

    (D) the worst in the world.

23. Which phrase is closest in meaning to the word "restrained" as it is used in line 11?

    (A) Put in prison

    (B) In handcuffs

    (C) Without education

    (D) With self-control

24. According to the passage, what caused the loss of money at the *Times*?

    (A) Other newspapers were more colorful.

    (B) Other newspapers had better reporters.

    (C) Other newspapers added a Sunday magazine.

    (D) Other newspapers were better managed.

25. What word or phrase does the word "his" as used in line 27 refer to?

    (A) Van Anda

    (B) Reporters

    (C) News of the day

    (D) International news

26. Where can the following sentence best be added to the passage?

    Their publishers ran sensational stories, not because they were true, but because they sold newspapers.

    (A) At the end of the first paragraph

    (B) After the word "City" in the second paragraph

    (C) At the end of the third paragraph

    (D) After the phrase "lawsuits" in the fourth paragraph

27. To improve its circulation, the management of the *Times* did all of the following EXCEPT:

    (A) emphasized good coverage of international news

    (B) added a Sunday magazine section

    (C) increased the number of lurid stories, even if they were not true

    (D) eliminated fiction from the paper

28. The passage implies that the newspaper's reputation

    (A) decreased when it lowered its price to a penny

    (B) grew because Adolph Ochs bought it in 1896

    (C) increased because of its coverage of the *Titanic*'s sinking

    (D) decreased because it could not compete with other New York papers

29. What word or phrase does the word "publication" as used in line 47 refer to?

(A) The *Times*

(B) "The Pentagon Papers"

(C) The Report

(D) The Constitution

30. According to the passage, the *Times* has a national edition that is

(A) protected by the Supreme Court

(B) printed in the form of a Sunday magazine

(C) shipped by train and air transport daily

(D) transmitted by satellite to regional printing plants

QUESTIONS 31–40 REFER TO THE FOLLOWING PASSAGE.

Pittsburgh, Pennsylvania, is located where the Allegheny and Monongahela rivers unite to form the Ohio River. Its fascinating history began in 1758 when
(5) General John Forbes and his British and colonial army captured Fort Duquesne from the French and renamed it Fort Pitt, for the British statesman William Pitt the Elder. After an agree-
(10) ment between the Native American tribes and William Penn's family, settlers began arriving. Pittsburgh was laid out (1764) by John Campbell in the area around the fort.
(15) Following the American Revolution, the town became an outfitting point for settlers traveling westward down the Ohio River. Pittsburgh's strategic location and wealth of natural resources
(20) spurred its commercial and industrial growth in the nineteenth century. A blast furnace, erected by George Anschutz about 1792, was the forerunner of the iron and steel industry that for
(25) more than a century was the city's economic power. By 1850, it was known as the "Iron City." The Pennsylvania Canal and the Portage Railroad, both completed in 1834, opened vital markets for
(30) trade and shipping.

After the American Civil War, great numbers of European immigrants swelled Pittsburgh's population, and industrial magnates such as Andrew
(35) Carnegie, Henry Clay Frick, and Thomas Mellon built their steel empires there. The city became the focus of historic friction between labor and management, and the American Federation
(40) of Labor was organized there in 1881. By 1900, the city's population had reached 321,616. Growth continued nearly unabated through World War II, and during the war years, Pittsburgh was a
(45) boom town.

During this period of economic and population growth, Pittsburgh became a grimy, polluted industrial city. After the war, however, the city undertook an
(50) extensive redevelopment program, with emphasis on smoke-pollution control, flood prevention, and sewage disposal. In 1957, it became the first American city to generate electricity by nuclear
(55) power. By the late 1970s and early 80s, the steel industry had virtually disappeared, but Pittsburgh successfully diversified its economy through more emphasis on light industries and on such
(60) high-technology industries as computer software, industrial automation (robotics), and biomedical and environmental technologies.

31. In the mid-eighteenth century, what two countries wanted to control the area now known as Pittsburgh?

(A) England and the United States

(B) England and France

(C) England and Germany

(D) England and Pennsylvania

32. When did settlers begin arriving in Pittsburgh?

    (A) After an agreement between the Indians and the Penn family

    (B) After the Allegheny and Monongahela rivers united

    (C) After the British captured Fort Pitt

    (D) After the American Revolution

33. Which phrase is closest in meaning to the phrase "outfitting point" as used in line 16?

    (A) A store that sells gasoline and oil

    (B) A location of food and water

    (C) A place to buy business suits and accessories

    (D) A source of equipment and supplies

34. What became the most important industry in Pittsburgh following the American Revolution?

    (A) The shipping industry

    (B) The iron and steel industry

    (C) The outfitting industry

    (D) The computer software industry

35. Which of the following phrases is closest in meaning to the phrase "vital markets" as used in line 29?

    (A) Hospitals and medical centers

    (B) Large stores for food and clothing

    (C) Places with customers for Pittsburgh's products

    (D) Native American tribes and military forts

36. According to the passage, who moved to Pittsburgh in great numbers after the Civil War?

    (A) Native American tribes

    (B) British soldiers

    (C) Confederate veterans

    (D) European immigrants

37. Which of the following phrases is closest in meaning to the phrase "focus of historic friction" as used in lines 37–38?

    (A) Center of an important conflict

    (B) Museum for historical photographs

    (C) Famous furniture factory

    (D) City of many professional sports

38. According to the passage, what can be inferred about Pittsburgh's population during World War II?

    (A) It did not grow.

    (B) It declined.

    (C) It grew enormously.

    (D) It stayed the same.

39. Between the Civil War and World War II, all of the following happened in Pittsburgh EXCEPT:

    (A) automobile factories produced most of the transportation for Americans

    (B) Carnegie, Frick, and Mellon created their steel empires

    (C) the American Federation of Labor was organized

    (D) the air became seriously polluted, and buildings were dirty

40. Where in the passage could the following sentence best fit?

    The elder Penn, who lived in Philadelphia, believed that peaceful settlements with the Indians would help his young colony prosper.

    (A) After the word "arriving" in the first paragraph

    (B) After the words "Ohio River" in the second paragraph

    (C) At the end of the third paragraph

    (D) After the words "polluted industrial city" in the fourth paragraph

QUESTIONS 41–50 REFER TO THE FOLLOWING PASSAGE.

The Missouri River is the longest tributary of the Mississippi River, and it begins its trip to join the Mississippi in the Rocky Mountains in Montana. The
(5) Missouri flows eastward to central North Dakota, where it turns southward across South Dakota, Nebraska, and Iowa. When it reaches Missouri, it turns eastward at Kansas City and meanders
(10) across central Missouri to join the Mississippi River, about 10 miles north of St. Louis, after traveling 2,315 miles.

Its drainage basin occupies about 529,400 square miles of the Great Plains.
(15) Elevations within its basin are extreme: from 14,000 feet above sea level in the Rockies near the Continental Divide to 400 feet where it joins the Mississippi. The flow of the Missouri changes fre-
(20) quently from 4,200 cubic feet per second to 900,000 cubic feet per second.

Its mouth was discovered in 1673 by the French explorers Jacques Marquette and Louis Joliet while they were canoe-
(25) ing down the Mississippi River. In the early 1700s, French fur traders began to navigate upstream. The first exploration of the river from its mouth to its headwaters was made in 1804–05 by
(30) Meriwether Lewis and William Clark. For many years, the river was, except for fur traders, little used by the earliest American settlers moving west. The American Fur Company began to use
(35) steamers on the river in 1830 but began to decline in the following year with the completion of the Hannibal and St. Joseph Railway to St. Joseph, Missouri.

For the first 150 years after settlement
(40) along the river, the Missouri was not developed as a useful waterway or as a source of irrigation and power. In 1940, a comprehensive program was started for flood control and water-resource de-
(45) velopment in the Missouri River basin. The Fort Peck Dam is one of the largest earthfill dams in the world. The entire system of dams and reservoirs has greatly reduced flooding on the Missouri
(50) and provides water to irrigate millions of acres of farmland. Electricity for many communities is generated along the river's upper course.

41. In which state does the Missouri begin its trip to the Mississippi?

(A) Iowa

(B) South Dakota

(C) North Dakota

(D) Montana

42. Which of the following is closest in meaning to the word "meanders" as used in line 9?

(A) Is harsh to the land it is in

(B) Follows a winding and turning course

(C) Causes a lot of damage with floods

(D) Flows slowly and gently

43. The passage implies that the elevation of the Missouri River's drainage basin

(A) remains level throughout the trip from Montana through Missouri

(B) rises almost 2,315 feet

(C) changes frequently

(D) drops more than 13,000 feet between the Rocky Mountains and its mouth on the Mississippi

44. Which of the following is the closest in meaning to the word "mouth" as it is used in line 22?

(A) Entrance to a harbor, valley, or cave

(B) The opening of a container

(C) Part of a river that flows into a lake or ocean

(D) Oral cavity

45. Where could the following sentence best be added to the passage?

    The speed of the river's current is just as extreme.

    (A) After the word "Iowa" in the first paragraph

    (B) After the word "Mississippi" in the second paragraph

    (C) After the word "upstream" in the third paragraph

    (D) At the end of the fourth paragraph

46. Who discovered the mouth of the Missouri River?

    (A) Meriwether Lewis and William Clark

    (B) French fur traders

    (C) Jacques Marquette and Louis Joliet

    (D) American fur traders

47. When were steamers first used on the Missouri River?

    (A) 1673

    (B) 1700

    (C) 1804

    (D) 1830

48. Which word does the word "power" as used in line 42 refer to?

    (A) Waterway

    (B) Irrigation

    (C) Development

    (D) Electricity

49. When was a flood control program for the Missouri River begun?

    (A) 1940

    (B) 1840

    (C) 1740

    (D) 1640

50. In the passage, all of the following topics are briefly discussed EXCEPT:

    (A) the geography of the Missouri River

    (B) the history of the Missouri River

    (C) tourism and recreation on the Missouri River

    (D) twentieth-century development of the Missouri River

ANSWER KEY AND EXPLANATIONS

1.	B	11.	C	21.	B	31.	B	41.	D
2.	D	12.	D	22.	A	32.	A	42.	B
3.	C	13.	D	23.	D	33.	D	43.	D
4.	B	14.	B	24.	A	34.	B	44.	C
5.	D	15.	A	25.	A	35.	C	45.	B
6.	A	16.	C	26.	B	36.	D	46.	C
7.	A	17.	C	27.	C	37.	A	47.	D
8.	B	18.	C	28.	C	38.	C	48.	D
9.	A	19.	C	29.	A	39.	A	49.	A
10.	C	20.	C	30.	D	40.	A	50.	C

1. **The correct answer is (B).** Choice (A) does not contain the most important facts about the career of Jonas Salk. Choice (C) contains information that is not mentioned in the passage. Choice (C) is incorrect; Salk was at the University of Pittsburgh.

2. **The correct answer is (D).** The other answer choices are incorrect definitions.

3. **The correct answer is (C).** The other answer choices contain words and phrases from the paragraph but are all incorrect.

4. **The correct answer is (B).** The sentence reads, "Working with scientists from other universities in a program to classify the various strains of the polio virus, Salk corroborated other studies in identifying three separate strains."

5. **The correct answer is (D).** Choice (A) is incorrect because Salk did not reject the studies; he used them. Choice (B) is incorrect because the text does not mention publishing until the third paragraph. Choice (C) is incorrect because *examined* is not close in meaning to *corroborate*.

6. **The correct answer is (A).** It is NOT true. All other answers are found in the second paragraph.

7. **The correct answer is (A).** *Findings* means the "information gained from research and experimentation." The correct answer is "the results of both tests."

8. **The correct answer is (B).** In the third paragraph, the text reports that the vaccine was injected by needle.

9. **The correct answer is (A).** This information is found in the last paragraph of the passage.

10. **The correct answer is (C).** The placement in the third paragraph is correct.

11. **The correct answer is (C).** The first two letters in choice (A) are the same as those in choice (B), but they do not make the words synonymous. Choice (B) uses a definition that might remind you of the word *assemble*. Choice (D) is the opposite of choice (B), but it is not the same as *resemble*.

12. **The correct answer is (D).** The other answer choices contain parts of synthesizers and violins.

13. **The correct answer is (D).** The other answer choices are not stated in the passage.

14. **The correct answer is (B).** The other answer choices are not stated in the passage.

15. **The correct answer is (A).** The meanings of the other answers have nothing to do with the word *coupled*.

16. **The correct answer is (C).** It is NOT used with a violin.

17. **The correct answer is (C).** The placement in the third paragraph is correct.

18. **The correct answer is (C).** The word *its* refers to the *body* of the violin in this instance.

19. **The correct answer is (C).** The other answer choices are not stated anywhere in the passage.

20. **The correct answer is (C).** All other answer choices are incorrect and are misstatements of parts of the passage.

21. **The correct answer is (B).** Choice (A) is incorrect; fiction is not published in the *Times*. Choice (C) is incorrect; the *Times* does not broadcast news on TV. Choice (C) is incorrect; see paragraph 4.

22. **The correct answer is (A).** See the last sentence of the first paragraph.

23. **The correct answer is (D).** Choices (A) and (B) can be used to mean restrained but not in the context of this sentence. Choice (C) is not related to any meaning of *restrained*.

24. **The correct answer is (A).** The other answer choices are not stated in the passage.

25. **The correct answer is (A).**

26. **The correct answer is (B).** The preceding sentence mentions how other newspapers have "lurid" stories. The sentence, "Their publishers ran sensational stories, not because they were true, but because they sold newspapers," gives further detail about the other newspapers' stories.

27. **The correct answer is (C).** All of the other answer choices are not true.

28. **The correct answer is (C).** Choice (A) is incorrect because the passage does not connect the paper's reputation to its price. Choices (B) and (D) are incorrect, because the passage does not connect the paper's reputation to Ochs's or the other New York papers.

29. **The correct answer is (A).** The word *publication* refers to the *Times*.

30. **The correct answer is (D).** The other answer choices are not stated in the passage.

31. **The correct answer is (B).** Choice (A) is incorrect; the United States did not exist in the mid-eighteenth century. Choice (C) is incorrect; Germany is not mentioned in the passage. Choice (D) is incorrect because Pennsylvania is not identified as a country in the passage.

32. **The correct answer is (A).** This is stated in the first paragraph.

33. **The correct answer is (D).** The passage mentions that travelers heading west would stop at the "outfitting point," and it makes sense that travelers would need *equipment and supplies* on their journey.

34. **The correct answer is (B).** See the second paragraph.

35. **The correct answer is (C).** *Vital* in this sentence means "of high importance." *Markets* are places where people can sell their products.

36. **The correct answer is (D).** No one mentioned in the other answers moved to Pittsburgh in great numbers after the Civil War.

37. **The correct answer is (A).** The other answer choices do not make sense within the context of the paragraph.

38. **The correct answer is (C).** See paragraph 3.

39. **The correct answer is (A).** The automobile industry is not mentioned in the passage.

40. **The correct answer is (A).** The sentence makes the most sense in this part of the passage.

41. **The correct answer is (D).** This is stated in the first sentence of the passage.

42. **The correct answer is (B).** When the word *meandering* is used to describe a river, it usually means that the river is "winding and turning," so choice (B) is the correct answer.

43. **The correct answer is (D).** This information can be inferred from the second paragraph of the passage.

44. **The correct answer is (C).** Choice (A) is incorrect, because the topic is a river, not a harbor, valley, or cave. Choices (B) and (D) are incorrect meanings for the context.

45. **The correct answer is (B).** This is where the sentence best fits into the passage.

46. **The correct answer is (C).** See paragraph 3.

47. **The correct answer is (D).** See paragraph 3.

48. **The correct answer is (D).** *Electricity* can also be thought of as "electric *power*."

49. **The correct answer is (A).** This is mentioned in the last paragraph of the passage.

50. **The correct answer is (C).** The other answer choices are all mentioned in the passage.

PART V

APPENDIXES

A Helpful Word List

Get into the habit of reading a little every day with your dictionary nearby. When you encounter a new word in a newspaper, magazine, or book, look it up. Then jot down the new word, its definition, and the sentence in which you encountered it in a notebook set aside for this purpose. Review your vocabulary notebook periodically—say, once a week. Your notebook will reflect the kinds of things you read and the words you find most difficult. The fact that you've taken the time and made the effort to write down the words and their meanings will help to fix them in your memory. Chances are good that you'll encounter a few words from your vocabulary notebook on the TOEFL.

abbreviate (verb) to make briefer, to shorten. *Because time was running out, the speaker had to abbreviate his remarks.* **abbreviation** (noun).

abrasive (adjective) irritating, grinding, rough. *The manager's rude, abrasive way of criticizing the workers was bad for morale.* **abrasion** (noun).

abridge (verb) to shorten, to reduce. *The Bill of Rights is designed to prevent Congress from abridging the rights of Americans.* **abridgment** (noun).

absolve (verb) to free from guilt, to exonerate. *The criminal jury absolved the man of the murder of his ex-wife.* **absolution** (noun).

abstain (verb) to refrain, to hold back. *After his heart attack, he was warned by the doctor to abstain from smoking, drinking, and overeating.* **abstinence** (noun), **abstemious** (adjective).

accentuate (verb) to emphasize, to stress. *The overcast skies and chill winds accentuated our gloomy mood.*

acrimonious (adjective) biting, harsh, caustic. *The election campaign became acrimonious, as the candidates traded insults and accusations.* **acrimony** (noun).

adaptable (adjective) able to be changed to be suitable for a new purpose. *Some scientists say that the mammals outlived the dinosaurs because they were more adaptable to a changing climate.* **adapt** (verb), **adaptation** (noun).

adulation (noun) extreme admiration. *Few young actors have received greater adulation than did Marlon Brando after his performance in* A Streetcar Named Desire. **adulate** (verb), **adulatory** (adjective).

adversary (noun) an enemy or opponent. *When the former Soviet Union became an American ally, the United States had lost a major adversary.*

adversity (noun) misfortune. *It's easy to be patient and generous when things are going well; a person's true character is revealed under adversity.* **adverse** (adjective).

aesthetic (adjective) relating to art or beauty. *Mapplethorpe's photos may be attacked on moral grounds, but no one questions their aesthetic value—they are beautiful.* **aestheticism** (noun).

affected (adjective) false, artificial. *At one time, Japanese women were taught to speak in an affected high-pitched voice, which was thought girlishly attractive.* **affect** (verb), **affectation** (noun).

aggressive (adjective) forceful, energetic, and attacking. *A football player needs a more aggressive style of play than a soccer player.* **aggression** (noun).

alacrity (noun) promptness, speed. *Thrilled with the job offer, he accepted with alacrity—"Before they can change their minds!" he thought.*

allege (verb) to state without proof. *Some have alleged that the actor was murdered, but all the evidence points to suicide.* **allegation** (noun).

alleviate (verb) to make lighter or more bearable. *Although no cure for AIDS has been found, doctors are able to alleviate the sufferings of those with the disease.* **alleviation** (noun).

ambiguous (adjective) having two or more possible meanings. *The phrase, "Let's table that discussion" is ambiguous; some think it means, "Let's discuss it now," while others think it means, "Let's save it for later."* **ambiguity** (noun).

ambivalent (adjective) having two or more contradictory feelings or attitudes; uncertain. *She was ambivalent toward her impending marriage; at times she was eager to go ahead, while at other times she wanted to call it off.* **ambivalence** (noun).

amiable (adjective) likable, agreeable, friendly. *He was an amiable lab partner, always smiling, on time, and ready to work.* **amiability** (verb).

amicable (adjective) friendly, peaceable. *Although they agreed to divorce, their settlement was amicable and they remained friends afterward.*

amplify (verb) to enlarge, expand, or increase. *Uncertain as to whether they understood, the students asked the teacher to amplify his explanation.* **amplification** (noun).

anachronistic (adjective) out of the proper time. *The reference in Shakespeare's* Julius Caesar *to "the clock striking twelve" is anachronistic, since there were no striking timepieces in ancient Rome.* **anachronism** (noun).

anarchy (noun) absence of law or order. *For several months after the Nazi government was destroyed, there was no effective government in parts of Germany, and anarchy ruled.* **anarchic** (adjective).

anomaly (noun) something different or irregular. *The tiny planet Pluto, orbiting next to the giants Jupiter, Saturn, and Neptune, has long appeared to be an anomaly.* **anomalous** (adjective).

antagonism (noun) hostility, conflict, opposition. *As more and more reporters investigated the Watergate scandal, antagonism between Nixon and the press increased.* **antagonistic** (adjective), **antagonize** (verb).

antiseptic (adjective) fighting infection; extremely clean. *A wound should be washed with an antiseptic solution. The all-white offices were bare and almost antiseptic in their starkness.*

apathy (noun) lack of interest, concern, or emotion. *American voters are showing increasing apathy over politics; fewer than half voted in the last election.* **apathetic** (adjective).

arable (adjective) able to be cultivated for growing crops. *Rocky New England has relatively little arable farmland.*

arbiter (noun) someone able to settle dispute; a judge or referee. *The public is the ultimate arbiter of commercial value: It decides what sells and what doesn't.*

arbitrary (adjective) based on random or merely personal preference. *Both computers cost the same and had the same features, so in the end I made an arbitrary decision about which to buy.*

arcane (adjective) little-known, mysterious, obscure. *Eliot's "Waste Land" is filled with arcane lore, including quotations in Latin, Greek, French, German, and Sanskrit.* **arcana** (noun, plural).

ardor (noun) a strong feeling of passion, energy, or zeal. *The young revolutionary proclaimed his convictions with an ardor that excited the crowd.* **ardent** (adjective).

arid (adjective) very dry; boring and meaningless. *The arid climate of Arizona makes farming difficult. Some find the law a fascinating topic, but for me it is an arid discipline.* **aridity** (noun).

ascetic (adjective) practicing strict self-discipline for moral or spiritual reasons. *The so-called Desert Fathers were hermits who lived an ascetic life of fasting, study, and prayer.* **asceticism** (verb).

assiduous (verb) working with care, attention, and diligence. *Although Karen is not a naturally gifted math student, by assiduous study she managed to earn an A in trigonometry.* **assiduity** (noun).

astute (adjective) observant, intelligent, and shrewd. *Alan's years of experience in Washington and his personal acquaintance with many political insiders make him an astute commentator on politics.*

atypical (adjective) not typical; unusual. *In* The Razor's Edge, *Bill Murray, best known as a comic actor, gave an atypical dramatic performance.*

audacious (adjective) bold, daring, adventurous. *Her plan to cross the Atlantic single-handed in a twelve-foot sailboat was audacious, if not reckless.* **audacity** (noun).

audible (adjective) able to be heard. *Although she whispered, her voice was picked up by the microphone, and her words were audible throughout the theater.* **audibility** (noun).

auspicious (adjective) promising good fortune; propitious. *The news that a team of British climbers had reached the summit of Everest seemed an auspicious sign for the reign of newly crowned Queen Elizabeth II.*

authoritarian (adjective) favoring or demanding blind obedience to leaders. *Despite Americans' belief in democracy, the American government has supported authoritarian regimes in other countries.* authoritarianism (noun)

belated (adjective) delayed past the proper time. *She called her mother on January 5 to offer her a belated "Happy New Year."*

belie (verb) to present a false or contradictory appearance. *Julie's youthful appearance belies her long, distinguished career in show business.*

benevolent (adjective) wishing or doing good. *In old age, Carnegie used his wealth for benevolent purposes, donating large sums to found libraries and schools.* **benevolence** (noun).

berate (verb) to scold or criticize harshly. *The judge angrily berated the two lawyers for their unprofessional behavior.*

bereft (adjective) lacking or deprived of something. *Bereft of parental love, orphans sometimes grow up insecure.*

bombastic (adjective) inflated or pompous in style. *Old-fashioned bombastic political speeches don't work on television, which demands a more intimate style of communication.* **bombast** (noun).

bourgeois (adjective) middle-class or reflecting middle-class values. *The Dadaists of the 1920s produced art deliberately designed to offend bourgeois art collectors, with their taste for respectable, refined, uncontroversial pictures.* **bourgeois** (noun).

buttress (noun) something that supports or strengthens. *The endorsement of the American Medical Association is a powerful buttress for the claims made about this new medicine.* **buttress** (verb).

camaraderie (noun) a spirit of friendship. *Spending long days and nights together on the road, the members of a traveling theater group develop a strong sense of camaraderie.*

candor (noun) openness, honesty, frankness. *In his memoir, the former defense secretary describes his mistakes with remarkable candor.* **candid** (adjective).

capricious (adjective) unpredictable, willful, whimsical. *The pop star has changed her image so many times that each new transformation now appears capricious rather than purposeful.* **caprice** (noun).

carnivorous (adjective) meat-eating. *The long, dagger-like teeth of the Tyrannosaurus make it obvious that this was a carnivorous dinosaur.* **carnivore** (noun).

carping (adjective) unfairly or excessively critical; querulous. *The newspaper is famous for its demanding critics, but none is harder to please than the carping McNamera, said to have single-handedly destroyed many acting careers.* **carp** (verb).

catalytic (adjective) bringing about, causing, or producing some result. *The conditions for revolution existed in America by 1765; the disputes about taxation that arose later were the catalytic events that sparked the rebellion.* **catalyze** (verb).

caustic (adjective) burning, corrosive. *No one was safe when the satirist H.L. Mencken unleashed his caustic wit.*

censure (noun) blame, condemnation. *The news that the senator had harassed several women brought censure from many people.* **censure** (verb).

chaos (noun) disorder, confusion, chance. *The first few moments after the boiler explosion were pure chaos: no one was sure what had happened, and the area was filled with people running and yelling.* **chaotic** (adjective).

circuitous (adjective) winding or indirect. *We drove to the cottage by a circuitous route so we could see as much of the surrounding countryside as possible.*

circumlocution (noun) speaking in a roundabout way; wordiness. *Legal documents often contain circumlocutions which make them difficult to understand.*

circumscribe (verb) to define by a limit or boundary. *Originally, the role of the executive branch of government was clearly circumscribed, but that role has greatly expanded over time.* **circumscription** (noun).

circumvent (verb) to get around. *When Jerry was caught speeding, he tried to circumvent the law by offering the police officer some money.*

clandestine (adjective) secret, surreptitious. *As a member of the underground, Balas took part in clandestine meetings to discuss ways of sabotaging the Nazi forces.*

cloying (adjective) overly sweet or sentimental. *The deathbed scenes in the novels of Dickens are famously cloying: as Oscar Wilde said, "One would need a heart of stone to read the death of Little Nell without laughing."*

cogent (adjective) forceful and convincing. *The committee members were won over to the project by the cogent arguments of the chairman.* **cogency** (noun).

cognizant (adjective) aware, mindful. *Cognizant of the fact that it was getting late, the master of ceremonies cut short the last speech.* **cognizance** (noun).

cohesive (adjective) sticking together, unified. *An effective military unit must be a cohesive team, all its members working together for a common goal.* **cohere** (verb), **cohesion** (noun).

collaborate (verb) to work together. *To create a truly successful movie, the director, writers, actors, and many others must collaborate closely.* **collaboration** (noun), **collaborative** (adjective).

colloquial (adjective) informal in language; conversational. *Some expressions from Shakespeare, such as the use of thou and thee, sound formal today but were colloquial English in Shakespeare's time.*

competent (adjective) having the skill and knowledge needed for a particular task; capable. *Any competent lawyer can draw up a will.* **competence** (noun).

complacent (adjective) smug, self-satisfied. *During the 1970s, American auto makers became complacent, believing that they would continue to be successful with little effort.* **complacency** (noun).

composure (noun) calm, self-assurance. *The company's president managed to keep his composure during his speech even when the TelePrompTer broke down, leaving him without a script.* **composed** (adjective).

conciliatory (adjective) seeking agreement, compromise, or reconciliation. *As a conciliatory gesture, the union leaders agreed to postpone a strike and to continue negotiations with management.* **conciliate** (verb), **conciliation** (noun).

concise (adjective) expressed briefly and simply; succinct. *Less than a page long, the Bill of Rights is a concise statement of the freedoms enjoyed by all Americans.* **concision** (noun).

condescending (adjective) having an attitude of superiority toward another; patronizing. *"What a cute little car!" she remarked in a condescending style. "I suppose it's the nicest one someone like you could afford!"* **condescension** (noun).

condolence (noun) pity for someone else's sorrow or loss; sympathy. *After the sudden death of the doctor, thousands of messages of condolence were sent to her family.* **condole** (verb).

confidant (noun) someone entrusted with another's secrets. *No one knew about Janee's engagement except Sarah, her confidant.* **confide** (verb), **confidential** (adjective).

conformity (noun) agreement with or adherence to custom or rule. *In my high school, conformity was the rule: everyone dressed the same, talked the same, and listened to the same music.* **conform** (verb), **conformist** (adjective).

consensus (noun) general agreement among a group. *Among Quakers, voting traditionally is not used; instead, discussion continues until the entire group forms a consensus.*

consolation (noun) relief or comfort in sorrow or suffering. *Although we miss our dog very much, it is a consolation to know that she died quickly, without suffering.* **console** (verb).

consternation (noun) shock, amazement, dismay. *When a voice in the back of the church shouted out, "I know why they should not be married!" the entire gathering was thrown into consternation.*

consummate (verb) to complete, finish, or perfect. *The deal was consummated with a handshake and the payment of the agreed-upon fee.* **consummate** (adjective), **consummation** (noun).

contaminate (verb) to make impure. *Chemicals dumped in a nearby forest had seeped into the soil and contaminated the local water supply.* **contamination** (noun).

contemporary (adjective) modern, current; from the same time. *I prefer old-fashioned furniture rather than contemporary styles. The composer Vivaldi was roughly contemporary with Bach.* **contemporary** (noun).

contrite (adjective) sorry for past misdeeds. *The public is often willing to forgive celebrities who are involved in some scandal, as long as they appear contrite.* **contrition** (noun).

conundrum (noun) a riddle, puzzle, or problem. *The question of why an all-powerful, all-loving God allows evil to exist is a conundrum many philosophers have pondered.*

convergence (noun) the act of coming together in unity or similarity. *A remarkable example of evolutionary convergence can be seen in the shark and the dolphin, two sea creatures that developed from different origins to become very similar in form.* **converge** (verb).

convoluted (adjective) twisting, complicated, intricate. *Tax law has become so convoluted that it's easy for people to accidentally violate it.* **convolute** (verb), **convolution** (noun).

corroborating (adjective) supporting with evidence; confirming. *A passerby who had witnessed the crime gave corroborating testimony about the presence of the accused person.* **corroborate** (verb), **corroboration** (noun).

corrosive (adjective) eating away, gnawing, or destroying. *Years of poverty and hard work had a corrosive effect on her beauty.* **corrode** (verb), **corrosion** (noun).

credulity (noun) willingness to believe, even with little evidence. *Con artists fool people by taking advantage of their credulity.* **credulous** (adjective).

criterion (noun) a standard of measurement or judgment. (The plural is criteria.) *In choosing a design for the new taxicabs, reliability will be our main criterion.*

critique (noun) a critical evaluation. *The editor gave a detailed critique of the manuscript, explaining its strengths and its weaknesses.* **critique** (verb).

culpable (adjective) deserving blame, guilty. *Although he committed the crime, because he was mentally ill he should not be considered culpable for his actions.* **culpability** (noun).

cumulative (adjective) made up of successive additions. *Smallpox was eliminated only through the cumulative efforts of several generations of doctors and scientists.* **accumulation** (noun), **accumulate** (verb).

curtail (verb) to shorten. *Because of the military emergence, all soldiers on leave were ordered to curtail their absences and return to duty.*

debased (adjective) lowered in quality, character, or esteem. *The quality of TV journalism has been debased by the many new tabloid-style talk shows.* **debase** (verb).

debunk (verb) to expose as false or worthless. *The magician loves to debunk psychics, mediums, clairvoyants, and others who claim supernatural powers.*

decorous (adjective) having good taste; proper, appropriate. *Most citizens believe the royal family's reserved and decorous style is appropriate.* **decorum** (noun).

decry (verb) to criticize or condemn. *Cigarette ads aimed at youngsters have led many to decry the marketing tactics of the tobacco industry.*

deduction (noun) a logical conclusion, especially a specific conclusion based on general principles. *Based on what is known about the effects of greenhouse gases on atmospheric temperature, scientists have made several deductions about the likelihood of global warming.* **deduce** (verb).

delegate (verb) to give authority or responsibility. *The president delegated the vice president to represent the administration at the peace talks.* **delegate** (noun).

deleterious (adjective) harmful. *About thirty years ago, scientists proved that working with asbestos could be deleterious to one's health, producing cancer and other diseases.*

delineate (verb) to outline or describe. *Naturalists had long suspected the fact of evolution, but Darwin was the first to delineate a process—natural selection—through which evolution could occur.*

demagogue (noun) a leader who plays dishonestly on the prejudices and emotions of his followers. *Senator Joseph McCarthy was labeled a demagogue who used the paranoia of the anti-Communist 1950s as a way of seizing fame and power in Washington.* **demagoguery** (noun).

demure (adjective) modest or shy. *The demure heroines of Victorian fiction have given way to today's stronger, more opinionated, and more independent female characters.*

denigrate (verb) to criticize or belittle. *The firm's new president tried to explain his plans for improving the company without seeming to denigrate the work of his predecessor.* **denigration** (noun).

depose (verb) to remove from office, especially from a throne. *Iran was formerly ruled by a monarch called the Shah, who was deposed in 1976.*

derelict (adjective) neglecting one's duty. *The train crash was blamed on a switchman who was derelict, having fallen asleep while on duty.* **dereliction** (noun).

derivative (adjective) taken from a particular source. *When a person first writes poetry, her poems are apt to be derivative of whatever poetry she most enjoys reading.* **derivation** (noun), **derive** (verb).

desolate (adjective) empty, lifeless, and deserted; hopeless, gloomy. *Robinson Crusoe was shipwrecked and had to learn to survive alone on a desolate island. The murder of her husband left Mary Lincoln desolate.* **desolation** (noun).

destitute (adjective) very poor. *Years of rule by a dictator who stole the wealth of the country had left the people of the Philippines destitute.* **destitution** (noun).

deter (verb) to discourage from acting. *The best way to deter crime is to insure that criminals will receive swift and certain punishment.* **deterrence** (noun), **deterrent** (adjective).

detractor (noun) someone who belittles or disparages. *The singer has many detractors who consider his music boring, inane, and sentimental.* **detract** (verb).

deviate (verb) to depart from a standard or norm. *Having agreed upon a spending budget for the company, we mustn't deviate from it; if we do, we may run out of money soon.* **deviation** (noun).

devious (adjective) tricky, deceptive. *The stockbroker's devious financial tactics were designed to enrich his firm while confusing or misleading government regulators.*

didactic (adjective) intended to teach, instructive. *The children's TV show* Sesame Street *is designed to be both entertaining and didactic.*

diffident (adjective) hesitant, reserved, shy. *Someone with a diffident personality should pursue a career that involves little public contact.* **diffidence** (noun).

diffuse (verb) to spread out, to scatter. *The red dye quickly became diffused through the water, turning it a very pale pink.* **diffusion** (noun).

digress (verb) to wander from the main path or the main topic. *My high school biology teacher loved to digress from science into personal anecdotes about his college adventures.* **digression** (noun), **digressive** (adjective).

dilatory (adjective) delaying, procrastinating. *The lawyer used various dilatory tactics, hoping that his opponent would get tired of waiting for a trial and drop the case.*

diligent (adjective) working hard and steadily. *Through diligent efforts, the townspeople were able to clear away the debris from the flood in a matter of days.* **diligence** (noun).

diminutive (adjective) unusually small, tiny. *Children are fond of Shetland ponies because their diminutive size makes them easy to ride.* **diminution** (noun).

discern (verb) to detect, notice, or observe. *I could discern the shape of a whale off the starboard bow, but it was too far away to determine its size or species.* **discernment** (noun).

disclose (verb) to make known; to reveal. *Election laws require candidates to disclose the names of those who contribute money to their campaigns.* **disclosure** (noun).

discomfit (verb) to frustrate, thwart, or embarrass. *Discomfited by the interviewer's unexpected question, Peter could only stammer in reply.* **discomfiture** (noun).

disconcert (verb) to confuse or embarrass. *When the hallway bells began to ring halfway through her lecture, the speaker was disconcerted and didn't know what to do.*

discredit (verb) to cause disbelief in the accuracy of some statement or the reliability of a person. *Although many people still believe in UFOs, among scientists the reports of "alien encounters" have been thoroughly discredited.*

discreet (adjective) showing good judgment in speech and behavior. *Be discreet when discussing confidential business matters—don't talk among strangers on the elevator, for example.* **discretion** (noun).

discrepancy (noun) a difference or variance between two or more things. *The discrepancies between the two witnesses' stories show that one of them must be lying.* **discrepant** (adjective).

disdain (noun) contempt, scorn. *The millionaire was disliked by many people because she treated "little people" with such disdain.* **disdain** (verb), **disdainful** (adjective).

disingenuous (adjective) pretending to be candid, simple, and frank. *When the Texas billionaire ran for president, many considered his "jest plain folks" style disingenuous.*

disparage (verb) to speak disrespectfully about, to belittle. *Many political ads today both praise their own candidate and disparage his or her opponent.* **disparagement** (noun), **disparaging** (adjective).

disparity (noun) difference in quality or kind. *There is often a disparity between the kind of high-quality television people say they want and the low-brow programs they actually watch.* **disparate** (adjective).

disregard (verb) to ignore, to neglect. *If you don't write a will, when you die, your survivors may disregard your wishes about how your property should be handled.* **disregard** (noun).

disruptive (adjective) causing disorder, interrupting. *When the senator spoke at our college, angry demonstrators picketed, heckled, and engaged in other disruptive activities.* **disrupt** (verb), **disruption** (noun).

dissemble (verb) to pretend, to simulate. *When the police questioned her about the crime, she dissembled innocence.*

dissipate (verb) to spread out or scatter. *The windows and doors were opened, allowing the smoke that had filled the room to dissipate.* **dissipation** (noun).

dissonance (noun) lack of music harmony; lack of agreement between ideas. *Most modern music is characterized by dissonance, which many listeners find hard to enjoy. There is a noticeable dissonance between two common beliefs of most conservatives: their faith in unfettered free markets and their preference for traditional social values.* **dissonant** (adjective).

diverge (verb) to move in different directions. *Frost's poem "The Road Less Traveled" tells of the choice he made when "Two roads diverged in a yellow wood."* **divergence** (noun), **divergent** (adjective).

diversion (noun) a distraction or pastime. *During the two hours he spent in the doctor's waiting room, his hand-held computer game was a welcome diversion.* **divert** (verb).

divination (noun) the art of predicting the future. *In ancient Greece, people wanting to know their fate would visit the priests at Delphi, who were supposedly skilled at divination.* **divine** (verb).

divisive (adjective) causing disagreement or disunity. *Throughout history, race has been the most divisive issue in American society.*

divulge (verb) to reveal. *The people who count the votes for the Oscar® awards are under strict orders not to divulge the names of the winners.*

dogmatic (adjective) holding firmly to a particular set of beliefs with little or no basis. *Believers in Marxist doctrine tend to be dogmatic, ignoring evidence that contradicts their beliefs.* **dogmatism** (noun).

dominant (adjective) greatest in importance or power. *The historian suggests that the existence of the frontier had a dominant influence on American culture.* **dominate** (verb), **domination** (noun).

dubious (adjective) doubtful, uncertain. *Despite the chairman's attempts to convince the committee members that his plan would succeed, most of them remained dubious.* **dubiety** (noun).

durable (adjective) long-lasting. *Denim is a popular material for work clothes because it is strong and durable.*

duress (noun) compulsion or restraint. *Fearing that the dean might expel him, he confessed to cheating on the test, not willingly but under duress.*

eclectic (adjective) drawn from many sources; varied, heterogeneous. *The Mellon family art collection is an eclectic one, including works ranging from ancient Greek sculptures to modern paintings.* **eclecticism** (noun).

efficacious (adjective) able to produce a desired effect. *Though thousands of people today are taking herbal supplements to treat depression, researchers have not yet proved them efficacious.* **efficacy** (noun).

effrontery (noun) shameless boldness. *The sports world was shocked when a pro basketball player had the effrontery to choke his head coach during a practice session.*

effusive (adjective) pouring forth one's emotions very freely. *Having won the Oscar® for Best Actress, Sally Field gave an effusive acceptance speech in which she marveled, "You like me! You really like me!"* **effusion** (noun).

egoism (noun) excessive concern with oneself; conceit. *Robert's egoism was so great that all he could talk about was the importance—and the brilliance—of his own opinions.* **egoistic** (adjective).

egregious (adjective) obvious, conspicuous, flagrant. *It's hard to imagine how the editor could allow such an egregious error to appear.*

elated (adjective) excited and happy; exultant. *When the Green Bay Packers' last, desperate pass was dropped, the elated fans of the Denver Broncos began to celebrate.* **elate** (verb), **elation** (noun).

elliptical (adjective) very terse or concise in writing or speech; difficult to understand. *Rather than speak plainly, she hinted at her meaning through a series of nods, gestures, and elliptical half-sentences.*

elusive (adjective) hard to capture, grasp, or understand. *Though everyone thinks they know what "justice" is, when you try to define the concept precisely, it proves to be quite elusive.*

embezzle (verb) to steal money or property that has been entrusted to your care. *The church treasurer was found to have embezzled thousands of dollars by writing phony checks on the church bank account.* **embezzlement** (noun).

emend (verb) to correct. *Before the letter is mailed, please emend the two spelling errors.* **emendation** (noun).

emigrate (verb) to leave one place or country to settle elsewhere. *Millions of Irish emigrated to the New World in the wake of the great Irish famines of the 1840s.* **emigrant** (noun), **emigration** (noun).

eminent (adjective) noteworthy, famous. *Vaclav Havel was an eminent author before being elected president of the Czech Republic.* **eminence** (noun).

emissary (noun) someone who represents another. *In an effort to close the construction deal, the former CEO was sent as an emissary to China to negotiate a contract.*

emollient (noun) something that softens or soothes. *She used a hand cream as an emollient on her dry, work-roughened hands.* **emollient** (adjective).

empathy (noun) imaginative sharing of the feelings, thoughts, or experiences of another. *It's easy for a parent to have empathy for the sorrow of another parent whose child has died.* **empathetic** (adjective).

empirical (adjective) based on experience or personal observation. *Although many people believe in ESP, scientists have found no empirical evidence of its existence.* **empiricism** (noun).

emulate (verb) to imitate or copy. *The British band Oasis admitted their desire to emulate their idols, the Beatles.* **emulation** (noun).

encroach (verb) to go beyond acceptable limits; to trespass. *By quietly seizing more and more authority, Robert Moses continually encroached on the powers of other government leaders.* **encroachment** (noun).

enervate (verb) to reduce the energy or strength of someone or something. *The stress of the operation left her feeling enervated for about two weeks.*

engender (verb) to produce, to cause. *Countless disagreements over the proper use of national forests have engendered feelings of hostility between ranchers and environmentalists.*

enhance (verb) to improve in value or quality. *New kitchen appliances will enhance your house and increase the amount of money you'll make when you sell it.* **enhancement** (noun).

enmity (noun) hatred, hostility, ill will. *Long-standing enmity, like that between the Protestants and Catholics in Northern Ireland, is difficult to overcome.*

enthrall (verb) to enchant or charm. *When the Swedish singer Jenny Lind toured America in the nineteenth century, audiences were enthralled by her beauty and talent.*

ephemeral (adjective) quickly disappearing; transient. *Stardom in pop music is ephemeral; most of the top acts of ten years ago are forgotten today.*

equanimity (noun) calmness of mind, especially under stress. *Roosevelt had the gift of facing the great crises of his presidency—the Depression, the Second World War—with equanimity and even humor.*

eradicate (verb) to destroy completely. *American society has failed to eradicate racism, although some of its worst effects have been reduced.*

espouse (verb) to take up as a cause; to adopt. *No politician in American today will openly espouse racism, although some behave and speak in racially prejudiced ways.*

euphoric (adjective) a feeling of extreme happiness and well-being; elation. *One often feels euphoric during the earliest days of a new love affair.* **euphorial** (noun).

evanescent (adjective) vanishing like a vapor; fragile and transient. *As she walked by, the evanescent fragrance of her perfume reached me for just an instant.*

exacerbate (verb) to make worse or more severe. *The roads in our town already have too much traffic; building a new shopping mall will exacerbate the problem.*

exasperate (verb) to irritate or annoy. *Because she was trying to study, Sharon was exasperated by the yelling of her neighbors' children.*

exculpate (verb) to free from blame or guilt. *When someone else confessed to the crime, the previous suspect was exculpated.* **exculpation** (noun), **exculpatory** (adjective).

exemplary (adjective) worthy to serve as a model. *The Baldrige Award is given to a company with exemplary standards of excellence in products and service.* **exemplar** (noun), **exemplify** (verb).

exonerate (verb) to free from blame. *Although he was suspected at first of being involved in the bombing, later evidence exonerated him.* **exoneration** (noun), **exonerative** (adjective).

expansive (adjective) broad and large; speaking openly and freely. *The actor's ranch is located on an expansive tract of land in Texas. Over dinner, she became expansive in describing her dreams for the future.*

expedite (verb) to carry out promptly. *As the flood waters rose, the governor ordered state agencies to expedite their rescue efforts.*

expertise (noun) skill, mastery. *The software company was eager to hire new graduates with programming expertise.*

expiate (verb) to atone for. *The president's apology to the survivors of the notorious Tuskegee experiments was his attempt to expiate the nation's guilt over their mistreatment.* **expiation** (noun).

expropriate (verb) to seize ownership of. *When the Communists came to power in China, they expropriated most businesses and turned them over to government-appointed managers.* **expropriation** (noun).

extant (adjective) currently in existence. *Of the seven ancient "Wonders of the World," only the pyramids of Egypt are still extant.*

extenuate (verb) to make less serious. *Karen's guilt is extenuated by the fact that she was only twelve when she committed the theft.* **extenuating** (adjective), **extenuation** (noun).

extol (verb) to greatly praise. *At the party convention, speaker after speaker rose to extol their candidate for the presidency.*

extricate (verb) to free from a difficult or complicated situation. *Much of the humor in the TV show I Love Lucy comes in watching Lucy try to extricate herself from the problems she creates by fibbing or trickery.* **extricable** (adjective).

extrinsic (adjective) not an innate part or aspect of something; external. *The high price of old baseball cards is due to extrinsic factors, such as the nostalgia felt by baseball fans for the stars of their youth, rather than the inherent beauty or value of the cards themselves.*

exuberant (adjective) wildly joyous and enthusiastic. *As the final seconds of the game ticked away, the fans of the winning team began an exuberant celebration.* **exuberance** (noun).

facile (adjective) easy; shallow or superficial. *The one-minute political commercial favors a candidate with facile opinions rather than serious, thoughtful solutions.* **facilitate** (verb), **facility** (noun).

fallacy (noun) an error in fact or logic. *It's a fallacy to think that "natural" means "healthful"; after all, the deadly poison arsenic is completely natural.* **fallacious** (adjective).

felicitous (adjective) pleasing, fortunate, apt. *The sudden blossoming of the dogwood trees on the morning of Matt's wedding seemed a felicitous sign of good luck.* **felicity** (noun).

feral (adjective) wild. *The garbage dump was inhabited by a pack of feral dogs, which had escaped from their owners and become completely wild.*

fervent (adjective) full of intense feeling; ardent, zealous. *In the days just after his religious conversion, his piety was at its most fervent.* **fervid** (adjective), **fervor** (noun).

flagrant (adjective) obviously wrong; offensive. *Nixon was forced to resign the presidency after a series of flagrant crimes against the U.S. Constitution.* **flagrancy** (noun).

flamboyant (adjective) very colorful, showy, or elaborate. *At Mardi Gras, partygoers compete to show off the most wild and flamboyant outfits.*

florid (adjective) flowery, fancy; reddish. *The grand ballroom was decorated in a florid style. Years of heavy drinking had given him a florid complexion.*

foppish (adjective) describing a man who is foolishly vain about his dress or appearance. *The foppish character of the 1890s wore bright-colored spats and a top hat; in the 1980s, he wore fancy suspenders and a shirt with a contrasting collar.* **fop** (noun).

formidable (adjective) awesome, impressive, or frightening. *According to his plaque in the Baseball Hall of Fame, pitcher Tom Seaver turned the New York Mets "from lovable losers into formidable foes."*

fortuitous (adjective) lucky, fortunate. *Although the mayor claimed credit for the falling crime rate, it was really caused by several fortuitous trends.*

fractious (adjective) troublesome, unruly. *Members of the British Parliament are often fractious, shouting insults and sarcastic questions during debates.*

fragility (noun) the quality of being easy to break; delicacy, weakness. *Because of their fragility, few stained glass windows from the early Middle Ages have survived.* **fragile** (adjective).

fraternize (verb) to associate with on friendly terms. *Although baseball players aren't supposed to fraternize with their opponents, players from opposing teams often chat before games.* **fraternization** (noun).

frenetic (adjective) chaotic, frantic. *The floor of the stock exchange, filled with traders shouting and gesturing, is a scene of frenetic activity.*

frivolity (noun) lack of seriousness; levity. *The frivolity of the Mardi Gras carnival is in contrast to the seriousness of the religious season of Lent which follows.* **frivolous** (adjective).

frugal (adjective) spending little. *With our last few dollars, we bought a frugal dinner: a loaf of bread and a piece of cheese.* **frugality** (noun).

fugitive (noun) someone trying to escape. *When two prisoners broke out of the local jail, police were warned to keep an eye out for the fugitives.* **fugitive** (adjective).

gargantuan (adjective) huge, colossal. *The building of the Great Wall of China was one of the most gargantuan projects ever undertaken.*

genial (adjective) friendly, gracious. *A good host welcomes all visitors in a warm and genial fashion.*

grandiose (adjective) overly large, pretentious, or showy. *Among Hitler's grandiose plans for Berlin was a gigantic building with a dome several times larger than any ever built.* **grandiosity** (noun).

gratuitous (adjective) given freely or without cause. *Since her opinion was not requested, her harsh criticism of his singing seemed a gratuitous insult.*

gregarious (adjective) enjoying the company of others; sociable. *Marty is naturally gregarious, a popular member of several clubs and a sought-after lunch companion.*

guileless (adjective) without cunning; innocent. *Deborah's guileless personality and complete honesty make it hard for her to survive in the harsh world of politics.*

gullible (adjective) easily fooled. *When the sweepstakes entry form arrived bearing the message, "You may be a winner!" my gullible neighbor tried to claim a prize.* **gullibility** (noun).

hackneyed (adjective) without originality, trite. *When someone invented the phrase, "No pain, no gain," it was clever, but now it is so commonly heard that it seems hackneyed.*

haughty (adjective) overly proud. *The fashion model strode down the runway, her hips thrust forward and a haughty expression, like a sneer, on her face.* **haughtiness** (noun).

hedonist (noun) someone who lives mainly to pursue pleasure. *Having inherited great wealth, he chose to live the life of a hedonist, traveling the world in luxury.* **hedonism** (noun), **hedonistic** (adjective).

heinous (adjective) very evil, hateful. *The massacre by Pol Pot of over a million Cambodians is one of the twentieth century's most heinous crimes.*

hierarchy (noun) a ranking of people, things, or ideas from highest to lowest. *A cabinet secretary ranks just below the president and vice president in the hierarchy of the executive branch.* **hierarchical** (adjective).

hypocrisy (noun) a false pretense of virtue. *When the sexual misconduct of the television preacher was exposed, his followers were shocked at his hypocrisy.* **hypocritical** (adjective).

iconoclast (noun) someone who attacks traditional beliefs or institutions. *The comedian enjoys his reputation as an iconoclast, though people in power often resent his satirical jabs.* **iconoclasm** (noun), **iconoclastic** (adjective).

idiosyncratic (adjective) peculiar to an individual; eccentric. *She sings pop music in an idiosyncratic style, mingling high-pitched whoops and squeals with throaty gurgles.* **idiosyncrasy** (noun).

idolatry (noun) the worship of a person, thing, or institution as a god. *In Communist China, Chairman Mao was the subject of idolatry; his picture was displayed everywhere, and millions of Chinese memorized his sayings.* **idolatrous** (adjective).

impartial (adjective) fair, equal, unbiased. *If a judge is not impartial, then all of her rulings are questionable.* **impartiality** (noun).

impeccable (adjective) flawless. *The crooks printed impeccable copies of the Super Bowl tickets, making it impossible to distinguish them from the real things.*

impetuous (adjective) acting hastily or impulsively. *Ben's resignation was an impetuous act; he did it without thinking, and he soon regretted it.* **impetuosity** (noun).

impinge (verb) to encroach upon, touch, or affect. *You have a right to do whatever you want, so long as your actions don't impinge on the rights of others.*

implicit (adjective) understood without being openly expressed; implied. *Although most clubs had no rules excluding blacks and Jews, many had an implicit understanding that no blacks or Jews would be allowed to join.*

impute (verb) to credit or give responsibility to; to attribute. *Although Sarah's comments embarrassed me, I don't impute any ill will to her; I think she didn't realize what she was saying.* **imputation** (noun).

inarticulate (adjective) unable to speak or express oneself clearly and understandably. *A skilled athlete may be an inarticulate public speaker, as demonstrated by many post-game interviews.*

incisive (adjective) expressed clearly and directly. *Franklin settled the debate with a few incisive remarks that summed up the issue perfectly.*

incompatible (adjective) unable to exist together; conflicting. *Many people hold seemingly incompatible beliefs: for example, supporting the death penalty while believing in the sacredness of human life.* **incompatibility** (noun).

inconsequential (adjective) of little importance. *When the stereo was delivered, it was a different shade of gray than I expected, but the difference was inconsequential.*

incontrovertible (adjective) impossible to question. *The fact that Sheila's fingerprints were the only ones on the murder weapon made her guilt seem incontrovertible.*

incorrigible (adjective) impossible to manage or reform. *Lou is an incorrigible trickster, constantly playing practical jokes no matter how much his friends complain.*

incremental (adjective) increasing gradually by small amounts. *Although the initial cost of the Medicare program was small, the incremental expenses have grown to be very large.* **increment** (noun).

incriminate (adjective) to give evidence of guilt. *The fifth amendment to the Constitution says that no one is required to reveal information that would incriminate him in a crime.* **incriminating** (adjective).

incumbent (noun) someone who occupies an office or position. *It is often difficult for a challenger to win a seat in Congress from the incumbent.* **incumbency** (noun), **incumbent** (adjective).

indeterminate (adjective) not definitely known. *The college plans to enroll an indeterminate number of students; the size of the class will depend on the number of applicants and how many accept offers of admission.* **determine** (verb).

indifferent (adjective) unconcerned, apathetic. *The mayor's small proposed budget for education suggests that he is indifferent to the needs of our schools.* **indifference** (noun).

indistinct (adjective) unclear, uncertain. *We could see boats on the water, but in the thick morning fog their shapes were indistinct.*

indomitable (adjective) unable to be conquered or controlled. *The world admired the indomitable spirit of Nelson Mandela; he remained courageous despite years of imprisonment.*

induce (verb) to cause. *The doctor prescribed a medicine which is supposed to induce a lowering of the blood pressure.* **induction** (noun).

ineffable (adjective) difficult to describe or express. *He gazed in silence at the sunrise over the Taj Mahal, his eyes reflecting an ineffable sense of wonder.*

inevitable (adjective) unable to be avoided. *Once the Japanese attacked Pearl Harbor, American involvement in World War Two was inevitable.* **inevitability** (noun).

inexorable (adjective) unable to be deterred; relentless. *It's difficult to imagine how the mythic character of Oedipus could have avoided his evil destiny; his fate appears inexorable.*

ingenious (adjective) showing cleverness and originality. *The Post-It note is an ingenious solution to a common problem—how to mark papers without spoiling them.* **ingenuity** (noun).

inherent (adjective) naturally part of something. *Compromise is inherent in democracy, since everyone cannot get his way.* **inhere** (verb), **inherence** (noun).

innate (adjective) inborn, native. *Not everyone who takes piano lessons becomes a fine musician, which shows that music requires innate talent as well as training.*

innocuous (adjective) harmless, inoffensive. *I was surprised that Andrea took offense at such an innocuous joke.*

inoculate (verb) to prevent a disease by infusing with a disease-causing organism. *Pasteur found he could prevent rabies by inoculating patients with the virus that causes the disease.* **inoculation** (noun).

insipid (adjective) flavorless, uninteresting. *Most TV shows are so insipid that you can watch them while reading without missing a thing.* **insipidity** (noun).

insolence (noun) an attitude or behavior that is bold and disrespectful. *Some feel that news reporters who shout questions at the president are behaving with insolence.* **insolent** (adjective).

insular (adjective) narrow or isolated in attitude or viewpoint. *New Yorkers are famous for their insular attitudes; they seem to think that nothing important has ever happened outside of their city.* **insularity** (noun).

insurgency (noun) uprising, rebellion. *The angry townspeople had begun an insurgency bordering on downright revolution; they were collecting arms, holding secret meetings, and refusing to pay certain taxes.* **insurgent** (adjective).

integrity (noun) honesty, uprightness; soundness, completeness. *"Honest Abe" Lincoln is considered a model of political integrity. Inspectors examined the building's support beams and foundation and found no reason to doubt its structural integrity.*

interlocutor (noun) someone taking part in a dialogue or conversation. *Annoyed by the constant questions from someone in the crowd, the speaker challenged his interlocutor to offer a better plan.* **interlocutory** (adjective).

interlude (noun) an interrupting period or performance. *The two most dramatic scenes in King Lear are separated, strangely, by a comic interlude starring the king's jester.*

interminable (adjective) endless or seemingly endless. *Addressing the United Nations, Castro announced, "We will be brief"—then delivered an interminable 4-hour speech.*

intransigent (adjective) unwilling to compromise. *Despite the mediator's attempts to suggest a fair solution, the two parties were intransigent, forcing a showdown.* **intransigence** (noun).

intrepid (adjective) fearless and resolute. *Only an intrepid adventurer is willing to undertake the long and dangerous trip by sled to the South Pole.* **intrepidity** (noun).

intrusive (adjective) forcing a way in without being welcome. *The legal requirement of a search warrant is supposed to protect Americans from intrusive searches by the police.* **intrude** (verb), **intrusion** (noun).

intuitive (adjective) known directly, without apparent thought or effort. *An experienced chess player sometimes has an intuitive sense of the best move to make, even if she can't explain it.* **intuit** (verb), **intuition** (noun).

inundate (verb) to flood; to overwhelm. *As soon as playoff tickets went on sale, eager fans inundated the box office with orders.*

invariable (adjective) unchanging, constant. *When writing a book, it was her invariable habit to rise at 6 and work at her desk from 7 to 12.* **invariability** (noun).

inversion (noun) a turning backwards, inside-out, or upside-down; a reversal. *Latin poetry often features inversion of word order; for example, the first line of Vergil's Aeneid: "Arms and the man I sing."* **invert** (verb), **inverted** (adjective).

inveterate (adjective) persistent, habitual. *It's very difficult for an inveterate gambler to give up the pastime.* **inveteracy** (noun).

invigorate (verb) to give energy to, to stimulate. *As her car climbed the mountain road, Lucinda felt invigorated by the clear air and the cool breezes.*

invincible (adjective) impossible to conquer or overcome. *For three years at the height of his career, boxer Mike Tyson seemed invincible.*

inviolable (adjective) impossible to attack or trespass upon. *In the president's remote hideaway at Camp David, guarded by the Secret Service, his privacy is, for once, inviolable.*

irrational (adjective) unreasonable. *Charles knew that his fear of insects was irrational, but he was unable to overcome it.* **irrationality** (noun).

irresolute (adjective) uncertain how to act, indecisive. *When McGovern first said he supported his vice president candidate "one thousand percent," then dropped him from the ticket, it made McGovern appear irresolute.* **irresolution** (noun).

jeopardize (verb) to put in danger. *Terrorist attacks jeopardize the fragile peace in the Middle East.* **jeopardy** (noun).

juxtapose (verb) to put side by side. *It was strange to see the actor Charlton Heston and musician Bob Dylan juxtaposed at the awards ceremony.* **juxtaposition** (noun).

languid (adjective) without energy; slow, sluggish, listless. *The hot, humid weather of late August can make anyone feel languid.* **languish** (verb), **languor** (noun).

latent (adjective) not currently obvious or active; hidden. *Although he had committed only a single act of violence, the psychiatrist who examined him said he had probably always had a latent tendency toward violence.* **latency** (noun).

laudatory (adjective) giving praise. *The ads for the movie are filled with laudatory comments from critics.*

lenient (adjective) mild, soothing, or forgiving. *The judge was known for his lenient disposition; he rarely imposed long jail sentences on criminals.* **leniency** (noun).

lethargic (adjective) lacking energy; sluggish. *Visitors to the zoo are surprised that the lions appear so lethargic, but in the wild lions sleep up to 18 hours a day.* **lethargy** (noun).

liability (noun) an obligation or debt; a weakness or drawback. *The insurance company had a liability of millions of dollars after the town was destroyed by a tornado. Slowness afoot is a serious liability in an aspiring basketball player.* **liable** (adjective).

lithe (adjective) flexible and graceful. *The ballet dancer was almost as lithe as a cat.*

longevity (noun) length of life; durability. *The reduction in early deaths from infectious diseases is responsible for most of the increase in human longevity over the past two centuries.*

lucid (adjective) clear and understandable. *Hawking's* A Short History of the Universe *is a lucid explanation of modern scientific theories about the origin of the universe.* **lucidity** (noun).

lurid (adjective) shocking, gruesome. *While the serial killer was on the loose, the newspapers were filled with lurid stories about his crimes.*

malediction (noun) curse. *In the fairy tale "Sleeping Beauty," the princess is trapped in a death-like sleep because of the malediction uttered by an angry witch.*

malevolence (noun) hatred, ill will. *Critics say that Iago, the villain in Shakespeare's* Othello, *seems to exhibit malevolence with no real cause.* **malevolent** (noun).

malinger (verb) to pretend illness to avoid work. *During the labor dispute, hundreds of employees malingered, forcing the company to slow production and costing it millions in profits.*

malleable (adjective) able to be changed, shaped, or formed by outside pressures. *Gold is a very useful metal because it is so malleable. A child's personality is malleable and deeply influenced by the things her parents say and do.* **malleability** (noun).

mandate (noun) order, command. *The new policy on gays in the military went into effect as soon as the president issued his mandate about it.* **mandate** (verb), **mandatory** (adjective).

maturation (noun) the process of becoming fully grown or developed. *Free markets in the former Communist nations are likely to operate smoothly only after a long period of maturation.* **mature** (adjective and verb), **maturity** (noun).

mediate (verb) to reconcile differences between two parties. *During the baseball strike, both the players and the club owners were willing to have the president mediate the dispute.* **mediation** (noun).

mediocrity (noun) the state of being middling or poor in quality. *The New York Mets, who'd finished in ninth place in 1968, won the world's championship in 1969, going from horrible to great in a single year and skipping mediocrity.* **mediocre** (adjective).

mercurial (adjective) changing quickly and unpredictably. *The mercurial personality of Robin Williams, with his many voices and styles, made him perfect for the role of the ever-changing genie in* Aladdin.

meticulous (adjective) very careful with details. *Repairing watches calls for a craftsperson who is patient and meticulous.*

mimicry (noun) imitation, aping. *The continued popularity of Elvis Presley has given rise to a class of entertainers who make a living through mimicry of "The King."* **mimic** (noun and verb).

misconception (noun) a mistaken idea. *Columbus sailed west under the misconception that he would reach the shores of Asia that way.* **misconceive** (verb).

mitigate (verb) to make less severe; to relieve. *Wallace certainly committed the assault, but the verbal abuse he'd received helps to explain his behavior and somewhat mitigates his guilt.* **mitigation** (noun).

modicum (noun) a small amount. *The plan for your new business is well designed; with a modicum of luck, you should be successful.*

mollify (verb) to soothe or calm; to appease. *Carla tried to mollify the angry customer by promising him a full refund.*

morose (adjective) gloomy, sullen. *After Chuck's girlfriend dumped him, he lay around the house for a couple of days, feeling morose.*

mundane (adjective) everyday, ordinary, commonplace. *Moviegoers in the 1930s liked the glamorous films of Fred Astaire because they provided an escape from the mundane problems of life during the Great Depression.*

munificent (adjective) very generous; lavish. *The billion-dollar donation to the United Nations is probably the most munificent act of charity in history.* **munificence** (noun).

mutable (adjective) likely to change. *A politician's reputation can be highly mutable, as seen in the case of Harry Truman—mocked during his lifetime, revered afterward.*

narcissistic (adjective) showing excessive love for oneself; egoistic. *Andre's room, decorated with photos of himself and the sports trophies he has won, suggests a narcissistic personality.* **narcissism** (noun).

nocturnal (adjective) of the night; active at night. *Travelers on the Underground Railroad escaped from slavery to the North by a series of nocturnal flights. The eyes of nocturnal animals must be sensitive in dim light.*

nonchalant (adjective) appearing to be unconcerned. *Unlike the other players on the football team, who pumped their fists when their names were announced, John ran on the field with a nonchalant wave.* **nonchalance** (noun).

nondescript (adjective) without distinctive qualities; drab. *The bank robber's clothes were nondescript; none of the witnesses could remember their color or style.*

notorious (adjective) famous, especially for evil actions or qualities. *Warner Brothers produced a series of movies about notorious gangsters such as John Dillinger and Al Capone.* **notoriety** (noun).

novice (noun) beginner, tyro. *Lifting your head before you finish your swing is a typical mistake committed by the novice at golf.*

nuance (noun) a subtle difference or quality. *At first glance, Monet's paintings of water lilies all look much alike, but the more you study them, the more you appreciate the nuances of color and shading that distinguish them.*

nurture (verb) to nourish or help to grow. *The money given by the National Endowment for the Arts helps nurture local arts organizations throughout the country.* **nurture** (noun).

obdurate (adjective) unwilling to change; stubborn, inflexible. *Despite the many pleas he received, the governor was obdurate in his refusal to grant clemency to the convicted murderer.*

objective (adjective) dealing with observable facts rather than opinions or interpretations. *When a legal case involves a shocking crime, it may be hard for a judge to remain objective in her rulings.*

oblivious (adjective) unaware, unconscious. *Karen practiced her oboe with complete concentration, oblivious to the noise and activity around her.* **oblivion** (noun), **obliviousness** (noun).

obscure (adjective) little known; hard to understand. *Mendel was an obscure monk until decades after his death, when his scientific work was finally discovered. Most people find the writings of James Joyce obscure; hence the popularity of books that explain his books.* **obscure** (verb), **obscurity** (noun).

obsessive (adjective) haunted or preoccupied by an idea or feeling. *His concern with cleanliness became so obsessive that he washed his hands twenty times every day.* **obsess** (verb), **obsession** (noun).

obsolete (adjective) no longer current; old-fashioned. *W. H. Auden said that his ideal landscape would include water wheels, wooden grain mills, and other forms of obsolete machinery.* **obsolescence** (noun).

obstinate (adjective) stubborn, unyielding. *Despite years of effort, the problem of drug abuse remains obstinate.* **obstinacy** (noun).

obtrusive (adjective) overly prominent. *Philip should sing more softly; his bass is so obtrusive that the other singers can barely be heard.* **obtrude** (verb), **obtrusion** (noun).

ominous (adjective) foretelling evil. *Ominous black clouds gathered on the horizon, for a violent storm was fast approaching.* **omen** (noun).

onerous (adjective) heavy, burdensome. *The hero Hercules was ordered to clean the Augean Stables, one of several onerous tasks known as "the labors of Hercules."* **onus** (noun).

opportunistic (adjective) eagerly seizing chances as they arise. *When the well-known movie star died suddenly, opportunistic publishers quickly released books about her life and death.* **opportunism** (noun).

opulent (adjective) rich, lavish. *The mansion of newspaper tycoon Hearst is famous for its opulent decor.* **opulence** (noun).

ornate (adjective) highly decorated, elaborate. *Baroque architecture is often highly ornate, featuring surfaces covered with carving, sinuous curves, and painted scenes.*

ostentatious (adjective) overly showy, pretentious. *To show off his wealth, the millionaire threw an ostentatious party featuring a full orchestra, a famous singer, and tens of thousands of dollars' worth of food.*

ostracize (verb) to exclude from a group. *In Biblical times, those who suffered from the disease of leprosy were ostracized and forced to live alone.* **ostracism** (noun).

pallid (adjective) pale; dull. *Working all day in the coal mine had given him a pallid complexion. The new musical offers only pallid entertainment: the music is lifeless, the acting dull, the story absurd.*

parched (adjective) very dry; thirsty. *After two months without rain, the crops were shriveled and parched by the sun.* **parch** (verb).

pariah (noun) outcast. *Accused of robbery, he became a pariah; his neighbors stopped talking to him, and people he'd considered friends no longer called.*

partisan (adjective) reflecting strong allegiance to a particular party or cause. *The vote on the president's budget was strictly partisan: every member of the president's party voted yes, and all others voted no.* **partisan** (noun).

pathology (noun) disease or the study of disease; extreme abnormality. *Some people believe that high rates of crime are symptoms of an underlying social pathology.* **pathological** (adjective).

pellucid (adjective) very clear; transparent; easy to understand. *The water in the mountain stream was cold and pellucid. Thanks to the professor's pellucid explanation, I finally understand relativity theory.*

penitent (adjective) feeling sorry for past crimes or sins. *Having grown penitent, he wrote a long letter of apology, asking forgiveness.*

penurious (adjective) extremely frugal; stingy. *Haunted by memories of poverty, he lived in penurious fashion, driving a twelve-year-old car and wearing only the cheapest clothes.* **penury** (noun).

perfunctory (adjective) unenthusiastic, routine, or mechanical. *When the play opened, the actors sparkled, but by the thousandth night their performance had become perfunctory.*

permeate (verb) to spread through or penetrate. *Little by little, the smell of gas from the broken pipe permeated the house.*

perceptive (adjective) quick to notice, observant. *With his perceptive intelligence, Holmes was the first to notice the importance of this clue.* **perceptible** (adjective), **perception** (noun).

perfidious (adjective) disloyal, treacherous. *Although he was one of the most talented generals of the American Revolution, Benedict Arnold is remembered today as a perfidious betrayer of his country.* **perfidy** (noun).

persevere (adjective) to continue despite difficulties. *Although several of her teammates dropped out of the marathon, Laura persevered.* **perseverance** (noun).

perspicacity (noun) keenness of observation or understanding. *Journalist Murray Kempton was famous for the perspicacity of his comments on social and political issues.* **perspicacious** (adjective).

peruse (verb) to examine or study. *Mary-Jo perused the contract carefully before she signed it.* **perusal** (noun).

pervasive (adjective) spreading throughout. *As news of the disaster reached the town, a pervasive sense of gloom could be felt everywhere.* **pervade** (verb).

phlegmatic (adjective) sluggish and unemotional in temperament. *It was surprising to see Tom, who is normally so phlegmatic, acting excited.*

placate (verb) to soothe or appease. *The waiter tried to placate the angry customer with the offer of a free dessert.* **placatory** (adjective).

plastic (adjective) able to be molded or reshaped. *Because it is highly plastic, clay is an easy material for beginning sculptors to use.*

plausible (adjective) apparently believable. *The idea that a widespread conspiracy to kill President Kennedy has been kept secret for over thirty years hardly seems plausible.* **plausibility** (noun).

polarize (adjective) to separate into opposing groups or forces. *For years, the abortion debate polarized the American people, with many people voicing extreme views and few trying to find a middle ground.* **polarization** (noun).

portend (verb) to indicate a future event; to forebode. *According to folklore, a red sky at dawn portends a day of stormy weather.*

potentate (noun) a powerful ruler. *Before the Russian Revolution, the Tsar was one of the last hereditary potentates of Europe.*

pragmatism (noun) a belief in approaching problems through practical rather than theoretical means. *Roosevelt's approach toward the Great Depression was based on pragmatism: "Try something." he said; "If it doesn't work, try something else."* **pragmatic** (adjective).

preamble (noun) an introductory statement. *The preamble to the Constitution begins with the famous words, "We the people of the United States of America . . ."*

precocious (adjective) mature at an unusually early age. *Picasso was so precocious as an artist that, at nine, he is said to have painted far better pictures than his teacher.* **precocity** (noun).

predatory (adjective) living by killing and eating other animals; exploiting others for personal gain. *The tiger is the largest predatory animal native to Asia. The corporation has been accused of predatory business practices that prevent other companies from competing with them.* **predation** (noun), **predator** (noun).

predilection (noun) a liking or preference. *To relax from his presidential duties, Kennedy had a predilection for spy novels featuring James Bond.*

predominant (adjective) greatest in numbers or influence. *Although hundreds of religions are practiced in India, the predominant faith is Hinduism.* **predominance** (noun), **predominate** (verb).

prepossessing (adjective) attractive. *Smart, lovely, and talented, she has all the prepossessing qualities that mark a potential movie star.*

presumptuous (adjective) going beyond the limits of courtesy or appropriateness. *The senator winced when the presumptuous young staffer addressed him as "Chuck."* **presume** (verb), **presumption** (noun).

pretentious (adjective) claiming excessive value or importance. *For an ordinary shoe salesman to call himself a "Personal Foot Apparel Consultant" seems awfully pretentious.* **pretension** (noun).

procrastinate (verb) to put off, to delay. *If you habitually procrastinate, try this technique: never touch a piece of paper without either filing it, responding to it, or throwing it out.* **procrastination** (noun).

profane (adjective) impure, unholy. *It seems inappropriate to have such profane activities as roller blading and disco dancing in a church.* **profane** (verb), **profanity** (noun).

proficient (adjective) skillful, adept. *A proficient artist, Louise quickly and accurately sketched the scene.* **proficiency** (noun).

proliferate (verb) to increase or multiply. *Over the past fifteen years, high-tech companies have proliferated in northern California, Massachusetts, and other regions.* **proliferation** (noun).

prolific (adjective) producing many offspring or creations. *With over three hundred books to his credit, Isaac Asimov was one of the most prolific writers of all time.*

prominence (noun) the quality of standing out; fame. *Kennedy's victory in the West Virginia primary gave him a position of prominence among the Democratic candidates for president.* **prominent** (adjective).

promulgate (verb) to make public, to declare. *Lincoln signed the proclamation that freed the slaves in 1862, but he waited several months to promulgate it.*

propagate (verb) to cause to grow; to foster. *John Smithson's will left his fortune for the founding of an institution to propagate knowledge, without saying whether that meant a university, a library, or a museum.* **propagation** (noun).

propriety (noun) appropriateness. *Some people had doubts about the propriety of former president Clinton's discussing his underwear on MTV.*

prosaic (adjective) everyday, ordinary, dull. *"Paul's Case" tells the story of a boy who longs to escape from the prosaic life of a clerk into a world of wealth, glamour, and beauty.*

protagonist (noun) the main character in a story or play; the main supporter of an idea. *Leopold Bloom is the protagonist of James Joyce's great novel* Ulysses.

provocative (adjective) likely to stimulate emotions, ideas, or controversy. *The demonstrators began chanting obscenities, a provocative act that they hoped would cause the police to lose control.* **provoke** (verb), **provocation** (noun).

proximity (noun) closeness, nearness. *Neighborhood residents were angry over the proximity of the sewage plant to the local school.* **proximate** (adjective).

prudent (adjective) wise, cautious, and practical. *A prudent investor will avoid putting all of her money into any single investment.* **prudence** (noun), **prudential** (adjective).

pugnacious (adjective) combative, bellicose, truculent; ready to fight. *Ty Cobb, the pugnacious outfielder for the Detroit Tigers, got into more than his fair share of brawls, both on and off the field.* **pugnacity** (noun).

punctilious (adjective) very concerned about proper forms of behavior and manners. *A punctilious dresser like James would rather skip the party altogether than wear the wrong color tie.* **punctilio** (noun).

pundit (noun) someone who offers opinions in an authoritative style. *The Sunday afternoon talk shows are filled with pundits, each with his or her own theory about this week's political news.*

punitive (adjective) inflicting punishment. *The jury awarded the plaintiff one million dollars in punitive damages, hoping to teach the defendant a lesson.*

purify (verb) to make pure, clean, or perfect. *The new plant is supposed to purify the drinking water provided to everyone in the nearby towns.* **purification** (noun).

quell (verb) to quiet, to suppress. *It took a huge number of police to quell the rioting.*

querulous (adjective) complaining, whining. *The nursing home attendant needed a lot of patience to care for the three querulous, unpleasant residents on his floor.*

rancorous (adjective) expressing bitter hostility. *Many Americans are disgusted by recent political campaigns, which seem more rancorous than ever before.* **rancor** (noun).

rationale (noun) an underlying reason or explanation. *At first, it seemed strange that several camera companies would freely share their newest technology; but their rationale was that offering one new style of film would benefit them all.*

raze (verb) to completely destroy; demolish. *The old Coliseum building will soon be razed to make room for a new hotel.*

reciprocate (verb) to make a return for something. *If you'll baby-sit for my kids tonight, I'll reciprocate by taking care of yours tomorrow.* **reciprocity** (noun).

reclusive (adjective) withdrawn from society. *During the last years of her life, actress Greta Garbo led a reclusive existence, rarely appearing in public.* **recluse** (noun).

reconcile (verb) to make consistent or harmonious. *Roosevelt's greatness as a leader can be seen in his ability to reconcile the demands and values of the varied groups that supported him.* **reconciliation** (noun).

recriminate (verb) to accuse, often in response to an accusation. *Divorce proceedings sometimes become bitter, as the two parties recriminate each other over the causes of the breakup.* **recrimination** (noun), **recriminatory** (adjective).

recuperate (verb) to regain health after an illness. *Although she left the hospital two days after her operation, it took her a few weeks to fully recuperate.* **recuperation** (noun), **recuperative** (adjective).

redoubtable (adjective) inspiring respect, awe, or fear. *Johnson's knowledge, experience, and personal clout made him a redoubtable political opponent.*

refurbish (verb) to fix up; renovate. *It took three days' work by a team of carpenters, painters, and decorators to completely refurbish the apartment.*

refute (adjective) to prove false. *The company invited reporters to visit their plant in an effort to refute the charges of unsafe working conditions.* **refutation** (noun).

relevance (noun) connection to the matter at hand; pertinence. *Testimony in a criminal trial may be admitted only if it has clear relevance to the question of guilt or innocence.* **relevant** (adjective).

remedial (adjective) serving to remedy, cure, or correct some condition. *Affirmative action can be justified as a remedial step to help minority members overcome the effects of past discrimination.* **remediation** (noun), **remedy** (verb).

remorse (noun) a painful sense of guilt over wrongdoing. *In Poe's story "The Tell-Tale Heart," a murderer is driven insane by remorse over his crime.* **remorseful** (adjective).

remuneration (noun) pay. *In a civil lawsuit, the attorney often receives part of the financial settlement as his or her remuneration.* **remunerate** (verb), **remunerative** (adjective).

renovate (verb) to renew by repairing or rebuilding. *The television program "The New This Old House" shows how skilled craftspeople renovate houses.* **renovation** (noun).

renunciation (noun) the act of rejecting or refusing something. *King Edward VII's renunciation of the British throne was caused by his desire to marry an American divorcee, something he couldn't do as king.* **renounce** (verb).

replete (adjective) filled abundantly. *Graham's book is replete with wonderful stories about the famous people she has known.*

reprehensible (adjective) deserving criticism or censure. *Although the athlete's misdeeds were reprehensible, not all fans agree that he deserves to be excluded from the Baseball Hall of Fame.* **reprehend** (verb), **reprehension** (noun).

repudiate (verb) to reject, to renounce. *After it became known that the congressman had been a leader of the Ku Klux Klan, most politicians repudiated him.* **repudiation** (noun).

reputable (adjective) having a good reputation; respected. *Find a reputable auto mechanic by asking your friends for recommendations based on their own experiences.* **reputation** (noun), **repute** (noun).

resilient (adjective) able to recover from difficulty. *A pro athlete must be resilient, able to lose a game one day and come back the next with confidence and enthusiasm.* **resilience** (adjective).

resplendent (adjective) glowing, shining. *In late December, midtown New York is resplendent with holiday lights and decorations.* **resplendence** (noun).

responsive (adjective) reacting quickly and appropriately. *The new director of the Internal Revenue Service has promised to make the agency more responsive to public complaints.* **respond** (verb), **response** (noun).

restitution (noun) return of something to its original owner; repayment. *Some Native American leaders are demanding that the U.S. government make restitution for the lands taken from them by white settlers.*

revere (verb) to admire deeply, to honor. *Millions of people around the world revered Mother Teresa for her saintly generosity.* **reverence** (noun), **reverent** (adjective).

rhapsodize (verb) to praise in a wildly emotional way. *That critic is such a huge fan of Toni Morrison that she will surely rhapsodize over the writer's next novel.* **rhapsodic** (adjective).

sagacious (adjective) discerning, wise. *Only a leader as sagacious as Nelson Mandela could have united South Africa so successfully and peacefully.* **sagacity** (noun).

salvage (verb) to save from wreck or ruin. *After the earthquake destroyed her home, she was able to salvage only a few of her belongings.* **salvage** (noun), **salvageable** (adjective).

sanctimonious (adjective) showing false or excessive piety. *The sanctimonious prayers of the TV preacher were interspersed with requests that the viewers send him money.* **sanctimony** (noun).

scapegoat (noun) someone who bears the blame for others' acts; someone hated for no apparent reason. *Although the shortstop's error was only one reason the Red Sox lost, many fans made him the scapegoat, booing him mercilessly.*

scrupulous (adjective) acting with extreme care; painstaking. *Disney theme parks are famous for their scrupulous attention to small details.* **scruple** (noun).

scrutinize (verb) to study closely. *The lawyer scrutinized the contract, searching for any sentence that could pose a risk for her client.* **scrutiny** (noun).

secrete (verb) to emit; to hide. *Glands in the mouth secrete saliva, a liquid that helps in digestion. The jewel thieves secreted the necklace in a tin box buried underground.*

sedentary (adjective) requiring much sitting. *When Officer Samson was given a desk job, she had trouble getting used to sedentary work after years on the street.*

sequential (adjective) arranged in an order or series. *The courses for the chemistry major are sequential; you must take them in the order, since each course builds on the previous ones.* **sequence** (noun).

serendipity (noun) the ability to make lucky accidental discoveries. *Great inventions sometimes come about through deliberate research and hard work, sometimes through pure serendipity.* **serendipitous** (adjective).

servile (adjective) like a slave or servant; submissive. *The tycoon demanded that his underlings behave in a servile manner, agreeing quickly with everything he said.* **servility** (noun).

simulated (adjective) imitating something else; artificial. *High-quality simulated gems must be examined under a magnifying glass to be distinguished from real ones.* **simulate** (verb), **simulation** (noun).

solace (verb) to comfort or console. *There was little the rabbi could say to solace the husband after his wife's death.* **solace** (noun).

spontaneous (adjective) happening without plan or outside cause. *When the news of Kennedy's assassination broke, people everywhere gathered in a spontaneous effort to share their shock and grief.* **spontaneity** (noun).

spurious (adjective) false, fake. *The so-called Piltdown Man, supposed to be the fossil of a primitive human, turned out to be spurious, although who created the hoax is still uncertain.*

squander (verb) to use up carelessly, to waste. *Those who had made donations to the charity were outraged to learn that its director had squandered millions on fancy dinners and first-class travel.*

staid (adjective) sedate, serious, and grave. *This college is no "party school"; the students all work hard, and the campus has a reputation for being staid.*

stagnate (verb) to become stale through lack of movement or change. *Having had no contact with the outside world for generations, Japan's culture gradually stagnated.* **stagnant** (adjective), **stagnation** (noun).

stimulus (noun) something that excites a response or provokes an action. *The arrival of merchants and missionaries from the West provided a stimulus for change in Japanese society.* **stimulate** (verb).

stoic (adjective) showing little feeling, even in response to pain or sorrow. *A soldier must respond to the death of his comrades in stoic fashion, since the fighting will not stop for his grief.* **stoicism** (noun).

strenuous (adjective) requiring energy and strength. *Hiking in the foothills of the Rockies is fairly easy, but climbing the higher peaks can be strenuous.*

submissive (adjective) accepting the will of others; humble, compliant. *At the end of Ibsen's play* A Doll's House, *Nora leaves her husband and abandons the role of submissive housewife.*

substantiated (adjective) verified or supported by evidence. *The charge that Nixon had helped to cover up crimes was substantiated by his comments about it on a series of audio tapes.* **substantiate** (verb), **substantiation** (noun).

sully (verb) to soil, stain, or defile. *Nixon's misdeeds as president did much to sully the reputation of the American government.*

superficial (adjective) on the surface only; without depth or substance. *Her wound was superficial and required only a light bandage. His superficial attractiveness hides the fact that his personality is lifeless and his mind is dull.* **superficiality** (noun).

superfluous (adjective) more than is needed, excessive. *Once you've won the debate, don't keep talking; superfluous arguments will only bore and annoy the audience.*

suppress (verb) to put down or restrain. *As soon as the unrest began, thousands of helmeted police were sent into the streets to suppress the riots.* **suppression** (noun).

surfeit (noun) an excess. *Most American families have a surfeit of food and drink on Thanksgiving Day.* **surfeit** (verb).

surreptitious (adjective) done in secret. *Many FBI agents believe the apartment houses a surreptitious drug-dealing business.*

surrogate (noun) a substitute. *When the congressman died in office, his wife was named to serve the rest of his term as a surrogate.* **surrogate** (adjective).

sustain (verb) to keep up, to continue; to support. *Because of fatigue, he was unable to sustain the effort needed to finish the marathon.*

tactile (adjective) relating to the sense of touch. *The thick brush strokes and gobs of color give the paintings of Van Gogh a strongly tactile quality.* **tactility** (noun).

talisman (noun) an object supposed to have magical effects or qualities. *Superstitious people sometimes carry a rabbit's foot, a lucky coin, or some other talisman.*

tangential (adjective) touching lightly; only slightly connected or related. *Having enrolled in a class on African-American history, the students found the teacher's stories about his travels in South America only of tangential interest.* **tangent** (noun).

tedium (noun) boredom. *For most people, watching the Weather Channel for 24 hours would be sheer tedium.* **tedious** (adjective).

temerity (noun) boldness, rashness, excessive daring. *Only someone who didn't understand the danger would have the temerity to try to climb Everest without a guide.* **temerarious** (adjective).

temperance (noun) moderation or restraint in feelings and behavior. *Most professional athletes practice temperance in their personal habits; too much eating or drinking, they know, can harm their performance.* **temperate** (adjective).

tenacious (adjective) clinging, sticky, or persistent. *Tenacious in pursuit of her goal, she applied for the grant unsuccessfully four times before it was finally approved.* **tenacity** (noun).

tentative (adjective) subject to change; uncertain. *A firm schedule has not been established, but the dance recital has been given the tentative date of January 20.*

terminate (verb) to end, to close. *The Olympic Games terminate with a grand ceremony attended by athletes from every participating country.* **terminal** (noun), **termination** (noun).

terrestrial (adjective) of the Earth. *The movie* Close Encounters of the Third Kind *tells the story of the first contact between beings from outer space and terrestrial humans.*

therapeutic (adjective) curing or helping to cure. *Hot-water spas were popular in the nineteenth century among the sickly, who believed that soaking in the water had therapeutic effects.* **therapy** (noun).

timorous (adjective) fearful, timid. *The cowardly lion approached the throne of the wizard with a timorous look on his face.*

toady (noun) someone who flatters a superior in hopes of gaining favor; a sycophant. *"I can't stand a toady!" declared the movie mogul. "Give me someone who'll tell me the truth—even if it costs him his job!"* **toady** (verb).

tolerant (adjective) accepting, enduring. *San Franciscans have a tolerant attitude about lifestyles: "Live and let live" seems to be their motto.* **tolerate** (verb), **toleration** (noun).

toxin (noun) poison. *DDT is a powerful toxin once used to kill insects but now banned in the U.S. because of the risk it poses to human life.* **toxic** (adjective).

tranquillity (noun) freedom from disturbance or turmoil; calm. *She moved from New York City to rural Vermont seeking the tranquillity of country life.* **tranquil** (adjective).

transient (adjective) passing quickly. *Long-term visitors to this hotel pay at a different rate than transient guests who stay for just a day or two.* **transience** (noun).

transgress (verb) to go past limits; to violate. *If that country has developed nuclear weapons, then it has transgressed the United Nation's rules against weapons development.* **transgression** (noun).

transitory (adjective) quickly passing. *Public moods tend to be transitory; people may be anxious and angry one month, but relatively content and optimistic the next.* **transition** (noun).

translucent (adjective) letting some light pass through. *Blocks of translucent glass let daylight into the room while maintaining privacy.*

transmute (verb) to change in form or substance. *In the middle ages, the alchemists tried to discover ways to transmute metals such as iron into gold.* **transmutation** (noun).

treacherous (adjective) untrustworthy or disloyal; dangerous or unreliable. *Nazi Germany proved to be a treacherous ally, first signing a peace pact with the Soviet Union, then invading. Be careful crossing the rope bridge; parts are badly frayed and treacherous.* **treachery** (noun).

tremulous (adjective) trembling or shaking; timid or fearful. *Never having spoken in public before, he began his speech in a tremulous, hesitant voice.*

trite (adjective) boring because of over-familiarity; hackneyed. *Her letters were filled with trite expressions, like "All's well that ends well," and "So far so good."*

truculent (adjective) aggressive, hostile, belligerent. *Hitler's truculent behavior in demanding more territory for Germany made it clear that war was inevitable.* **truculence** (noun).

truncate (verb) to cut off. *The manuscript of the play appeared truncated; the last page ended in the middle of a scene, halfway through the first act.*

turbulent (adjective) agitated or disturbed. *The night before the championship match, Martina was unable to sleep, her mind turbulent with fears and hopes.* **turbulence** (noun).

unheralded (adjective) little known, unexpected. *In a year of big-budget, much-hyped mega-movies, this unheralded foreign film has surprised everyone with its popularity.*

unpalatable (adjective) distasteful, unpleasant. *Although I agree with the candidate on many issues, I can't vote for her, because I find her position on capital punishment unpalatable.*

unparalleled (adjective) with no equal; unique. *His victory in the Masters golf tournament by a full twelve strokes was an unparalleled accomplishment.*

unstinting (adjective) giving freely and generously. *Eleanor Roosevelt was much admired for her unstinting efforts on behalf of the poor.*

untenable (adjective) impossible to defend. *The theory that this painting is a genuine Van Gogh became untenable when the artist who actually painted it came forth.*

untimely (adjective) out of the natural or proper time. *The untimely death of a youthful Princess Diana seemed far more tragic than Mother Teresa's death of old age.*

unyielding (adjective) firm, resolute, obdurate. *Despite criticism, he was unyielding in his opposition to capital punishment; he vetoed several death penalty bills as governor.*

usurper (noun) someone who takes a place or possession without the right to do so. *Kennedy's most devoted followers tended to regard later presidents as usurpers, holding the office they felt he or his brothers should have held.* **usurp** (verb), **usurpation** (noun).

utilitarian (adjective) purely of practical benefit. *The design of the Model T car was simple and utilitarian, lacking the luxuries found in later models.*

utopia (noun) an imaginary, perfect society. *Those who founded the Oneida community dreamed that it could be a kind of utopia—a prosperous state with complete freedom and harmony.* **utopian** (adjective).

validate (verb) to officially approve or confirm. *The election of the president is validated when the members of the Electoral College meet to confirm the choice of the voters.* **valid** (adjective), **validity** (noun).

variegated (adjective) spotted with different colors. *The brilliant, variegated appearance of butterflies makes them popular among collectors.* **variegation** (noun).

venerate (verb) to admire or honor. *In Communist China, Chairman Mao Zedong was venerated as an almost god-like figure.* **venerable** (adjective), **veneration** (noun).

verdant (adjective) green with plant life. *Southern England is famous for its verdant countryside filled with gardens and small farms.* **verdancy** (noun).

vestige (noun) a trace or remainder. *Today's tiny Sherwood Forest is the last vestige of a woodland that once covered most of England.* **vestigial** (adjective).

vex (verb) to irritate, annoy, or trouble. *Unproven for generations, Fermat's last theorem was one of the most famous, and most vexing, of all mathematical puzzles.* **vexation** (noun).

vicarious (adjective) experienced through someone else's actions by way of the imagination. *Great literature broadens our minds by giving us vicarious participation in the lives of other people.*

vindicate (verb) to confirm, justify, or defend. *Lincoln's Gettysburg Address was intended to vindicate the objectives of the Union in the Civil War.*

virtuoso (noun) someone very skilled, especially in an art. *Vladimir Horowitz was one of the great piano virtuosos of the twentieth century.* **virtuosity** (noun).

vivacious (adjective) lively, sprightly. *The role of Maria in "The Sound of Music" is usually played by a charming, vivacious young actor.* **vivacity** (noun).

volatile (adjective) quickly changing; fleeting, transitory; prone to violence. *Public opinion is notoriously volatile; a politician who is very popular one month may be voted out of office the next.* **volatility** (noun).

whimsical (adjective) based on a capricious, carefree, or sudden impulse or idea; fanciful, playful. *The book is filled with the kind of goofy jokes that are typical of the author's whimsical sense of humor.* **whim** (noun).

zealous (adjective) filled with eagerness, fervor, or passion. *A crowd of the candidate's most zealous supporters greeted her at the airport with banners, signs, and a marching band.* **zeal** (noun), **zealot** (noun), **zealotry** (noun).

Applying to Colleges and Universities in the U.S.

Daniel M. Lundquist
Vice President for Admissions and Financial Aid
Union College

Robert Hunter
Director of Academic Services
World Education Services

HIGHER EDUCATION IN THE UNITED STATES

More than 565,000 international students now study in more than 2,500 of 3,800 colleges and universities in the United States. The opportunity to choose from such a large range of institutions and programs is one of the greatest advantages of the U.S. educational system. American schools range from large research universities with more than 20,000 students to small colleges with fewer than 1,000 students; from universities with graduate and professional studies in medicine, law, and many other fields, to schools offering only the two-year associate degree; from urban schools in large cities to rural institutions located far from metropolitan areas.

Admission to a college or university typically follows satisfactory completion of twelve years of elementary and secondary education for students educated in the United States. The twelve-year cycle is usually broken down as follows:

* A five-year primary program beginning at about age six, generally called elementary school

* A three-year intermediate program, generally called middle school

* A four-year secondary program, generally called high school

The admission requirements for students educated outside the U.S. educational system will vary from school to school. The educational preparation that is required to apply to a university in your own country will usually enable you to apply to a U.S. college or university.

appendix b

A number of secondary-level programs in other countries are seen as being at a "higher level" than the typical secondary-level program in the United States. Some U.S. colleges and universities will give advanced-standing credit toward an undergraduate academic degree for these programs. Since U.S. colleges and universities have the authority to determine their own admission and advanced-standing policies, you should always ask each school what specific educational qualifications it requires from students educated in your country.

Types of U.S. Institutions of Higher Education

Two-year institutions, which are sometimes referred to as community or junior colleges, award the associate degree—Associate of Arts (A.A.) or Associate of Science (A.S.)—following successful completion of a specific two-year, full-time program. There are two basic types of programs at two-year institutions. Some programs are strictly academic and designed to prepare students for transfer to four-year institutions with bachelor's degree programs. Others are more practical or applied and provide career training in specific areas. This second type does not usually prepare students for transfer to a four-year institution, although some of the credits earned may still be accepted by a four-year institution. A small number of two-year institutions offer the final two years of the undergraduate program only, awarding the bachelor's degree rather than the associate degree. Most two-year institutions are publicly supported by the state and local communities, although some are private. Some private two-year colleges are proprietary, or run for a profit.

The college or university (sometimes called an institute when it emphasizes engineering or other technical courses) awards the bachelor's degree. The Bachelor of Arts (B.A.) and Bachelor of Science (B.S.) degrees are the two most frequently awarded, but a variety of bachelor's degrees by other names are also granted. Bachelor's degrees are typically awarded following successful completion of a four-year, full-time program. Bachelor's degree programs in some fields of study or at some institutions can be longer than four years. There are both public and private colleges and universities in the United States, and some have a religious affiliation.

Characteristics of U.S. Colleges

Publicly supported schools are generally state colleges or universities or two-year community colleges. These institutions receive most of their funding from the states in which they are located. Students who are residents of the sponsoring state can usually attend these schools for lower fees than students coming from other states or from outside the United States.

Private schools generally have higher costs because they do not receive the same primary funding from the state and federal government. All students at private institutions pay similar fees no matter where they are from.

Colleges and universities with religious affiliations are private. Most of them are Christian (Roman Catholic and Protestant), although there are a small number of Jewish and Islamic institutions. Many of these colleges have very active relationships with the religious institution that sponsors them, and religious life may play a large role on the campus at these schools. Others have a much looser historical affiliation, rather than an active relationship with a specific religion. You do not need to be a member of a particular church or religious group to attend a religiously affiliated college in the United States. Enrollment in these institutions will not usually interfere with your own religious views.

However, there are a few exceptions. Some colleges that emphasize in their literature that they are Christian are organized according to fundamentalist principles. Students from a Christian fundamentalist or evangelical background will be very comfortable on a campus where Bible study may be required and social life is strictly regulated. Read the literature of these colleges very carefully. They may offer the setting you seek, but they may not.

The only way that proprietary institutions are different from the other types of schools is that they are privately owned and run for a profit. They are "educational businesses" that offer services and courses similar to those at other institutions. Their programs tend to focus on technical and preprofessional courses of study.

Almost all colleges in the United States are coeducational, which means that both men and women attend. There are a small number of single-sex schools, some for men and some for women. Faculty, administration, and staff members will likely be of both sexes at any college.

The U.S. educational system is flexible in many ways. The first one to two years of most undergraduate degree programs focus primarily on basic introductory course work and general education in the arts and sciences. This exposes students to a variety of academic disciplines and shows them how these fields are related. Students entering the U.S. system from educational systems in other countries may feel that they have completed these general education requirements at home through previous study at the secondary level. However, general and liberal arts studies at the undergraduate level in the U.S. provide international students with an understanding of the bases and values of U.S. society, a perspective that is likely missing in similar courses taught in another culture. The final two years of most undergraduate programs focus on the major subject of concentration.

In summary, the structure of the U.S. system of higher education provides students with an opportunity to take a wide variety of courses and explore different interests but also includes in-depth study in a specific field. These choices and the broadly based education they result in are among the most attractive reasons for studying in the United States.

The Academic Calendar

American colleges operate on three main types of calendars that divide the year into terms: the semester, trimester, and quarter systems. The academic year is approximately nine months long no matter how it is divided. The semester system divides that nine months in half, resulting in fall and spring semesters. Schools that use the trimester and quarter systems divide the same nine months into three 3-month terms. The summer term is the fourth quarter in the quarter system, and enrollment in classes is optional. For most institutions the academic year runs from late August or September to May or June. Many schools operate all year long, and students can often take courses over the summer term for an additional fee.

There are usually two examination periods in each term, one in the middle and one at the end. Holiday schedules vary with each school, but there are usually a number of short holidays in each term, a longer break in December and January, and a weeklong vacation period in early spring. International students who want or need to stay on campus during holiday periods should find out from the housing office if this is possible and if there is any additional charge.

Faculty Members and Methods of Instruction

Students and faculty members typically interact less formally in U.S. undergraduate programs than they do elsewhere in the world. They often develop close relationships or friendships. The size of the institution and the size of the class will be important factors. Professors sometimes ask students to join them for lunch or participate with them in community activities. Each professor has his or her own personality and style but, in general, faculty members at U.S. schools are more accessible than faculty members in many other countries.

The classroom experience is frequently characterized by discussion between the professor and the students. A portion of a student's grade for a course is often determined by the quality of participation in class discussions. It is unusual to find a course where the entire grade is based on one examination at the end of the term. International students should be prepared to participate in class discussions since classmates and professors will expect it. Most faculty members are aware that cultural factors and English language skills may initially make participation difficult for international students. With time, most international students find that this participation adds a great deal to the learning process.

There are three basic methods of instruction. Large introductory-level courses are usually taught through lectures at which several hundred students gather to hear a professor speak. The small class or seminar includes a group of 5 to 30 students. This method is generally used in more advanced courses and allows for more interaction between the students and the professor. Laboratory sections are similar to seminars and are usually required with courses in the sciences or applied fields like computer science or engineering.

Almost all colleges offer opportunities for students to work individually with professors in tutorials or independent study courses.

Academic and Personal Advising Systems

An attractive feature of U.S. higher education is the support and counseling that students receive.

International or Foreign Student Adviser. Most U.S. colleges and universities have an international office with trained professionals available to counsel students from other countries on a broad range of matters, including:

- Orientation to campus and community life
- Immigration and visa
- Employment and practical training
- Off-campus and social activities and opportunities
- Personal and health concerns
- General academic planning
- Financial problems

Faculty Adviser. At most schools, each student is assigned a faculty adviser. The assignment is usually based on the student's field of study. Faculty advising includes the following areas:

- Requirements for degrees
- Selection of academic courses
- Academic performance and progress

Peer Counselor. Many colleges have developed a system of peer counseling for students. The counselors are upperclass students and provide the student viewpoint on academic and personal matters.

Outside the Classroom

An important part of your educational experience in the United States will be participation in nonacademic, social, and extracurricular activities on campus. Many opportunities are available for students to become involved in sports, student government, music, drama, and other organized and individual activities. Such activities are designed to contribute to your personal growth, provide recreation, create opportunities to meet new people with similar interests, and help prepare you for future leadership roles upon graduation. Participation in these activities is not required to obtain a U.S. degree. These are optional activities, but they play a central role in campus life at U.S. colleges and universities.

HOW TO DETERMINE WHICH COLLEGES ARE BEST FOR YOU

Choosing which colleges and universities to apply to is a difficult task when you are not familiar with the United States and its system of education. With so many institutions to choose from, it is necessary to approach your choice in a logical way to arrive at a list of schools that would be best for you.

Now, consider the following list when looking at colleges. How important is each one to you? Rank them in order from one through eight, according to your own priorities.

Cost

Look for the total cost of tuition, fees, and room and board. You will need additional funds for books and other living expenses. If you need financial aid, are grants available? Compare the number of international students enrolled to the number of awards given and the average amount granted. This will give you an idea about the possibility of receiving one of these awards and how much it might help you to meet your need.

Enrollment

Look at the total and undergraduate enrollments. Is this the right size school for you? Find the percentage of international students and how many countries are represented. Does it have the blend of U.S. and international students you are looking for?

Entrance Difficulty

Find the entrance difficulty for U.S. students. Compare the number of international students who applied to the number accepted. This will tell you how difficult it is to gain admission.

Location

Consider where the institution is located. What is the climate in that area of the country? Is the campus setting urban, suburban, small-town, or rural? Would you be happy living in this type of area?

Housing

Is on-campus housing available and guaranteed? Is it available during the summer and during breaks if you need it?

Library Holdings and Facilities

Refer to the information on library holdings and other facilities, such as laboratories, computer labs, and athletic facilities, to make certain they meet your needs.

Type of Institution

Is it a two-year or four-year institution? Is it public or private? Is it religious or proprietary? These are all important factors to consider in the decision-making process.

English as a Second Language (ESL) Program

Is there an intensive English language program available (if needed)?

Decide what you want and need concerning each of the previous items. Review the institutions on your first list. Eliminate those that do not meet the criteria that are important to you. For example, if you cannot afford more than $10,000 each year, eliminate those institutions with combined tuition and fees and room and board that come close to that amount, unless you are especially interested in a particular institution and it offers financial aid for which you are confident you will qualify. If you want to attend an institution in a particular state or area of the United States, eliminate those schools that do not fit that category. If you are sure that you want to attend a large public institution, you can eliminate the schools that do not match this criterion. You should now have a much shorter list of colleges that may be good choices for you.

Select seven to ten institutions that seem to meet your needs the best. This is your second list. Be sure to request application materials as early as possible. It is best to start this process sixteen months before the date you intend to enter college.

While you wait for the answers to your requests for further information, determine which standardized admission tests you need to take. Most schools require the College Board's SAT or the American College Testing's ACT Assessment (ACT). A few require the College Board's SAT Subject Tests. In addition, the Test of English as a Foreign Language (TOEFL) is generally required for international students who do not speak English as a native language. You will want to avoid having to take additional tests after receiving application materials from individual institutions because it will slow down the application process.

Review the materials that you receive and any information on these schools that is available in the advising office in your school or the center where you received this publication. Reduce your list to three to five colleges and universities by reviewing the following information:

- Detailed description of the overall academic program
- Specific course offerings and faculty information
- Academic facilities (libraries, computer, and laboratory facilities)
- Detailed description of the campus and surrounding community
- Housing, financial aid, and ESL (if needed)
- Extracurricular, cultural, and religious activities that are important to you

This is your third and final list for application purposes.

APPLYING

Once again, be sure to request application materials as early as possible. It is best to start this process sixteen months before the date you intend to enter college. In addition, the way you complete your application and present yourself is very important and will play a big part in determining the outcome of your efforts to gain admission. If you want to find a college or university that is able to meet your needs, it is very important for you to be completely honest and sincere in the information you provide to them.

Carefully read the application and information that you have received from each school. It will tell you how the school sees itself, its mission, philosophy, and educational goals. Once you know what a specific college values and emphasizes, you will have some idea of what aspects of your own background and goals to emphasize as you prepare your application. More important, getting a broad sense of the school will help you determine if it is a place where you would fit in and be comfortable and happy. Admission officers will be doing exactly what you did to prepare for applying. They will attempt to determine how your abilities, goals, and interests match what they have to offer and what kind of contributions you might be able to make to the college and its students. You should present yourself in your best light, but do not give incorrect information. Admission officers can usually tell when an application statement does not sound like the truth. In addition, the legal implications of giving false information about yourself can be very serious.

A complete application that is ready to be evaluated by the admission committee typically contains the following:

- Fully completed preliminary (if required) and final application forms
- Teacher recommendations (if required)
- Secondary school report (if required)
- Transcripts and academic records
- TOEFL or other English language proficiency test scores (if required and applicable)
- Standardized test scores (SAT, ACT, and SAT Subject Tests if applicable)
- Nonacademic information as requested by the college or university
- Financial aid application (if applicable)
- Application fee

Preliminary Applications

Some colleges require international applicants to complete a preliminary application. If a school uses this process, you will receive a preliminary application with the materials they send to you. The preliminary application helps admission officers determine whether or not you will be a likely candidate before you go through the more complicated process of completing the final application form.

The preliminary application will request basic information about you and may also ask for a brief statement of your goals. Your statement should indicate the reasons why you feel the school would be a good place for you and what contributions you can make to life on campus. Return the preliminary application as quickly as possible.

If the admission officer finds that your goals, abilities, and general background are compatible with what that particular college is looking for, you will be sent the final application to complete. If it is determined that you are not a competitive candidate, you will be notified of this decision and can then focus your attention and energy on the other schools you have selected.

Final Applications

It is important to complete the final application and provide all the required information and documents the college has requested as quickly as possible. The sooner the college receives your application and all the required supporting documents, the sooner they will be reviewed and evaluated. An application submitted early can only help your chance of being offered admission and will give you extra time to supply additional information if it is requested.

Personal Information

The personal information requested on an application form is an important part of the complete application package. You will likely be asked to answer a variety of questions about yourself—your abilities, goals, special talents, and why you wish to attend that particular college. Many international applicants have wonderfully rich backgrounds and experiences they can share.

Most admission officers will take into account that you are from another culture and, if applicable, that English is not your native language. Share your experiences and your enthusiasm as clearly as you can. Samples of your writing, art work, or tapes of musical performances, as applicable to the program of study you wish to pursue, may be included if you wish. If any portion of the application does not apply to you, note that on the form, along with an explanation. For example, many secondary schools in other countries have fewer school-sponsored activities than U.S. high schools. Some schools do not award academic honors. These situations should be explained.

Keep in mind that the personal information asked for on the application will provide admission officers with the information they need to get to know you as a person, not just your academic achievements and test results. Make the most of this opportunity.

Teacher Recommendations

Policies regarding teacher recommendations vary from college to college, but you should be prepared to have at least one teacher provide a reference for you. Select someone who knows you well and has taught you in a subject that is related to the course of study you are thinking of following at college. If you are undecided about a specific course of study, then it is wise to select a teacher who knows you well and has a high regard for you academically and personally.

You have the option of making these recommendations confidential between the letter writer and the college. Many teachers, headmasters, principals, and tutors will often write a more open recommendation if they know it will be confidential.

Secondary School Reports and Transcripts

The school report and the transcript of your academic record are essential to the evaluation of your academic abilities. The report form should be filled out by the official in your school who is responsible for college placement. This is usually a counselor, principal, headmaster, or careers master. This form should introduce you in the context of your whole school experience in relationship to the other students in your class. Admission committees will be interested in learning how you have performed in your own educational system. The school report should talk about your accomplishments and provide a prediction of your chances for success in university-level studies.

Your official transcript or academic record is the objective part of your application. Academic records vary greatly from one education system to the next. Systems of evaluation or grading and the formats used to present this information also differ widely. Ask your school to include a guide to the grading standards used in the educational system in your country and for your school specifically. If your school ranks students by their level of academic achievement, make certain the ranking is included with the information they send. It will provide an easily understood picture of how well you have done. If your school does not rank students, an estimate of your rank (for example, top 10 percent) would be helpful. Admission officers will want to know how you have performed over time, so be sure to have records sent that describe your academic performance for the past three to four years. If there is a national school-leaving certificate examination at the end of secondary education in your country (such as British GCSE's or British-based O and A Levels, French Baccalaureat, German Abitur, Hong Kong Certificate of Education, etc.), have official results sent as soon as they are available.

If your transcripts, academic records, and leaving-certificate examination results are not in English, make sure that you have officially certified literal English translations of all documents sent along with the official documents in the original language.

TOEFL or Other English Language Proficiency Test Scores

Your ability to speak, write, and understand English is an absolute requirement to be considered for direct admission to most degree programs in the United States. If English is not your native language, language proficiency can be demonstrated in several ways. The Test of English as a Foreign Language (TOEFL) is the most widely accepted test of proficiency. If English is not your native language but most of your formal schooling has been in English-speaking schools, you may not be required to take an examination. The policies regarding English language proficiency vary from institution to institution. Be sure that you know the policies and requirements of each school that you are considering.

If you know that your English ability is not up to acceptable standards, you may wish to consider intensive study of English in your country or in the United States. There are many English as a second language (ESL) programs available in the United States. Entrance requirements are minimal, and students are placed at the correct level of study through testing of their ability. Programs may last from five weeks to as long as a year. Sometimes a student is admitted to a college conditionally, pending study in an intensive English language program. U.S. consular officials abroad will frequently not grant an F-1 (student) visa for admission to an ESL program in the United States unless the visa applicant also has conditional admission to a full-time undergraduate program.

Many international students arriving in the United States for the first time are surprised to learn that they must take an additional test in English even though they had already submitted results from the TOEFL or other approved English proficiency examination. Retesting is sometimes done to enable academic counselors to make the best course placements and to determine if some additional English language training might be useful.

Standardized Test Scores

Many U.S. colleges and universities require all applicants to take either the College Board's SAT or the American College Testing's ACT Assessment (ACT). A few may also require three of the College Board's SAT Subject Tests. These examinations may present problems for some international applicants. The context and format of the tests are often unfamiliar to them, and sometimes it is difficult to find a testing center that is close enough to home. If information on these examinations is not available at your secondary school, it can be obtained by writing directly to the Educational Testing Service, Rosedale Road, Princeton, New Jersey 08541 U.S.A. (SAT, SAT Subject Tests, TOEFL) or logging on to their Web site at www.ets.org. You can also write to American College Testing, P.O. Box 168, Iowa City, Iowa 52243-0168 U.S.A. (ACT) or log on to their Web site at www.act.org.

Students often express concern over taking these tests. You should not allow these worries to grow into any unwarranted anxiety over how well you will score. Most U.S. admission officers are aware of the difficulties that tests like these present to students educated outside of the U.S. system or whose native language is not English. They will take this into account. Universities generally place greater weight on the quantitative (mathematics) sections of these tests, particularly for applicants who do not speak English as their native language. The tests are only one part of the academic evaluation, and admission committees will place the results of your examinations in the proper context.

If you are applying to a college that requires any of these standardized tests, you should make certain you know the school's requirements and expectations for level of performance. These vary from one school to the next. Another important point is that you may take the tests several times. Your performance may improve as you become more familiar and more comfortable with them. Most U.S. students begin taking these tests almost two years before they plan to enter college. If you are beginning the application process that early, it would be wise to do the same.

Nonacademic Information

While academic ability is certainly the most important factor, other factors can also play a large role and will be considered in the admission process. Since a college education is primarily an academic experience, it is important that a candidate have the academic preparation necessary to succeed at the schools to which he or she is applying. Once a candidate has demonstrated the necessary academic ability, however, the admission officer focuses attention on the nonacademic factors that set that candidate apart from the rest of the applicants. The deciding factor in an admission decision can be the nonacademic information. (However, some candidates with extremely strong academic backgrounds may be admitted almost solely on the basis of their academic achievement and potential. This type of candidate usually has a combination of very high grades, excellent standardized test scores, and enthusiastic school support.)

Financial Aid

You must submit a financial aid application if you intend to seek financial assistance for your undergraduate studies. Unfortunately, assistance for non-U.S. citizens is generally quite limited. The policies regarding financial aid vary considerably. Find out early what the policies are at the colleges that interest you. You should also explore the possibilities for aid available through the government of your home country.

The Application Fee

An application fee is usually required to cover the cost of processing your application. The fee at most colleges is around $50 and is typically payable in U.S. dollars only. Some colleges will waive the fee for very needy students.

Check each college's application requirements. Complete all forms and submit the application package as early as possible.

Timing

Timing can be one of the most difficult problems that international applicants face. Make certain that you have carefully read all of the information provided by the institution. Make a list of all of the deadlines that exist for various steps in the admission process for each institution to which you are applying. The list can be used as a quick resource in the future to make sure that you do not miss any important deadlines. Send all items and correspondence by air mail, and mail them as far before the deadlines as possible. Most schools will send a card acknowledging receipt of your application and will also inform you if any required items are missing from your application package.

It's a good idea to include several mailing labels filled out with your address with your application. The admissions office will appreciate your thoroughness.

Interviews

A final step in the application process may be an interview with a college representative. The interviewer may be an admissions officer or a graduate of the institution who is living in your area. Many U.S. colleges send representatives abroad to meet with prospective students, and an increasing number of graduates are available to meet with international students in their home countries. These meetings provide an excellent opportunity for you to learn more about the institutions that interest you. They also give the interviewer a chance to get an impression of you and how your abilities, goals, and interests match those of the institution. The interviews are generally informal and should be viewed as an opportunity to exchange information. A written summary of the meeting is typically sent to the college, but it does not usually play a large role in the actual decision to admit or reject an applicant.

Some U.S. colleges and universities use what are called "third-party" representatives or recruiters to interview prospective students in other countries. When these representatives are not actual members of the staff, faculty, or alumni of the institution, you should be extremely careful in evaluating the information you receive. Promises of admission expressed before the college receives detailed information about your academic background may indicate that the institution has lower standards than you wish to find in a U.S. college. When you are not dealing directly with an actual faculty or staff member or an alumnus of a college or university, you should seek additional information about the institution before making a final decision concerning your application.

Be sure to check with each institution to determine its policy regarding interviews and to find out if an interviewer is available in your area.

There is one final suggestion about presenting yourself to a U.S. college or university. Most colleges are looking for a varied student population that comes from many backgrounds and represents many different academic interests and personal qualities. Don't forget to stress the unique experience you will bring to the school.

WHAT TO DO WHEN YOU HAVE BEEN ACCEPTED

Once you have received acceptances from the colleges that you applied to, there are several important steps that must be taken.

Saying Yes or No

Each college will tell you exactly what steps to follow to confirm your acceptance of their offer of admission and how to prepare for the first term. This information will be included with the letter of admission or in materials that will be sent to you shortly thereafter. You must respond with a "yes" or "no" to each offer of admission. You will usually be required to submit a financial deposit to the institution that you plan to attend. This deposit will range from about $50 to $500 (higher in a few cases) and is used to guarantee your place in the class. As soon as you decide which college you want to attend, make sure to send your replies of both yes and no to all of the colleges that accepted you. Make sure that you do not miss any deadlines.

You may receive a letter that informs you that you are on a "waiting list." This generally means that the admission office determined that you were qualified for admission but there was not enough room to admit all qualified applicants. If you are placed on a waiting list at a college you wish to attend, you will be asked to respond "yes" or "no" to the offer of staying on the waiting list. If you say yes, you may be offered admission later if space becomes available. If you have been placed on a waiting list at your first-choice college and offered admission by your second-choice school, you may wish to consider taking the following steps:

- Notify the second-choice school that you accept its offer of admission and submit any required deposit.
- Write to your first-choice school and confirm that you want to remain on the waiting list.

If you are offered a place at your first-choice college later, you can withdraw from your place at your second-choice school (but you will have to forfeit your deposit) and then attend the college you wanted to go to most. If you are not offered a place at your first-choice college, you can still attend your second-choice school when the academic term begins.

Student Visas

The rules and regulations governing the entrance of all international students into the United States are complicated. If you have any questions about matters relating to immigration rules and regulations, you should check with the international student adviser at the college you plan to attend. He or she is specially trained and kept informed of the latest information on laws, work permits, health insurance, and other matters relating to international students and their dependents. It is your responsibility, however, to maintain your status by obtaining your forms at the correct time, keeping your passport valid six months beyond the date of completion of your program, and maintaining enrollment with a full course load.

For more information on student visas, go to http://www.UnitedStatesVisas.gov/studying.html.

Fees and Other Expenses

A few U.S. institutions require international students to pay the entire year's fees in advance. U.S. consular officers in some countries have begun to ask for proof of such advance payment before issuing a visa. Many have found this necessary to protect both the student and the institution. Problems have sometimes arisen from currency restrictions imposed by the government of the student's home country and sometimes from the actions of dishonest students. The solution for some colleges has been to institute a policy of prepayment of fees. Each institution will inform you if prepayment is required. Institutions with prepayment policies will not send the forms you need to obtain a visa until payment has been received.

Those colleges that do not require a full prepayment of fees may have several options for fee payment. Most colleges send bills twice a year, once in the summer before school begins and again in the winter to cover the second half of the year's fees. Some colleges will allow you to pay the annual fee in one large payment or to spread out your bill in monthly installments. You will be billed for the cost of tuition, general activities (to fund student organizations), health insurance if required, and housing and meal costs if you have chosen to live and eat on campus. Extra costs, such as those for books and supplies, recreational expenses, and travel will not be billed by the college, but you should make sure to include them when determining your budget for the year.

Another important item in financial planning is health and accident insurance. Most colleges require that all students be covered by a policy that will help with payment of medical or hospital bills if they are sick or injured while in the United States. There is no national health-care plan in the United States. All medical bills must be paid by the individual or through an insurance policy. Health care in the United States is very expensive, and the approximately $800 per year that students must pay to be insured is very reasonable. Information on insurance policies and how to obtain proper coverage will be supplied by the international student office at the college you choose to attend. Health insurance will not cover pre-existing conditions or dental care. Even if your college does not require you to take health insurance, you should not plan to live in the United States without it.

Housing

Each college has its own policies regarding living on campus and will usually offer a range of housing options. It is important for you to study all of the housing information you receive. This will typically be sent to you with your letter of admission or shortly afterward. Some colleges require all first-year students to live on campus in college housing. You will generally be asked to indicate your first, second, and third choices from among the options available. If the type of room you want most is not available, the housing office can then provide you with a desirable alternative from your second or third choice. A small number of colleges do not offer on-campus or college-sponsored housing. If this is the case, they will usually help international students locate suitable housing through community organizations that are set up for this purpose.

A free publication titled *Getting Ready to Go: Practical Information for Living and Studying in the United States* is avalable from most EducationUSA advising centers. It will help you plan your arrival in the United States.

HOW U.S. COLLEGES AND UNIVERSITIES EVALUATE ACADEMIC CREDENTIALS

Dale Edward Gough
Director, International Education Service
American Association of Collegiate Registrars and Admissions Officers (AACRAO)

If you are a student preparing to apply for admission to colleges and universities in the United States, it is important for you to understand the procedures that most U.S. institutions follow when evaluating your academic credentials in order to decide whether or not to admit you.

In your country, it is probably the ministry of education, or some similar body, that determines the eligibility of applicants from outside your education system. In the U.S. there is no ministry of education to make such decisions. Each college or university is free to set its own standards for admission, and it is the responsibility of the institution to review your previous education and academic performance to determine if you meet those standards.

U.S. colleges and universities are generally classified as highly selective, selective, somewhat selective, or open admission (institutions that can admit students regardless of their previous academic performance). The level of selectivity that an institution follows is based on many factors, and since each college and university has its own admission criteria, your academic credentials may meet the standards at some institutions but not at others.

Many institutions have their own staff members evaluate or assess your previous education. Other institutions might require you to send your academic records to an outside agency that specializes in providing evaluations of non-U.S. education. Sometimes an institution specifies a particular agency, or it might provide you with a list of several agencies and ask you to choose one. However, these agencies do not make the decision whether or not to admit you. They assess your previous education and provide the institution with their evaluation. The institution then makes the decision regarding your admission.

Pay close attention to the instructions on each application you submit and follow the instructions carefully. If you apply to more than one institution, you will probably be required to follow different instructions for each one. Do not assume that all institutions' requirements are the same.

Here are some things to keep in mind when applying:

- You will need to have an official copy of all your previous academic records (often referred to in application materials as an "official transcript") sent to the institution (and to the reviewing agency, if one is being used). "Official" records mean that the school where you studied must send a copy of your academic record directly to the institution (and to the agency, if one is being used). You, as the applicant, should not mail such records to the institution. If you do, the records might not be considered "official."

- Academic records that are not in English need to be translated, and both the original-language records and the translation must be sent. Pay particular attention to the instructions regarding translations. Some institutions and agencies might allow you to do the translation yourself if you are sufficiently proficient in English. However, others might require an official translation or one done by an authorized or licensed translator. Follow instructions carefully to avoid unnecessary delays.

- Standardized tests are an important part of the application process for U.S. institutions. If you were educated in a system that uses external national examinations, such as the Baccalaureat from France or "Ordinary" or "Advanced" level examinations from the United Kingdom, you will need to send copies of the results of these examinations. If you are applying as a first-year student at the undergraduate (bachelor's degree) level, you may also need to take certain standardized tests that are often required of U.S. applicants, such as the SAT or the ACT Assessment. Schools will instruct you as to which test(s) to take and how to make arrangements for testing.

- If English is not your native language, or if you have not been educated in a country or region where English is a native language, you may be required to submit the results of an English language proficiency test, such as the Test of English as a Foreign Language (TOEFL).

- If you need an F-1 or M-1 (student) visa or a J-1 (exchange visitor-student) visa, you will need to present evidence that you have adequate financial support for the entire period of your anticipated study. Most U.S. colleges and universities will ask you to complete a form regarding the financial support for your studies, or they will tell you what documentation is required. Usually, you will have to complete a form outlining the sources of your financial support as well as provide verification of such support. Again, carefully follow all instructions regarding documentation.

- Deadlines are extremely important! Pay close attention to any deadlines listed on the application forms. The admission of international students to U.S. institutions does take more time than the admission of U.S. students, and most schools have an earlier international application deadline. U.S. colleges and universities receive thousands of applications from international students each year. In order to be considered for admission for the term in which you want to begin your studies, it is essential that your application and all materials be received before the deadline.

Studying in the United States will be an exciting and rewarding experience. To start off in the best possible way, carefully follow the instructions of each institution in which you are interested. If you have any questions about the application process or what materials you need to provide, contact the institution for clarification or assistance.

UNDERSTANDING ACCREDITATION

Kristine Luken Program Specialist
U.S. Department of Education

Accreditation in the United States is a voluntary, nongovernmental process in which an institution agrees to be evaluated and/or have its programs evaluated by an accrediting agency against standards for measuring quality. The goal of accreditation is to ensure that the education provided by institutions of higher education meets acceptable levels of quality.

Accrediting agencies are nongovernmental, private educational associations that carry out the function of accrediting institutions and programs to determine their quality. Institutions and programs that request an agency's evaluation and meet its evaluation criteria are then accredited by that agency.

Having a basic understanding of accreditation—what it is and what it means—will help you to make choices that will bring you closer to meeting your career goals.

Recognized vs. Unrecognized Accrediting Agencies

Accrediting agencies fall into two categories: recognized and unrecognized. It is important to understand the difference between the two categories.

Recognized Accrediting Agencies

The U.S. Department of Education does not accredit institutions; rather, it determines which accrediting agencies receive recognition by the Department. Accrediting agencies may voluntarily seek recognition from the Secretary of Education, but it is not a requirement that they do so. Recognition by the Department is limited to those agencies that accredit institutions that need the recognition in order to participate in federal programs, such as the Federal Student Financial Aid Program. While some recognized accrediting agencies may accredit foreign institutions, those accrediting activities are outside the authority and review of the Department. An accrediting agency that meets the Department's criteria for recognition is believed to be a reliable authority on the quality of education or training provided by the institutions it accredits in the United States and its territories.

Accrediting agencies recognized by the Department of Education can have a regional or national scope: regional agencies accredit degree-granting institutions within six geographic regions of the United States, and national agencies accredit institutions or programs all across the United States. Agencies that meet these criteria are placed on the Department's List of Nationally Recognized Accrediting Agencies, available at http://www.ed.gov/admins/finaid/accred/accreditation_pg6.html#NationallyRecognized.

The Council for Higher Education Accreditation (CHEA), a private, nongovernmental agency, also recognizes organizations that accredit institutions and programs. CHEA recognizes many types of accrediting organizations, including some of the same accrediting agencies that the Department of Education recognizes. In order to be eligible for CHEA recognition, accrediting organizations must demonstrate that their mission and goals are consistent with those of CHEA and that a majority of the institutions and programs accredited by the organization award degrees. CHEA's List of Participating and Recognized Organizations can be found at http://www.chea.org/directories/index.asp.

Unrecognized Accrediting Agencies

Just as there are recognized accrediting agencies, there are unrecognized accrediting agencies. Accreditation standards of unrecognized accrediting agencies have not been reviewed by the Department of Education or CHEA. There are a variety of reasons why an agency may be unrecognized. For example, the agency may be working toward recognition with the Department or CHEA, or it may not meet the criteria for recognition by either organization.

Unrecognized accrediting agencies should be viewed with caution until their reputation can be determined. If an agency is unrecognized, this does not necessarily mean that they do not have high standards of quality. But it is important to know that many employers in the United States only recognize degrees earned from institutions accredited by an accrediting agency recognized by the Department or CHEA.

For more information about recognized and unrecognized accrediting agencies, as well as fraud and abuse related to accreditation, visit the U.S. Network for Education Information Web site at http://www.ed.gov/about/offices/list/ous/international/usnei/us/edlite-accreditation.html.

Accredited vs. Unaccredited Institutions

It is not enough to know the meaning of recognized and unrecognized accrediting agencies; it is also important to know the difference between accredited and unaccredited institutions.

Accredited Institutions

Accredited institutions have agreed to be reviewed and/or have their programs reviewed to determine the quality of education and training being provided. If an institution is accredited by an agency recognized by the Department of Education or CHEA, its teachers, course work, facilities, equipment, and supplies are reviewed on a routine basis to ensure that students receive a high-quality education and get what they pay for. Attending an accredited institution is often a requirement for employment in the United States and can be helpful if you plan to transfer academic credits to another institution, such as graduate school.

Any institution can claim to be accredited. It is important that you take the time to learn about the accrediting agency and its reputation. To find out if the institution you are interested in is accredited by an agency recognized by the Department, review the Department's database of postsecondary institutions and programs at http://www.ope.ed.gov/accreditation/.

Unaccredited Institutions

Unaccredited institutions are not reviewed against a set of standards in order to determine the quality of their education and training. This does not mean that an unaccredited institution is of poor quality, but earning a degree from an unaccredited institution may create problems for a student.

Some employers, institutions, and licensing boards only recognize degrees earned from institutions accredited by an accrediting agency recognized by the Department. With that in mind, it is recommended that a student check with other institutions regarding their transfer-of-credit policy to determine whether they would accept the degree and/or credits earned from any institution in which the student is considering enrolling.

In some states, it can even be *illegal* to use a degree from an institution that is not accredited by an accrediting agency recognized by the Department unless approved by the state licensing agency.

It is important to determine if a degree from an unaccredited institution will allow you to achieve your educational and career goals. To learn more about the issues and problems that may arise from pursuing an unaccredited degree, read over the frequently asked questions developed by Degree.net at http://www.degree.net/guides/accreditation_faqs.html.

Fake Accrediting Agencies

Fake accrediting agencies offer accreditation for a fee without doing an in-depth review of the school's programs or teachers. Their accreditation has nothing to do with ensuring that students receive a high-quality education and is worthless and meaningless.

Fake accrediting agencies may adopt names that are similar to other well-known accrediting agencies, sprinkle the names of legitimate institutions in their list of accredited members, and even use all the right-sounding words in their marketing materials to describe their accrediting standards and review process. These are just some of the ways fake accrediting agencies try to confuse students and make them believe they are legitimate.

So, do not be misled by a name or a slick marketing technique; always do your homework on any institution you want to attend. Remember, it is not enough to know that an institution is accredited. You also need to find out as much as you can about the accrediting agency. Your efforts will be worth your time.

U.S. and Foreign Diploma Mills

A familiar definition of diploma mill is "an organization that awards degrees without requiring students to meet educational standards for those degrees."

Diploma mills are not accredited by a nationally recognized agency. You will not find the institution's accrediting agency on the Department's list of Nationally Recognized Accrediting Agencies or on CHEA's List of Participating and Recognized Organizations. Instead, diploma mills often claim accreditation by a fake accrediting agency to attract more students to their degree programs and make themselves seem legitimate.

Remember: In some states it can be illegal to use a degree from an institution that is not accredited by a nationally recognized accrediting agency unless approved by the state licensing agency.

Not only are U.S. diploma mills a problem, but foreign diploma mills selling their degrees in the United States are a problem too. Some of these foreign diploma mills even claim to have approval from the education ministry of their country to offer degrees, when, in reality, they are operating without the knowledge of the country. Often these institutions use the name of the foreign education ministry in their marketing materials to make themselves seem legitimate. What the institution is trying to do is make students believe that its programs have been reviewed and meet some level of quality when, in fact, they do not.

Before taking the offer to enroll in a foreign institution, find out as much as you can about the accreditor and the institutions it accredits, as well as the recognition process of the foreign education ministry. This information will give you a better picture of the institution and its reputation. To review a list of agencies that license and regulate higher education in Canada and other countries, visit www.degree.net/guides/checking_out2.html.

The .edu Extension in Internet Addresses

Not all institutions in the United States that use the .edu extension as a part of their Internet address are necessarily legitimate institutions. Before the Department of Commerce created more strict requirements, some questionable institutions were approved to use .edu in their address. New requirements allow only those institutions accredited by an agency recognized by the Department of Education to use it. However, institutions that were approved to use it before the new requirements were put into place can still use it, which means there could still be some illegitimate institutions with .edu in their address. Whether an institution uses the .edu extension or not, it is important to know as much as possible about the institution before enrolling.

FINANCING YOUR U.S. EDUCATION

Nancy W. Keteku
Regional Educational Advising Coordinator for Africa

Education in the United States can be expensive. However, higher education is the most important investment you will ever make. You should start your financial planning at the same time you select the colleges to which you will apply; that is, about one year prior to enrollment.

Financing your college education is a four-pronged effort, consisting of

- assessing your personal and family funds;
- identifying financial assistance for which you are eligible;
- compiling effective applications; and
- reducing educational costs.

First, you need to confer with your parents and other family sponsors to find out how much money they can commit each year to your education. Try to raise as much money as possible from family sources, because most scholarship awards are highly competitive and cover only part of the total educational and living costs.

At the same time, conduct research in your own country to find possible funding from local government, business, or foundation sources. Although these sources are not found in all countries, you may be able to reduce your educational cost through scholarships from local organizations.

If your family and local funds do not cover the cost of a U.S. education, you will need to look for financial assistance from other sources, such as American colleges and universities. However, when searching, do not assume that all institutions award financial aid. In fact, only about 50 percent of the institutions offering bachelor's degrees provide financial assistance to students who are not citizens or permanent residents of the United States, and most of them provide only partial assistance. Keep in mind that financial aid for U.S. students is different from financial aid for international students. Be sure to inform the admissions office of your country of citizenship and request information on financial aid available to non-U.S. citizens.

CAN I AFFORD COLLEGE?

You have probably heard about scholarships and financial aid. So what's the difference? A scholarship is a financial award based on merit in areas like academics, athletics and performing arts, or community service and leadership. Financial aid is based on a student's financial need, as documented by family income, assets, and other factors. Although different in many ways, most scholarships and financial aid are extremely competitive and require an exemplary academic record. Consult with your educational adviser on how to research available financial aid for international students. You will discover that most financial awards cover only a portion of the total cost of attendance. Thus, the more money you can raise from family sources, the better your chances are of attending the college or university of your choice.

As you do your research, make a list of the colleges and universities you would like to attend. Write down the annual cost of each (tuition, fees, insurance, room and board, books, and clothing), and then enter the total financial aid award offered by each of the institutions. In this way, you can quickly see where your best chances lie, and you can eliminate the institutions where you would not stand a good chance of attending based on the financial aid you would receive. When planning your finances, consider these ways to reduce your costs:

- Look for institutions that offer the highest quality education at the lowest price.

- Try to complete a four-year bachelor's degree in three years. This will save you thousands of dollars. Students can accelerate their programs by earning transfer credit for college-level courses completed in the home country; taking courses at a nearby community college—if tuition is lower and credits are transferable; attending summer school; and taking one additional course each semester.

- Find out if the institution offers scholarship assistance based on your first-year grades. A superior academic record could save you thousands of dollars.

- Live off campus with a relative or friend.

- Attend a community college for the first two years and then transfer to a four-year institution to complete your degree.

Here are some additional pointers on financing your U.S. education:

- International students often ask about full scholarships, which cover the entire cost of education, except for airfare. These awards are both rare and competitive. The total number of full scholarships offered to incoming international students each year is about 2,000, offered by only about 200 colleges in the United States. There are usually 20 highly qualified international students competing for each major scholarship. To compete successfully for a full scholarship, you must be one of the top students in your country, have a high grade point average (GPA), score well on the SAT and TOEFL, and demonstrate outstanding performance in other areas, such as leadership.

- International students also ask about financial assistance from foundations, organizations, and the U.S. government. These types of financial aid are rarely awarded to international students because there is very little aid available through such sources, and it is usually earmarked for advanced graduate students. Fewer than 5 percent of international undergraduates are financed through these sources. Again, your educational adviser can tell you whether or not there are special funds available for students from your country.

- Financial aid is awarded at the beginning of the academic year (August–September) and is rarely available for students entering in January. Note: Aid is more likely to be available to first-year students than to those transferring from other institutions. If you are already enrolled in a university at home and wish to transfer to a university in the United States, ask the admission office about its policy on financial aid for international transfer students.

- You may be able to negotiate a loan to cover part of your education. Your educational adviser will have a list of reputable loan programs for which you are eligible. These loans usually require both a creditworthy U.S. citizen to act as a cosigner and proof of enrollment in a U.S. university. Before taking a loan, make sure you know how you are going to repay it and how a loan will affect your plans for graduate study and returning home.

- Working can help pay part of your education. However, immigration regulations permit international students to work only part-time and only on campus. After your first year of study, you may apply to the Bureau of U.S. Citizenship and Immigration Services (USCIS) (formerly INS) for permission to work off campus, but there is no guarantee that this will be granted and you cannot work off campus for more than twelve months. Understanding the various regulations from the USCIS can be difficult, so you should carefully review the information found at http://uscis.gov/graphics/index.htm.

TIPS FROM THE EXPERTS

Here are some questions that international education advisers in various countries are frequently asked about studying in the U.S.

Q When should I start the application process if I am interested in studying in the U.S.?

A You should start the application process a year and a half before your planned arrival at a U.S. college campus. The academic year generally runs from September to May or June. So if you plan to enroll in September, you should begin contacting schools in March, April, or May of the previous year.

Q What are the best colleges in the U.S.?

A "Best" is a relative term. In the U.S. there is a very wide range of colleges offering diverse opportunities. What is best for you may not be best for another student. It is not advisable to go by so-called ranking only. You need to make a list of your own priorities, do a realistic self-assessment, and then do research in order to find the "best" colleges for you.

Q How does one select a U.S. college or university?

A Students select institutions based on some combination of the following: their academic and career goals; the type of institution they want (specialized colleges, liberal arts colleges, institutes of technology, colleges with a religious affiliation, single-gender colleges); the availability, level, and quality of programs in their fields of interest and specializations; the geographic location and setting (rural, suburban, or city-based); climate; costs; the nature of and availability of financial aid; size (number of students and student-faculty ratio); diversity on campus (including the number of international students); availability of special programs such as interdisciplinary studies and internship opportunities; and student life and campus activities.

Q What do colleges look for when making their admission decisions?

A Colleges look for a variety of factors, such as a good academic record, English language proficiency, acceptable standardized test scores, an effective statement of purpose or essay, strong letters of recommendation, proof of financial support, and other program-specific requirements.

Q Does the U.S. welcome international students?

A The U.S. is known for its diversity of peoples and cultures. U.S. universities value the perspectives brought to their classrooms and research and heartily welcome international students.

Q What attracts international students to higher education in the U.S.?

A International students are attracted to the availability of a large variety of majors and specializations, the U.S. system of accreditation, flexibility in the educational system, merit-based admission and financial assistance, and the marketability of the degree. Students enjoy their experience in a proven educational system in a country with a diverse culture and a modern outlook.

Q What is the cost of higher education in the U.S.?

A The cost of studying at a U.S. college or university is anywhere from $20,000 to more than $50,000 per year. This includes tuition, fees (including computer, lab, or other facilities usage), food, and on-campus or off-campus housing. Additional expenses include books and supplies, transportation, insurance, and personal expenses.

Q What financial aid opportunities are available for international students?

A Financial aid is very competitive at the undergraduate level. Scholarships, which are given to top students only, are very rare for international students. Financial assistance from foundations, organizations, and the U.S. government is also rarely awarded to international undergraduate students. Less than 5 percent of international undergraduates are financed through these sources. Your educational adviser will be able to tell you whether there are special funds available for students from your country.

Q What tests do I need to take and what are the minimum scores required for admission?

A Many colleges and universities require the SAT or the ACT Assessment for undergraduate admission. Also, international students whose native language is not English are required to take an English language proficiency test. The Test of English as a Foreign Language (TOEFL) is the most widely accepted test. There are many competitive colleges and universities that require SAT Subject Test scores in addition to the SAT. The Subject Tests are in subjects such as biology, history, math, chemistry, and physics. You need to check with the colleges and universities you are applying to and ask if they require any Subject Tests.

Each college or university has different score requirements for standardized tests. You can strengthen your application by obtaining excellent scores.

Q When should I take the tests?

A When applying for standardized tests, keep in mind the time period during which the test scores will be valid. For instance, TOEFL scores are valid for only two years. Try to take tests by October if you plan to study in the United States in September of the following year. Another thing to take into consideration is that many colleges have financial aid deadlines as early as December, January, or February for enrollment in September, and if you are applying for financial aid, you must make sure that all items in your application packet, including your test scores, reach the colleges and universities of your choice before then. But do not take a test unless you feel prepared to do so. Time yourself and take a lot of practice tests to get used to the pattern of questions and the timing.

Q How important are standardized test scores?

A Standardized test scores are only one part of the application procedure and not the sole decision-making factor in the admissions process. They are a valuable tool in assessing the potential of students applying from varied educational backgrounds to succeed in the higher educational system of the U.S. While the format of each test varies, most focus on measuring the verbal, analytical, problem-solving, and quantitative skills of students. The level of skills required in a particular program may vary by the field of study and by the school or department. The ability of an international student to succeed in a particular program or school is determined only after a comprehensive review of the entire application packet.

Q What is a grade point average?

A A grade point average (GPA) is the most common method of measuring a student's academic performance. For each course, grades are awarded on a scale of A to D and F. At the end of each term, letter grades are converted into numerals on a 4.0 scale (A = 4, B = 3, C = 2, D = 1, F = 0) and each numeral grade is multiplied by the number of credits each course is worth. These numbers are added together and then divided by the total number of credits taken to determine the student's GPA for that term. A GPA is calculated for each term, cumulated each year, and a final GPA is calculated. (Note: Most programs use a GPA scale of 4.0, although a few schools use a scale of 5.0.) A C average or better is generally expected of undergraduate students.

Q What are credits?

A Students receive their degree by completing a specified number of credits. One credit is roughly equivalent to one hour of class time per week. Each course earns a specified number of credits (usually 3 or 4). Sometimes the terms "semester hours," "quarter hours," or "units" are used instead of "credits" or "credit hours."

Q What is the academic year for colleges in the U.S.?

A The academic year usually runs from mid-August to the end of May. However, it varies for each college or university. It may be divided into semesters, quarters, or trimesters. In addition, many schools provide a summer term of six to eight weeks. Students sometimes take summer courses to lower their course load during the regular terms or to earn their degrees more quickly. There are at least two main breaks during the academic year: two to four weeks in December and January and about a week in the spring (called Spring Break).

Q What is the difference between applying for the fall and spring semesters?

A As stated above, the academic year begins with the fall semester, which is when most students are admitted. Orientation programs are held with this in mind, and some prerequisite courses may only be offered in the fall. However, students can apply for initial admission in the spring semester if admissions have been opened up by a particular school or department. One thing to keep in mind, though, is that since most allocations for financial aid are made for fall enrollment, those who start in the spring are less likely to receive financial assistance.

Q What is a transcript, and what does "official transcript" mean?

A A transcript is a detailed account of a student's educational record that lists courses taken and the grades received. An official transcript is issued by the school awarding the grades/degree and is certified by the designated issuing authority of that school. The official transcript must be issued in a sealed envelope with the school's stamp and the official's signature or initials across the flap.

Q What does the application packet contain?

A The application packet contains a completed application form with the application fee, official transcripts, official test scores, an essay or statement of purpose, letters of recommendation, proof of adequate financial resources, an affidavit of support, request for financial assistance (if applicable), and any supplemental materials.

Q Should I have a native speaker or a company write my application essay?

A The essay is the one section of the application that gives admissions officers a chance to get to know your personality and nonacademic background. Don't waste the chance to show them how unique you are by having someone else write your essay. Only you can distinguish yourself from the hundreds of other students; at highly selective schools, the essay can be the deciding factor between two similar applicants. The essay is not a list of achievements or an autobiography. Depending on the question asked, focus on one event, book, or person that affected your view of the world. Talk about something personal, good or bad, and write so that the admission officers will remember you.

Q What should be included in recommendation letters?

A Recommendation letters can be a critical factor in the selection process and should discuss the following:

- The content of the course the student took and the methods of teaching that were used

- The student's performance in the class, including a comparison to other students in the class

- The student's attitude toward learning, including evidence of his or her motivation, commitment, curiosity, independence, and creative thinking

- The student's character, strengths, and uniqueness

- Prediction about the student's impact (academic, personal, and/or extracurricular) on a college or community

Q What are some useful tips for potential U.S.-bound students?

A Be clear about your objectives. Consult different resources to gather information. Plan well in advance. Work systematically, keeping academic strengths as priorities. Make intelligent use of available information. And while you are in the U.S., work hard, learn about the country, and promote understanding about your home country.

Q Where can I get more information about higher education in the U.S.?

A To learn more about studying in the U.S., visit

> www.petersons.com
> www.educationUSA.state.gov
> www.ed.gov
> www.finaid.org
> www.studyUSA.com
> www.ets.org
> www.collegeboard.com

NOTES

NOTES

NOTES

NOTES

Peterson's
Book Satisfaction Survey

Give Us Your Feedback

Thank you for choosing Peterson's as your source for personalized solutions for your education and career achievement. Please take a few minutes to answer the following questions. Your answers will go a long way in helping us to produce the most user-friendly and comprehensive resources to meet your individual needs.

When completed, please tear out this page and mail it to us at:

> Publishing Department
> PETERSON'S, A Nelnet Company
> 2000 Lenox Drive
> Lawrenceville, NJ 08648

You can also complete this survey online at **www.petersons.com/booksurvey.**

1. **What is the ISBN of the book you have purchased? (The ISBN can be found on the book's back cover in the lower right-hand corner.)** _____

2. **Where did you purchase this book?**
   - ❑ Retailer, such as Barnes & Noble
   - ❑ Online reseller, such as Amazon.com
   - ❑ Petersons.com
   - ❑ Other (please specify) _____

3. **If you purchased this book on Petersons.com, please rate the following aspects of your online purchasing experience on a scale of 4 to 1 (4 = Excellent and 1 = Poor).**

	4	3	2	1
Comprehensiveness of Peterson's Online Bookstore page	❑	❑	❑	❑
Overall online customer experience	❑	❑	❑	❑

4. **Which category best describes you?**
   - ❑ High school student
   - ❑ Parent of high school student
   - ❑ College student
   - ❑ Graduate/professional student
   - ❑ Returning adult student
   - ❑ Teacher
   - ❑ Counselor
   - ❑ Working professional/military
   - ❑ Other (please specify) _____

5. **Rate your overall satisfaction with this book.**

Extremely Satisfied	Satisfied	Not Satisfied
❑	❑	❑

6. Rate each of the following aspects of this book on a scale of 4 to 1 (4 = Excellent and 1 = Poor).

	4	3	2	1
Comprehensiveness of the information	❏	❏	❏	❏
Accuracy of the information	❏	❏	❏	❏
Usability	❏	❏	❏	❏
Cover design	❏	❏	❏	❏
Book layout	❏	❏	❏	❏
Special features (e.g., CD, flashcards, charts, etc.)	❏	❏	❏	❏
Value for the money	❏	❏	❏	❏

7. This book was recommended by:
❏ Guidance counselor
❏ Parent/guardian
❏ Family member/relative
❏ Friend
❏ Teacher
❏ Not recommended by anyone—I found the book on my own
❏ Other (please specify) _____

8. Would you recommend this book to others?

Yes	Not Sure	No
❏	❏	❏

9. Please provide any additional comments.

_____

_____

_____

_____

_____

Remember, you can tear out this page and mail it to us at:

Publishing Department
PETERSON'S, A Nelnet Company
2000 Lenox Drive
Lawrenceville, NJ 08648

or you can complete the survey online at **www.petersons.com/booksurvey**.

Your feedback is important to us at Peterson's, and we thank you for your time!

If you would like us to keep in touch with you about new products and services, please include your e-mail here: _____